Building
Colonial Furnishings,
Miniatures,
& Folk Art

Erna Zuterman

1975.
In memoriam

Deerfield Village, Deerfield, Massachusetts.

An
Early
American
Society
Book

The editors of *Early American Life*, the Society's official magazine, have checked this book for historical and, where possible, factual accuracy. Opinions and interpretations expressed within its pages have been left as written by the author. It is the objective of the Society to sponsor and recommend books that it feels have lasting value to persons interested in colonial and early American times—books that are both entertaining and enlightening.

Robert G. Miner
President and Editor of Publications

Building Colonial Furnishings, Miniatures, & Folk Art

Joseph Daniele

Stackpole Books

BUILDING COLONIAL FURNISHINGS, MINIATURES, AND FOLK ART

Copyright © 1976 by Joseph W. Daniele

Published by
STACKPOLE BOOKS
Cameron and Kelker streets
Harrisburg, Pa. 17105

Printed in the U.S.A.

Library of Congress Cataloging in Publication Data

Daniele, Joseph William.
  Building colonial furnishings, miniatures, and
folk art.

  1. Furniture making. 2. Furniture, Colonial—
United States. 3. Miniature objects—United States.
4. Folk art—United States. I. Title.
TT200.D36   684.1'042'0974   76-17006
ISBN 0-8117-0451-3

To Jean
my co-author

It was her love of colonial furnishings that got me started; her guidance and understanding that kept me going; and her assistance that helped me finish this book.

Contents

SECTION TWO

SECTION THREE

SECTION FOUR

Tavern Side Table
Fireside Settle
Corner Wall Cupboard
Flat Wall Cupboard
Small Gateleg Table
Rocking Settee (Mammy Bench)
Trestle-leg Cradle
Tall Poster or Canopy Bed
Child's Trundle Bed

SECTION EIGHT

Preface

Many items of furniture go under the name "Colonial." Very often the term is applied by modern manufacturers with little thought to authenticity of design. Colonial styling, like the American character, is made up of many facets—some concrete and some abstract—all mixing and blending to form the final outcome. Colonial styling incorporates Dutch, German, English, and French influences, the English influence predominating. Each group added its unique customs or heritage to pieces they made, adding to the development of colonial furniture as we now know it.

Colonial furniture is mainly a product of New England, for several reasons. The southern settlements quickly developed materials for trade: cotton, tobacco, rice, and indigo were just a few of the items exported. Therefore, they established a mercantile relationship whereby they could afford to import finished English goods in return or could have local cabinetmakers produce copies of fine English furnishings. New England had little to export with the exception of timber, and this lack of a balance in trade forced the early settlers to be self-sufficient. Soap, candles, tools, clothing, and household furnishings were all made by the individual families for their own use.

Colonial furniture, therefore, was a necessity, made by local people, based upon traditional designs, but not contained by a strict adherence to contemporary pieces found in Europe. The individuality of interpretation, design, and simple but sturdy construction are the most outstanding features of colonial furniture. Each piece carried the personality of its maker, reflecting pride in construction and ownership. Perhaps this is why so many pieces have endured for over 300 years— that pride having been passed from generation to generation.

New England had great forests of pine, and furniture of this wood soon filled the early homes.

No matter what new styles appear, the beauty of pine furniture, dark from age, cut and gouged from years of usage, never dulls to the aesthetic eye. Colonial pieces are just as desirable today as they were when first made. These pieces are too beautiful to lose, and this book was created by a desire to carry on the line. I hope you will use this book as the early colonists relied upon memory: as a starting place. The finished pieces should be an extension of your personality, so *do* change the design, size, or intended purpose to suit yourself. The furniture then represents a double pleasure—the enjoyment of creating something yourself with your own hands, and the pride of ownership; a feeling that cannot be achieved by purchasing readymade furniture in a showroom.

JOSEPH WILLIAM DANIELE

Acknowledgments

Obtaining the historical background and general information required for this type of book was possible only with the help of many people, some associated with restoration settlements, and some private collectors. I would like to offer my sincere appreciation and gratitude to the following people and institutions for their assistance:

Colonial Williamsburg, Williamsburg, Virginia
Copper City Realty Inc., Lancaster, Pennsylvania
Deft Wood Finishing Products, Alliance, Ohio
Library of Congress, Washington, D. C.
Metropolitan Museum of Art, New York, New York
Mystic Seaport, Mystic, Connecticut
National Gallery of Art, Index of American Design, Washington, D. C.
Newburyport Historical Society, Newburyport, Massachusetts
Mr. and Mrs. Frank Okarmus, Springfield, Massachusetts
Old Sturbridge Village, Sturbridge, Massachusetts
Pennsylvania Farm Museum, Lancaster, Pennsylvania
Philadelphia Free Library, Philadelphia, Pennsylvania
Philadelphia Museum of Art, Philadelphia, Pennsylvania
United States Naval Academy, Annapolis, Maryland
Shelburne Museum, Shelburne, Vermont
Smithsonian Institution, Washington, D. C.
Strawbery Banke, Portsmouth, New Hampshire

Introduction

No other furniture has equalled the colonial style in warmth and charm. This furniture has uniqueness that developed from the determination of the frontier population, people who came to the New World because they wanted political and religious freedom. The search for freedom extended also into their furnishings. Unafraid to make a dangerous sea journey to a foreign land and to make a home and new life with only their two hands, they developed a strong sense of self-determinism. Whatever they needed, they made for themselves—homes, farms, defense, furnishings, and government. Such determinism found expression also in their household items.

Colonists were non-conformists, and as they would not become obsequious to foreign monarchs, so too they would not be confined by stereotyped furniture designs. As the colonies progressed, so too did the furnishings. Furniture made from rough planks cut in a pit saw developed into folk art. Individual interpretations of classical European designs and improvisation of personal wants and desires, along with the constant interaction of various ethnic backgrounds met and developed a style of fluidity, grace, warmth, and character. The colonial style does not contain a great array of fancy turns or intricate scrolls. It is plain, simple, and serviceable. All of the designs in this book were chosen because they typify the true spirit of colonial styling. All pieces were developed from priceless antique prototypes found in several museums around the eastern seaboard. We cannot hope to own the originals, but we can do the next best thing; make our own reproductions or adaptations that follow the originals in design and intention.

This book has been laid out in sections or groupings wherein all projects shown have a common factor. Several variants are offered on some plans so that you will have a choice. You will notice that small changes have been made from time to time on some of the projects, more or less interjecting my own personality on the original pieces. In colonial times this was called "bespoke" work. This means that the person who wanted the piece made would tell the cabinetmaker or joiner just what he wanted. Often the finished product was a compromise between the two people involved. The piece was then spoken about—a type of verbal list of specifications. I recommend that you do the same thing; use this book as our forefathers used their concept of design; as a starting place. Feel free to impose your own individuality upon the plans, thus the piece becomes truly yours in every way.

I have included a brief historical background for

each piece. Some have interesting stories concerning their origins, and others have descriptions of the process of their development or evolution. Too often we lose sight of the original intent or purpose, thereby losing an insight into our heritage.

Section One is concerned with various methods used in construction, including making doors and drawers. There are also remarks about finishing furniture, including staining, distressing, sealing, and finishing. Do not feel that the offered methods are the only ones that will work; rather they are offered as a basis—methods that have worked for both my students and for me.

Section Two on colonial joinery, offers several types of cupboards. A hutch dresser, server, dry sink, and an apothecary chest are included.

Section Three centers on tables used in early times. Different types and adaptations are offered in order to give you a wide selection. Coffee tables, an end table, and dining room table are included.

Section Four deals with colonial timepieces, ranging from a small steeple clock to a grandmother's clock. All of the items represented are based upon known museum pieces.

Section Five includes large furniture, having plans for three different types of desks. A difficult item to fit in with colonial styles, all of the desks offered here were developed from authentic designs. Also included in this section are a chandelier and an authentic spinning wheel.

Section Six, on folk art, contains various wall pieces, from tavern signs to decoys and a large carved eagle. These items are very often hard to find, and this section should be a help in your search for authentically styled accessories.

Section Seven is devoted to miniatures: A scale model of the Fenno House in Old Sturbridge Village is given along with plans for furnishings and accessories. Directions are given also for conversion of any plan to full-size or doll-size pieces, as well as the reverse—any full-sized plan may be converted to miniature with these simple instructions. A ladder-back chair, trestle-leg cradle, fireside settle, and a canopy bed are only a few of the items included.

Section Eight is a list of possible suppliers of components for some of the projects. Most of these parts can be purchased locally, however the list in this section is intended as insurance on the availability of needed special items.

With only a few exceptions, all of the projects can be made with common hand and power tools. A great deal of woodworking skill is not needed to construct these pieces because they are designed as simply as possible to eliminate complex joinery. The early settlers learned that the ship-lap joint would endure, and most of the projects use this type of joint. The ship-lap joint is not difficult to make and it insures a lasting, authentic type of joinery.

The wide range of projects covered offers something for everyone and every need. You can develop your own adaptations from the historical pictures included, or obtain different ideas through visits to your local museums. The variations are countless. The colonial style of furniture and furnishings is timeless, mainly because of the individualism of each piece. Because most colonial furnishings were based upon reflections and memories, the plans for furnishings included in this collection were designed in the same manner.

At times several museum-piece styles were combined to produce the final drawing. At other times, remembrance of colonial stories, told by museum settlement curators or guides, became the main idea behind the design. Such concrete and abstract influences meshed and merged together, much like the original human ethnic blending, to produce these plans. Most are not direct line-for-line copies, but are the result of individual interpretation of 18th-century styling.

In the working drawings, only the critical measurements are given as firm. The irregular curves, cyma curves, scrolls, or turnings are dimensioned in one-inch grids. Such cuts are seldom absolute, they are more likely to be suggestions. They were included as possible ideas for the reader upon which to base his own designs.

This book was developed, above all else, for *individual interpretation* of colonial styling. The desired result is a form of uniqueness, so that the finished product is an extension of you, your personality, and your particular requirements.

Construction Hints

STOCK SELECTION

Each project has a material list with suggested sizes and species of wood. In all but a few, the suggested material is pine. This was done for several reasons: A great deal of the early furnishings were constructed from pine, and its use here will make your piece more authentic; also, pine is easy to work with and does not require special tools. More important, pine is available at a nominal cost nationwide through local lumber supply outlets.

If other species of wood are more to your personal preference and are available, by all means use it. I once saw an 18th-century spinning wheel in a museum that contained six different species of wood. Colonial craftsmen used whatever was on hand that suited their needs, and this should be your guideline.

Plywood

Plywood is a modern invention undreamed of in colonial times. The main advantage of using plywood is the availability of all thicknesses in large sheets. Plywood is very stable and will not shrink or expand.

Several designs in this book call for parts made from plywood, however, in each case the plywood is used for drawer bottoms, dust panels, or project backs. Plywood should *never* be used where the edges or its unique grain will be seen, or this will detract from the colonial design.

Stock Dimensions

The material list gives the largest size of each piece required. A word of caution should be

noted regarding modern lumber sizes. When the material list states one-inch-wide stock it follows the ordering or purchase practice of lumberyards where, in reality, the stock thickness is only ¾" thick. The working drawings made allowances for this discrepancy in thickness only. All other sizes are exact and not lumberyard sizes. To illustrate this point, if a 1" x 6" was purchased in a local lumberyard, the actual board size would be ¾" x 5½".

Some projects call for extra thick stock, such as 1¼", 1½", or 2" boards. Many lumber supply outlets refer to such sizes in quarters. Thus 1¼" becomes five quarters, 1½" is six quarters and so on.

Many larger supply outlets have these thicknesses as stock items, or will order such material for you. A list of possible suppliers has been included in the book for reader assistance in obtaining parts or materials. (See *Section Eight*.)

Gluing Stock

Pine boards today do not come overly wide, therefore several must be glued together to make up the required widths needed. Because pine "works," special care should be given to making these glue joints. A plain butt joint, as a rule, will

18

open under strain. One method to overcome this tendency is to glue in dowel pins about 12 inches on centers. The doweling helps to hold the joints together.

There are several excellent ready-to-use glues on the market, the most common being the white liquid type. (Elmer's is a well known brand.) This glue affords excellent holding power and requires only a short clamping time, usually four to six hours. The commercial liquid hide glues, such as Franklin Glues, have greater adhesive strength but they require a 24-hour clamp time. Either glue will work well, it becomes just a matter of personal choice.

There are a few important rules to gluing stock that should not be ignored:

1. *All* excess glue *must be removed* as soon as possible after joining, and before it can dry, so that the surface will accept staining and finishing. The glue will dry rock-hard and often almost invisible, but the glazed surface will not accept a stain coat. The result will be a white streak that could ruin many hours of work.

2. Do not "starve" the glue joint by squeezing out the glue through excessive clamp pressure. The best way to prevent glue-starved joints is to apply the adhesive to both pieces to be joined and then allow "set time." Set time means to allow the glue to set before clamping. A general rule is five minutes set time on soft woods, such as pine, and eight minutes for hard woods.

Fig. 1–2. Thomas Lee House, Lyme, Connecticut.

CLAMPING

When clamping stock together, do not try to make up for poor joint fits with clamp pressure. This will put undue strain on the joint, which will then often fail after drying. Dry-fit the joint to achieve perfect fit. Then glue and clamp the stock.

When several bar clamps are used, it is recommended that the clamps be alternated one up and the next one down. This procedure will help prevent buckling. (See Fig. 1–3.) The force of the bar clamps will have a tendency to force the joint to bulge or buckle. It is recommended that in addition to alternating the bar clamp positions that straight edges and "C" clamps be used on the ends. (See Fig. 1–3.)

JOINING BOARDS

Butt Joint

The most common joint is a plain butt joint. This is where two boards are glued together. It is the weakest joint to use and is not recommended for any joint that will receive pressure. The whole idea of a good joint is to increase the surface areas that come together under glue and pressure, or to introduce a third material to counteract the strain.

The dowel, spline, or half-lap joints are recommended, and they can be made with a minimum of special power tools.

Dowel Joint

Drill holes for the dowel pins in the edges of the pieces to be joined. A doweling jig is a big help in this operation. If a doweling jig is not available, make your own by soldering two thumbtacks back to back. Stick one tack in the edge of a board and when the other board to be joined is brought up tight, the other end of the tack will mark it in the exact spot. Once the holes are drilled, apply glue to all of the parts and allow the glue to become tacky. (This will prevent glue-starved joints created by too much clamp pressure.) Insert the dowels in one piece, line up the other pieces, and join them. Clamp the pieces together and wipe off excess glue. Allow 24 hours drying time.

Half-Lap Joint (Rabbet Joint)

Another way of joining pieces is the lap-joint method. A rabbet of any depth may be cut along the center joints, just as long as they complement each other. Most often the lap joint is made by cutting rabbets one-half the thickness of the stock. Example: A ¾″ board will have a rabbet thickness of ⅜ of an inch. When the two boards are glued together they will equal the original thickness of the stock. (See Fig. 1–5.)

After the rabbets are cut, dry-fit both pieces to check the alignment. Apply glue to all areas and allow the glue to become tacky. Clamp the pieces together for 24 hours. (Dowel pins, if holes are

Fig. 1–4. Gluing boards with dowels.

21

Fig. 1–5   Half-lap joint (rabbet joint).

Fig. 1–6.   Spline joint.

22

drilled prior to rabbeting, may be placed through both parts of the joint for added strength.)

The spline joint is made by cutting matching dados in the edges of the two boards to be glued. The dados can be cut any depth desired and most often the dado width is one-third the board thickness. Cut a spline (See Fig. 1–6), to fit into the two dados. Glue all members to be joined and allow the glue to set the suggested time.

Install the spline into the dados and clamp the boards together. Wipe off all excess glue while still wet.

FRAMING JOINTS

Secondary to edge joinery but just as important for good construction are the common joints used for framing. These are the joints used to frame the stiles and rails on cabinet fronts, door frames, and drawer dividers.

The prime purpose of framing joints is to create a large surface area for fastening and reinforcement. All of the following joints are easily made on common hand or power tools, yet meet the criteria for proper construction.

Butt Joint

The plain butt joint is the weakest method used in framing. This joint is made by butting one piece of stock to another at a right angle. Very little surface contact is made and the end grain will not glue satisfactorily. If this type of joint is used, it is recommended that the joint be reinforced with a glue block screwed onto the rear surface area to secure it.

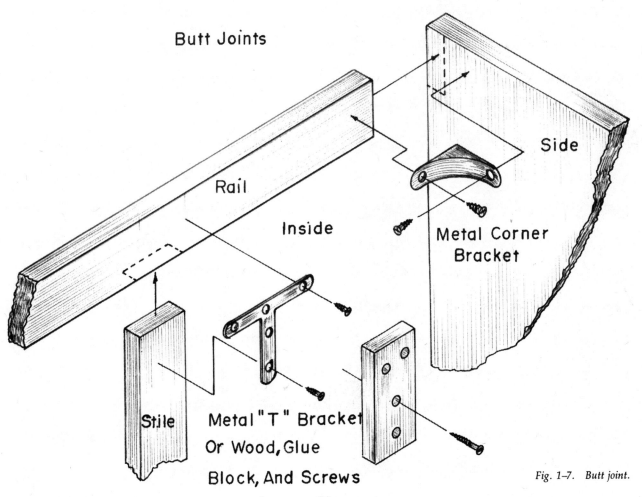

Butt Joints

Rail

Inside

Side

Metal Corner Bracket

Stile   Metal "T" Bracket Or Wood, Glue Block, And Screws

Fig. 1–7. Butt joint.

MITER JOINTS

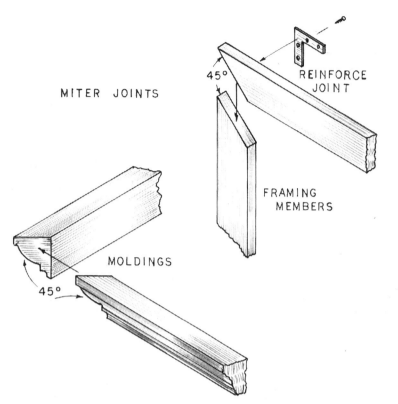

45°

REINFORCE
JOINT

FRAMING
MEMBERS

MOLDINGS

45°

Fig. 1–8. Miter joints.

Half-Lap Joint

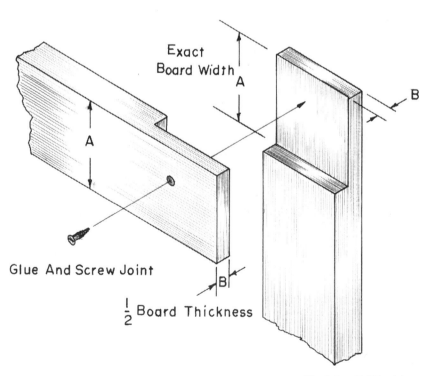

Exact
Board Width

A

B

A

Glue And Screw Joint

B

$\frac{1}{2}$ Board Thickness

Fig. 1–9. Half-lap joint.

24

Miter Joints

A miter joint is one in which the two pieces to be joined are cut at an angle, usually 45°. Once again, because the joining surfaces are end grains, this type of joint is very weak without additional reinforcement. Secondly, the "feather" or top edges of a miter joint have a tendency to shrink and open up. It is recommended that the miter joint be used only on outside corners for moldings.

Half-Lap Joint

The half-lap joint is one of the strongest right-angle joints in framing. This joint is made by re- moving one half the board thickness from each piece to be fastened, for the full width. This joint offers a broad surface for gluing and screwing.

To make a good half-lap joint, mark the pieces to be fastened, and remove one-half the board thickness in a male/female mortise and tenon con- struction. Glue the two parts and secure together with screws or clamps. (See Fig. 1–9.)

T-Lap Joints

When the half-lap joint occurs in the center of framing members, it is called a T-lap joint. The construction is similar to the half-lap joint, and it is secured in the same manner. (See Fig. 1–10.)

"T" Half-Lap

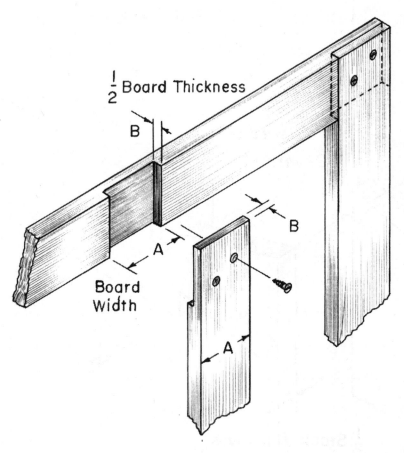

Fig. 1–10. T-lap joint.

25

Wedge Lap Joints

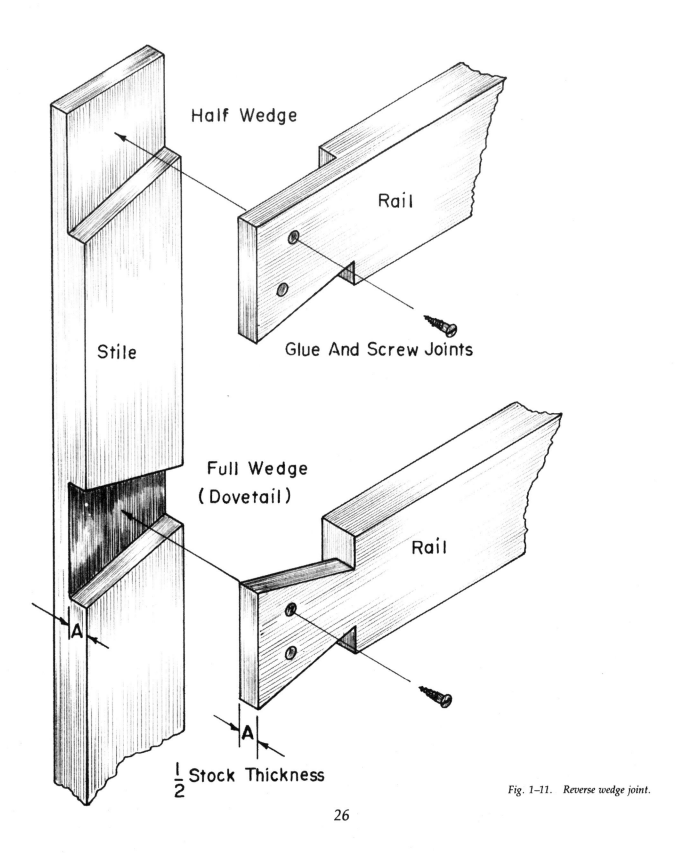

Half Wedge

Rail

Stile

Glue And Screw Joints

Full Wedge
(Dovetail)

Rail

A

$\frac{1}{2}$ Stock Thickness

Fig. 1–11. Reverse wedge joint.

26

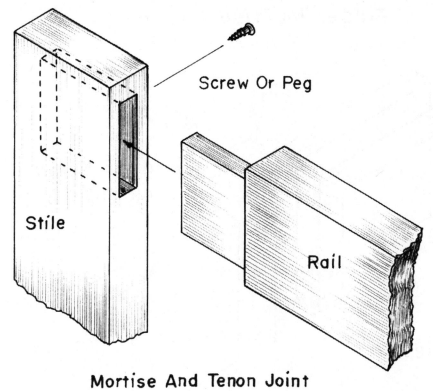

Screw Or Peg

Stile

Rail

Mortise And Tenon Joint

Fig. 1–12. Mortise and tenon joint.

Dovetail (Reverse Wedge)
Lap Joint

The dovetail or reverse wedge half-lap joint is made by cutting the male/female mortise and tenon section in the shape of a large key. The tenon section is made first and its shape marked on the mortise section. Remove the material from the female section and join together with glue and screws.

The dovetail half-lap joint is excellent for securing any downward force or strain on framing members. (See Fig. 1–11.)

Mortise & Tenon Joint

The mortise and tenon or "finger" joint has superior holding qualities, but is more difficult to construct. A tenon is a male projection that fits into a female recess or mortise. The tenon is most often made on a table saw, and the mortise is made by a mortise attachment on a drill press. Mortises can be made by means of a hand drill and chisel if preferred. Mark out the size of the intended mortise hole on the female member. Drill a line-series of holes to the desired depth. With a sharp butt chisel, cut away the stock between the drilled holes. Mark the male member from the actual mortise hole and cut the tenon with a "back" saw or table saw. It is recommended that the tenon be cut slightly oversize so that it can be custom fitted to the mortise for a tight contact. Wood pegs may be inserted for extra strength if desired. (See Fig. 1–13.)

DRAWER CONSTRUCTION

The most difficult operation in making furniture is drawer construction. Drawers are made up of several interlocking pieces: The front, back, sides, bottom, guides, and raised panels. All of these pieces have to fit together perfectly to operate in a pre-made opening.

27

Finger Mortise And Tenon Joint

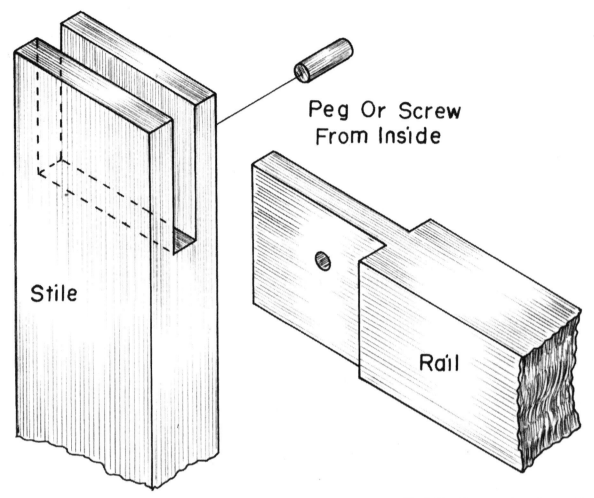

Stile

Peg Or Screw From Inside

Rail

Fig. 1–13.   Finger mortise and tenon joint.

Drawers, because of operational forces and function, require solid construction. Plain butt joint construction will not endure a great deal of wear, and is therefore recommended only on very small projects, such as a spice box.

Dovetail joints are excellent, but they require a high degree of skill to make by hand with a back saw, or with special power tools and jigs. Any of the drawers shown may be made with dovetail joints if you prefer, and if you have available tools, although dovetailing is not a necessity. (See Fig. 1–14.)

A rabbet construction will afford a happy medium between the butt joint and the dovetail joint for serviceable drawers. The rabbet construction can be made on a table saw, and it affords cross-nailing, thereby making it a solid, functional drawer, able to withstand normal stress and strain.

To make a drawer unit, two basic cuts will be employed, the rabbet end joint and the dado. The rabbet is a right angle or L-shaped cut, and the dado is a U-shaped slot. (See Fig. 1–15.)

Typical Drawer Construction

Measure the size of the drawer opening and cut the drawer stock to the required size. Determine

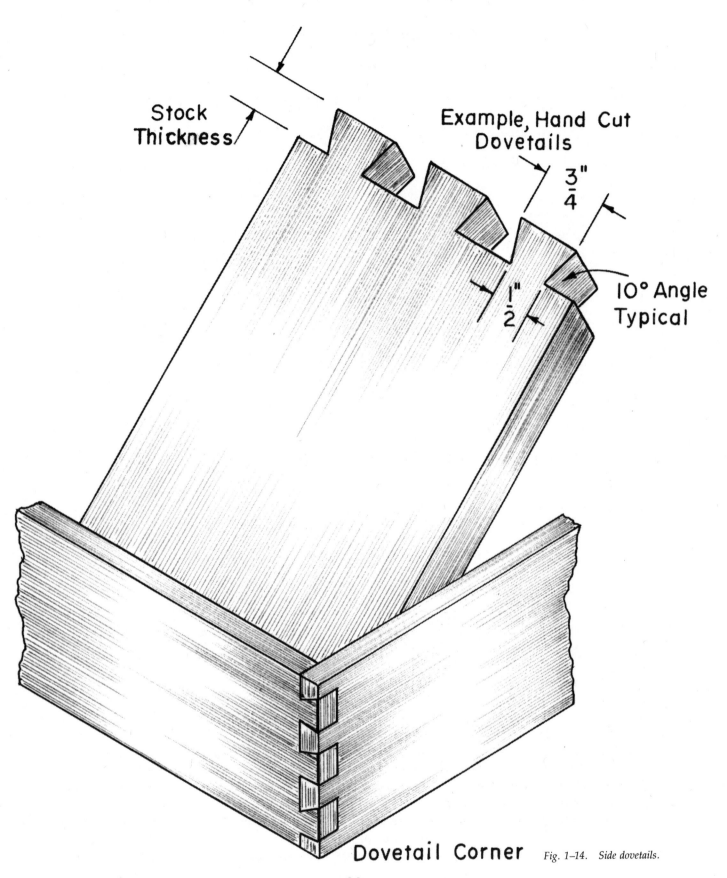

Stock
Thickness

Example, Hand Cut
Dovetails

$\frac{3}{4}$"

$\frac{1}{2}$"

10° Angle
Typical

Dovetail Corner

Fig. 1–14. Side dovetails.

29

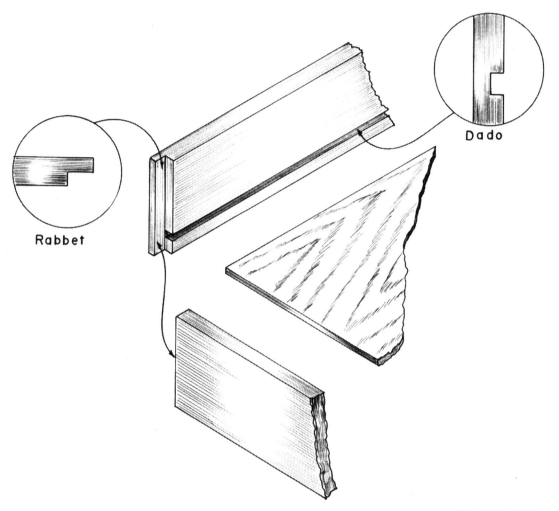

Fig. 1–15. Rabbets and dado.

what style of drawer front you want to use, either a flush or overlap construction, before cutting.

Notice that the side pieces in the rabbet joint drawer are a square cut. The rabbets are cut into the front and rear pieces so that the end grains do not show. As a rule, the rabbet depth is one-half the thickness of the drawer stock. For example, for a drawer thickness of ¾ inch, the rabbet cut would be ⅜" x ¾". A dado is cut into all four pieces about ⅝" up from the bottom to receive the ¼" plywood or hardboard bottom. The dado is ⅜", the same depth as the rabbet.

Cross-nail the drawer rear and the two drawer side-pieces together. Cut the plywood or hardwood drawer bottom to size. Insert the

drawer bottom into the pre-made dados. Fit the drawer front to the side pieces and the extending drawer bottom, and cross-nail into the rabbet joints.

Drawer Fronts

Most drawers call for a ⅜" offset or lap-over. To do this, the drawer front must be cut ¾" larger than the drawer opening. A ⅜" x ⅜" rabbet is cut in on all four sides. This will give a ⅜" overset or lap-over to the drawer front all around. If the drawer front shrinks later on, it will still cover the opening.

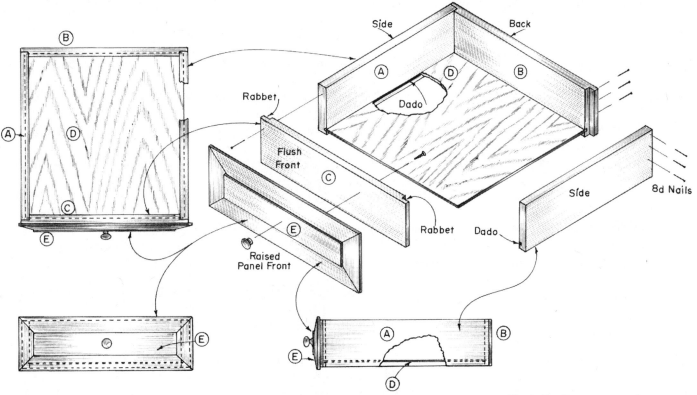

Fig. 1–16. *Drawer construction.*

RAISED PANEL DRAWER FRONTS

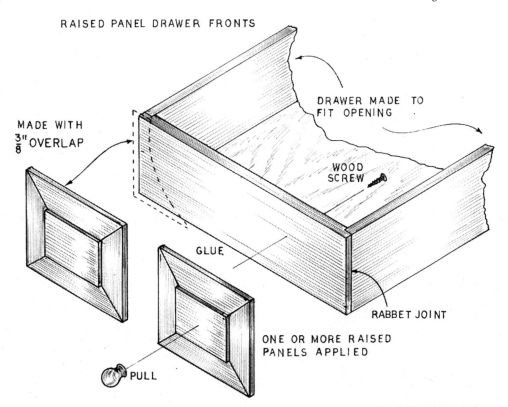

Fig. 1–17. *False raised panel drawer fronts.*

Raised Panels

Many of the drawings call for raised panel fronts. When raised panels are used, the drawer front is cut to the exact size of the opening. False drawer fronts or raised panels are cut (see Fig. 1–17), and these panels are glued and screwed to the regular drawer front piece.

The fronts or raised panels are cut so that a ⅜" offset or lap-over is achieved on the top, bottom, and sides. The space between the raised panels should be equal to the space of the rails or stiles. Figure 1–17 shows a drawer with two raised panels. The panels overlap the top and bottom plus the outside edges. The space between the two panels will be about 1¼", or the same amount that would show if a 2" rail had been used with a ⅜" lap-over on two drawers.

DRAWER GUIDES

The finest constructed drawer in the world will not operate correctly without proper drawer guides. A drawer guide supports the weight of the drawer and whatever it contains, but even more important, the guide creates a clear, easy track for smooth operation in a given direction.

There are several good methods of installing shop-made drawer guides, and each one is designed for an express purpose. Several commercial companies sell pre-made, all-purpose drawer guides that give perfect alignment and fingertip control. It is the drawer guide that makes a square and proper fit in the opening, and extra care should be given to this operation in construction.

Center Drawer Guide Assembly

This type of guide is used for center support of an open space. The center drawer guide, sometimes called an inverted "T," serves a dual purpose. First, the wide center board supports the drawer and contents in the opening. Secondly, the "T" body and drawer guide rider insure proper operation.

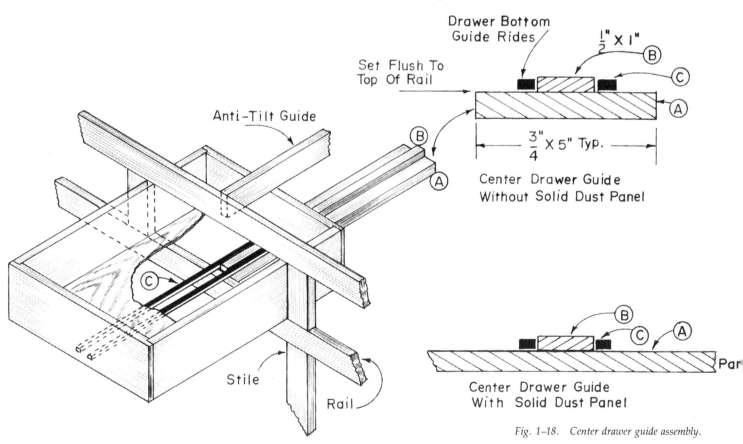

Fig. 1–18. Center drawer guide assembly.

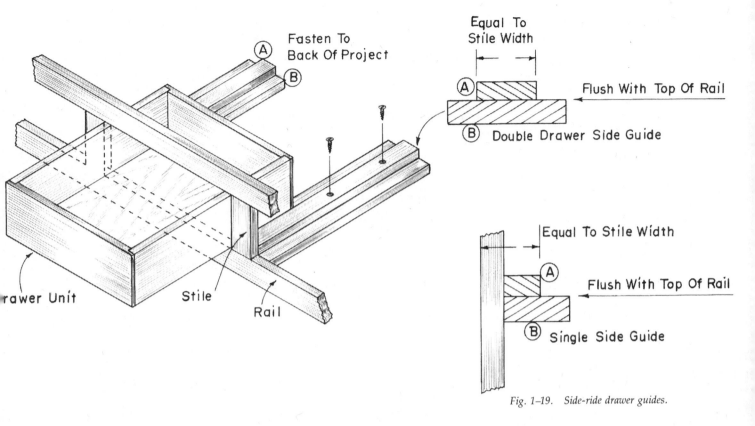

The center guide is made by installing a flat board 4 to 6 inches wide between the project front and back pieces, flush with the bottom of the drawer opening. The "T" strip, most often 1/2" x 1", is nailed in the center. A notch is cut into the back of the drawer the exact size of the strip. Small guide-ride strips are glued on each side of the drawer bottom. The guide-rides insure that the drawer will follow the "T" strip. A tilt-prevent guide is installed on top of the drawer opening. This will prevent the drawer from riding off the given track.

If a full dust panel is used between the drawer opening and the space below, the "T" body may be installed directly to this member. Drawer units can be squared to the drawer opening by moving the "T" body side to side, if necessary.

Side-Ride Drawer Guides

Side drawer guides are used for wide or large drawers, offering more support than a central drawer guide.

To make side guides, install a 1" x 4" wood member on each side of the project, flush with the bottom of the drawer opening (Part B). These are the drawer supports. Install Parts A, the drawer guides, to the supports. These pieces should be placed so as to confine the drawer proper to fit squarely and level in the opening. The sides of the drawer will ride against Part A. It is recommended that an anti-tilt guide be installed flush with the top center of the opening. (See Fig. 1–18).

Tabletop Rabbet Guides

The rabbet guide is designed for light drawers (such as the lower drawer in the cobbler's bench), that operate directly under a tabletop without any side pieces.

To make a rabbet guide, install small strips to the top sides of the drawer unit. 3/8" x 3/8" or 1/2" x 1/2", Parts B, are typical. Cut a matching size rabbet into two strips of wood so that an "L" shape

33

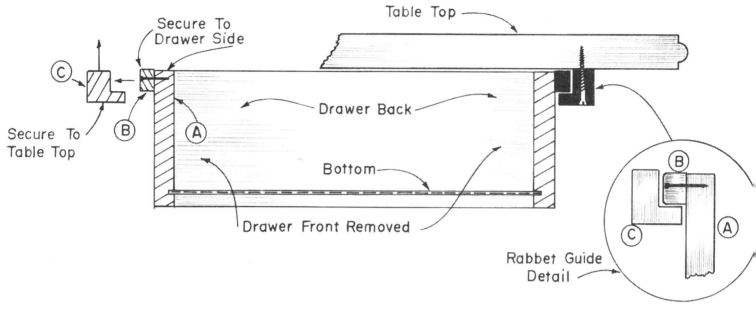

Secure To
Drawer Side

Table Top

Secure To
Table Top

Drawer Back

Bottom

Drawer Front Removed

Rabbet Guide
Detail

Fig. 1–20.   *Tabletop rabbet guides.*

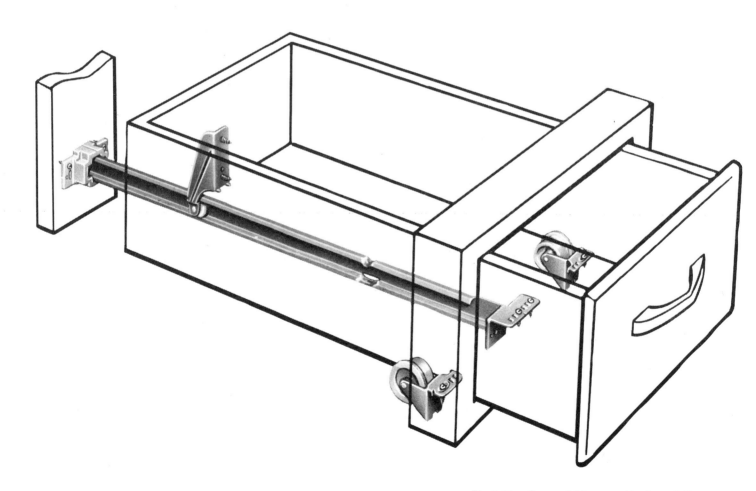

Fig. 1–21.   *Commercial drawer guide, Amerock Corp.*

is obtained. The strips on the drawer will ride in the rabbets, Parts C.

Install the rabbet strips under the tabletop as shown in Figure 1–20.

Commercial Drawer Guide

This adjustable, self-contained drawer guide was developed for use in kitchen cabinets, but it works well for any drawer. This guide has a metal track that is easily cut to the desired length. A bracket that contains a nylon wheel is attached to the rear of the drawer. The wheel runs in the track for guidance and support. Small rollers are installed in each corner for the drawer sides to ride upon.

If commercial guides are used, you should notice that the center track and side rollers take some space away from the actual opening, thus the drawer unit will be smaller in height than the opening. It would be best, in this case, to make the drawer units after the hardware has been installed. These guides work best when a false drawer front is used.

RAISED PANELS

A raised panel is one that is higher in its center, usually with rather wide beveled edges.

The amount the center is raised and its length will vary somewhat depending upon the size of the panel to be used. Figure 1–22 gives a general size used on large drawers and door units. Smaller drawer units will have smaller cuts.

Cutting Raised Panels

To cut raised panels, set the table saw blade at a 15° angle and raise the height to 1¼". Set the rip fence ¼" away from the top of the blade. Cut all four edges of the panel on this setting.

The second cut is made by bringing the saw blade back to a 90° or zero setting. Set the height of the blade to intersect the first angle cut, which should be ¼" (Fig. 1–24).

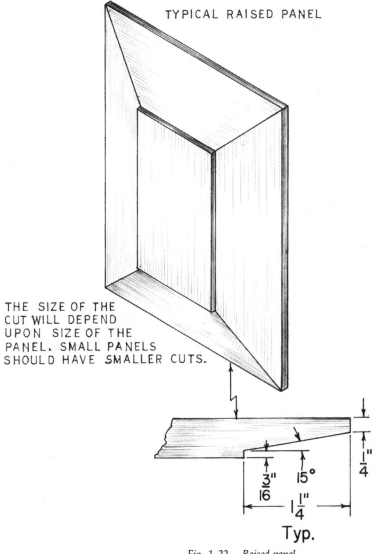

TYPICAL RAISED PANEL

THE SIZE OF THE CUT WILL DEPEND UPON SIZE OF THE PANEL. SMALL PANELS SHOULD HAVE SMALLER CUTS.

$\frac{3}{16}$" 15° $\frac{1}{4}$" $1\frac{1}{4}$"

Typ.

Fig. 1–22. Raised panel.

Set the rip fence 1¼" away from the blade (the height of the first angle cut). Cut the panel on the flat on all four sides with this setting. Sand the panel smooth, and it is ready for installation. This panel is used plain for drawer fronts, or enclosed in a frame for usage as a door panel.

DOOR FRAMING

To use the raised panel as a door unit, determine the total size of the door by allowing ¾" more than the door opening in width and height.

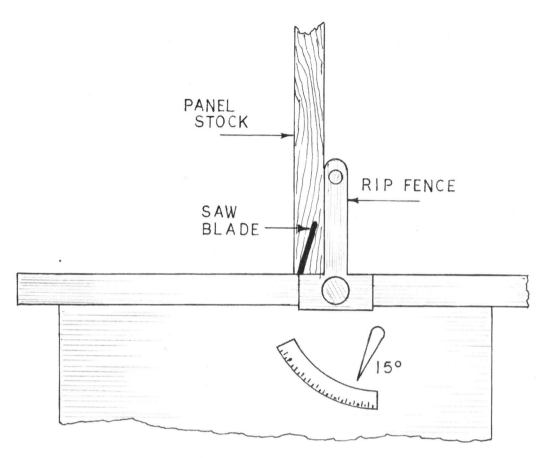

PANEL
STOCK

RIP FENCE

SAW
BLADE

15°

FIRST CUT: SET SAW BLADE TO 15°.
SET BLADE HEIGHT TO $1\frac{1}{2}$ INCHES.
CUT ALL FOUR EDGES AT THIS SETTING.

Fig. 1–23.   First saw setting for cutting raised panels.

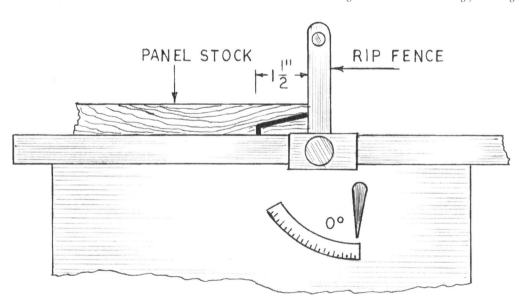

PANEL STOCK

RIP FENCE

$1\frac{1}{2}''$

0°

SECOND CUT: SET RIP FENCE OVER TO THE
HEIGHT AMOUNT OF THE FIRST CUT ($1\frac{1}{2}''$) AND
SET BLADE HEIGHT TO INTERSECT FIRST CUT.

Fig. 1–24.   Second saw setting for cutting raised panels.

Most of the raised panel door units call for a 1⅝"
by ¾" frame. The frames may be made in any one
of three ways.

Door Frame With
Mortise and Tenon Joints

Figure 1–25 shows a door frame made with a
tenon that is the same width as the ends of the
raised panel to be used. This tenon is longer than
the amount the panel will extend into the frame to
insure stronger holding power.

A dado is cut into the inside edges of all four
pieces of the door frame. The width of the dado is
determined by the size of the edge of the raised
panel. Cut tenons into the top and bottom pieces
of the frame. Assemble the door frame, leaving
out the top piece. Insert the precut raised panel,
and attach the top piece of the door frame. This
door unit is then cut with ⅜" x ⅜" rabbet on the
back outer edges, and is installed in the opening
with either ⅜" inset or offset hinges.

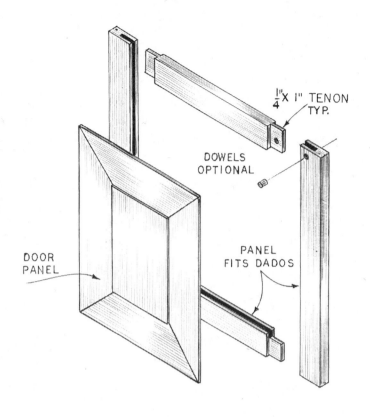

MORTISE AND TENON FRAME

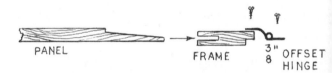

Fig. 1–25. Door frame with mortise and tenon.

REINFORCED MITER JOINTS

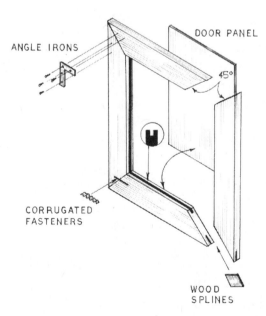

Fig. 1–26. Door frame with miter joints (reinforced).

Door Frame With Miter Joints

Another method of making the door unit is that
of using mitred (45°), joints in place of the mortise
and tenon joints. The miter joint is not as strong
as the tenon joint, but is easier to make. However-
er, strength may be added in any of the three
ways suggested in Figure 1–26. The same measurements are used as in the tenon method. Cut a
dado inside the frame pieces to receive the raised
panel. Miter-cut all four pieces of the frame. As-

37

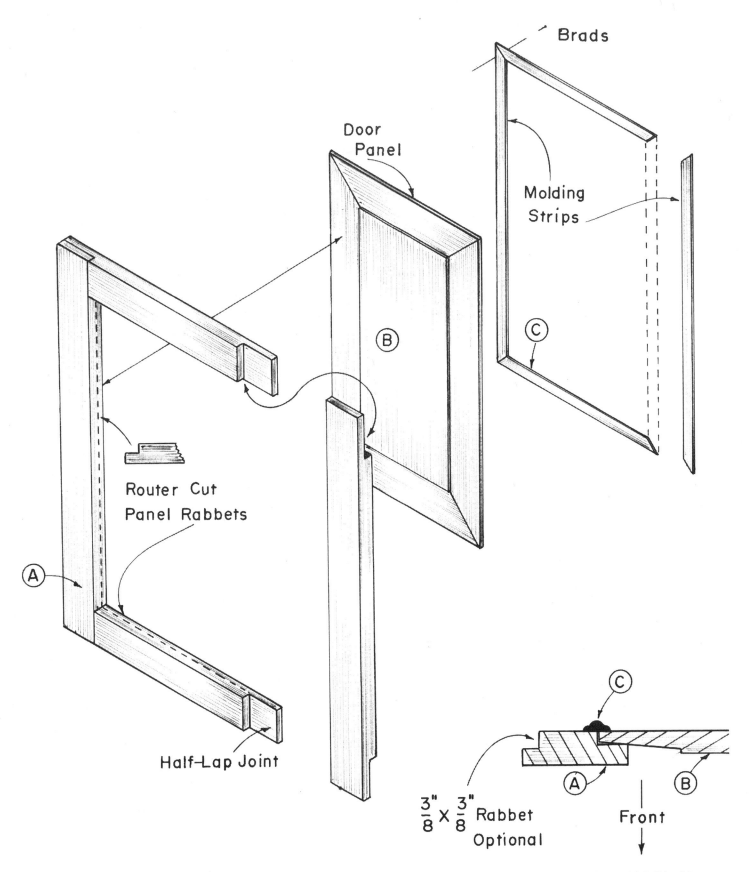

Brads

Door
Panel

Molding
Strips

B

C

Router Cut
Panel Rabbets

A

Half-Lap Joint

C

A   B

$\frac{3}{8}" \times \frac{3}{8}"$ Rabbet
Optional

Front

Fig. 1–27. Door frame with half-lap joints.

semble the frame over the raised panel like a picture frame. Cut the required ⅜" x ⅜" rear rabbet and install with offset or inset hardware.

Door Frame With
Half-Lap Joints

Perhaps the best method is the old standby, the half-lap. Measure the frame from stock ¾" wider and higher than the opening. Cut a half-lap joint on each end and construct a frame (See Fig. 1–9, framing joints, for details.)

Glue and secure the frame joints. When the glue has dried, cut a rabbet on the rear inside edges to receive the raised panel. A rabbet bit in an electric router is recommended.

Insert the pre-made raised panel into the rabbet. Cover the opening between panel and frame with thin flat moldings. Cut a ⅜" x ⅜" rabbet on the outside edges of the door frame and install the unit into its opening with ⅜" offset hinges.

HARDWARE

Flush doors, those made the exact size of the opening, when made of pine, will soon shrink, and within a few months be ⅛" to ¼" undersize. In view of this fact a ⅜" offset door is recommended for most of the projects. If you want the whole hinge to show, use a ⅜" offset hinge. Many companies make these hinges in the butterfly, "H", "H and L", and spearpoint design. However, if you want very little hinge to show, use a ⅜" inset hinge. Door or drawer pulls can be purchased to match the hinges. The door catches may be friction or magnetic.

LEG FASTENING

Because this book is based upon colonial furniture, the legs on the items included are plain round, not lathe-turned. Round legs on the cobbler's bench and other projects are fastened by drilling a hole in the leg support or scab to match

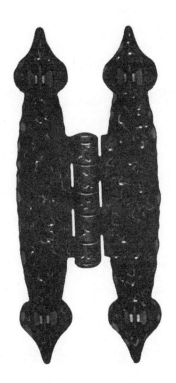

Fig. 1–29. Flush hinge, Amerock Corp.

Fig. 1–30. Flush "H and L" hinge, Amerock Corp.

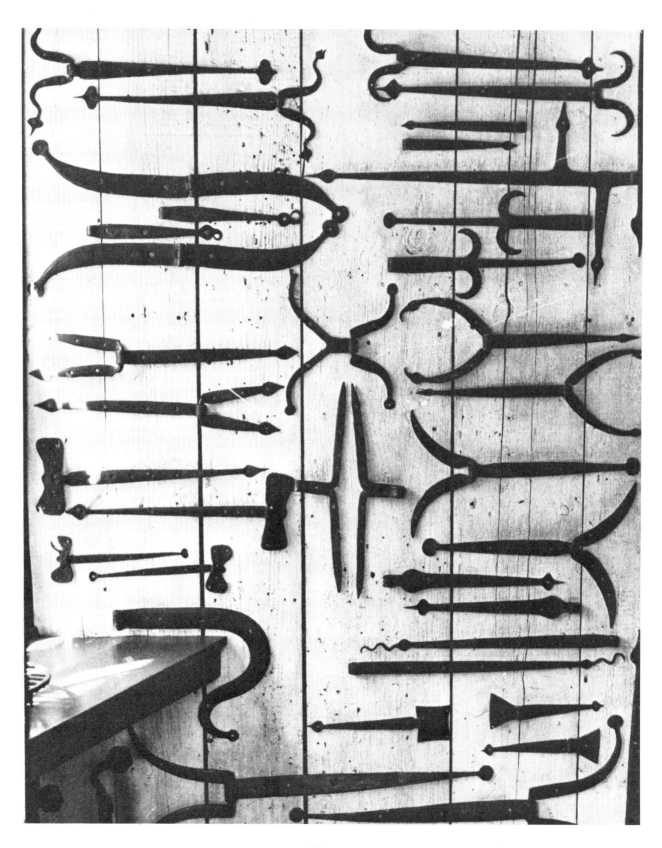

Fig. 1–28. Hardware, Old Sturbridge Village, Sturbridge, Massachusetts.

Fig. 1–31.   *Flush strap hinge, Amerock Corp.*

the size of the leg. Fit the leg into the hole. Adjust the fit with a rasp or file if necessary.

Cut a V-like slot across the top of the leg as shown in Figure 1–33. Cut a wedge a little shorter than the depth of the V-slot cut in the leg. Glue the leg into the pre-drilled hole, and glue and drive the wedge into the slot. A cross-dowel pin may be installed if so desired; many colonial pieces had such pins. After the glue has dried, trim off the wedge flush with the top of the leg support.

FRAME CONSTRUCTION

Many items require framing much like kitchen

Fig. 1–32.   *Offset (³⁄₈″) "H" hinge, Amerock Corp.*

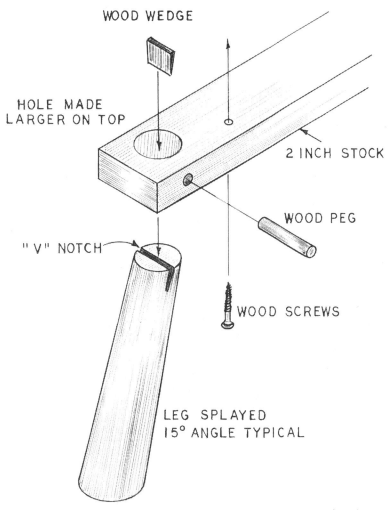

WOOD WEDGE

HOLE MADE
LARGER ON TOP

2 INCH STOCK

WOOD PEG

"V" NOTCH

WOOD SCREWS

LEG SPLAYED
15° ANGLE TYPICAL

Fig. 1–33. Leg fastening.

Lower Skirt Boards

The cyma curve found on most colonial furniture serves two functions. It gives the piece a classic form, and it also creates a leg for the unit. A full board will warp, causing a long piece of stock to rock on the high point. The cyma curve scroll in the skirt board relieves this by making the skirt into two short legs. Notice in Figure 1–35, the skirt is cut so that only the two extreme ends bear the weight of the object. Similar but smaller cuts are made on the side pieces so that the result is four leg-like structures instead of three solid boards.

FINISHING

There are as many methods of finishing furniture as there are people making it. The method given here is one that has been found to produce the best results with the least amount of special tools, skill, and time involved.

Distressing

Distressing is a means of intentionally cutting or marking the new piece in order to reproduce the wear on the original old pieces. If you have not tried this method before, practice on a piece of scrap wood. Stain and lacquer this piece of scrap in order to see the final result. Distress marks are more pronounced after staining and finishing.

Distressing can be extreme or minimal. For light distressing, strike the surface a few times with a rock at random locations, or roll the rock across the piece. Staining will bring out the grooves and digs made by the rock. For heavy distressing, cut 1″ x 1/32″ slots into the surface of the furniture about 1/16″ deep. Do not overdo it. The appearance of wormholes can be achieved by using an awl or a nail. Punch clusters of angled holes in several places. These punched holes, after staining, will appear as wormholes. When you are finished distressing the furniture, sand the unit completely, rounding out all cuts and dents. The square edges of authentic colonial pieces are always rounded off, much like stair treads, by the many years of wear.

cabinet work. Colonial craftsmen did not try to hide all end grains, nor should you.

In Figure 1–34 the side pieces have been glued up to the desired width. (¾″ plywood, cut to size, may be substituted.) A ¼″ x ⅜″ rabbet is cut at the rear inside edge to take the back piece of ¼″ plywood or hardboard. The front rails and stiles are nailed, glued, or screwed to the side pieces. Drawer guides are screwed to the side pieces where needed. The drawer guides should be a little shorter than the side pieces because they will shrink less than the side pieces and will push out the rails or stiles. The center drawer guide serves a double purpose; to keep the drawer unit steady and to help secure the top piece. Any method of framing will serve the purpose, and Figure 1–34 is given only as an example. Half-lap joints between the rails and stiles will be excellent for framing.

CABINET CONSTRUCTION

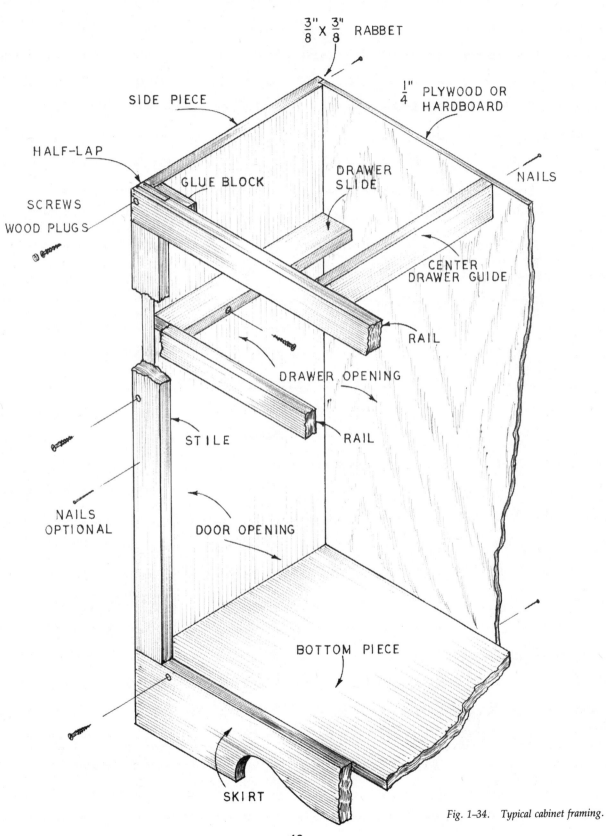

$\frac{3"}{8}$ X $\frac{3"}{8}$ RABBET

SIDE PIECE

$\frac{1}{4}"$ PLYWOOD OR HARDBOARD

HALF-LAP

GLUE BLOCK

DRAWER SLIDE

NAILS

SCREWS
WOOD PLUGS

CENTER DRAWER GUIDE

RAIL

DRAWER OPENING

STILE

RAIL

NAILS OPTIONAL

DOOR OPENING

BOTTOM PIECE

SKIRT

Fig. 1–34. Typical cabinet framing.

43

Staining

Any oil-based or water-based stain will do. Most of the pieces illustrated were finished with an oil stain called "Old Pine," which is a very dark stain. Many paint companies sell stains under names such as antique pine, Salem maple, or nutmeg maple, to name a few. Once you have chosen a stain, try some on a scrap piece of wood, because the woods will take the stain differently, depending upon the openness of the grain. Remember that the lacquer finish will change the stain by giving depth to the finish.

Apply the stain according to manufacturer's directions, allowing a little time for penetration. Pine soaks up stain much quicker than hardwoods, so do not wait too long before wiping off the excess stain. Wipe the project down with a rag to achieve an even coat. Allow stain to dry for 24 hours before sealing.

Painting

Some projects, such as the signboards and weathervanes, call for painting in colors. All of the painted objects in this book were painted with a latex wall paint; however, any water-based paint will do. The Deft® Company makes many water-based stains and colors that may be used, and I find that I have always had good results with them. They are available in small amounts, are inexpensive and will not dry up with limited usage. If you have a favorite brand, by all means continue to use it.

Sealer Coat

Lacquer applied over an *oil-based* paint will "lift" the finish, however, it may be applied directly to water-based paints with no difficulty. If an oil-based paint is used, the surface must be sealed before any lacquer or Deft® is applied. To seal an oil-based paint, apply one or two coats of white shellac, cut 50/50 with alcohol. Lacquer or Deft® may then be applied with no problems.

This coat locks in the stain or color. More important, pine wood, even when sanded smooth, still has small hair-like fibers that lie down under sanding, thus cannot be sanded off. The sealer coat stiffens these fibers, and a light sanding after sealing removes them completely. The sealer coat may be any brushing lacquer, Deft®, or cut shellac.

Glazing

Glazing is used on some items, a good example being the signboard. The glaze is made up of one part flat black paint and one part turpentine. Wipe this glaze onto the project after the sealer coat has dried. Let it stand for a few minutes for penetration and wipe down with a cloth. The flat black glaze will dull the bright colors and give the project a weathered look. Cover this glaze with another sealer coat of shellac or lacquer. Sand lightly when it is dry.

Finish

After the sealer coats have dried, apply the finish. A very satisfactory finish can be achieved by using several coats of Deft®, lacquer, or similar finish. Sand between every two coats. A white powder will result from this sanding; wipe the white powder off and apply two more coats before sanding again. Deft® and most lacquers dry very quickly, so that you can often apply two or even four coats a day. Allow two hours between coats. Build up your finish with at least six to eight coats.

Final Steps

When the last coat of finish has dried overnight, rub the entire piece with a mixture of lemon oil and fine pumice or rottenstone. Fine steel wool may be used in place of the pumice if you desire. Be sure to rub in the direction of the

SKIRT BOARDS

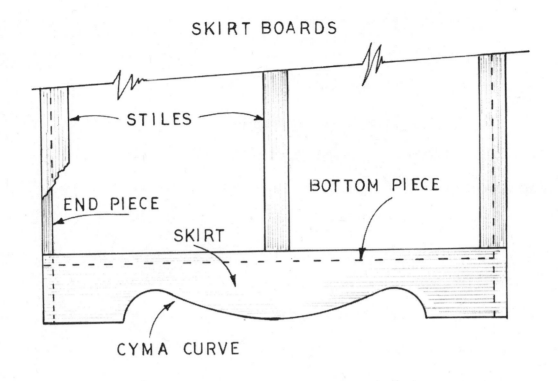

STILES

END PIECE

BOTTOM PIECE

SKIRT

CYMA CURVE

ALTERNATE DESIGNS

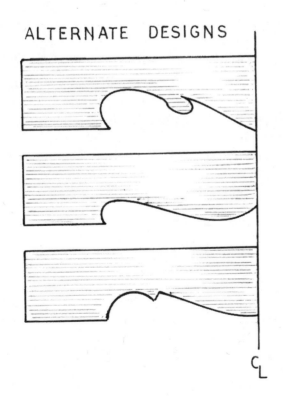

C_L

SMALL END
SHAKER
DESIGN

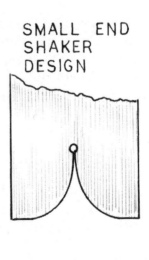

Fig. 1–35. Cyma curve skirt board.

Fig. 1–36. Decorated chest, Storrowton Village, Springfield, Massachusetts.

grain. The old saying about hand-rubbed finishes still holds true. Rubbing the oil and pumice into the furniture with the palm of the hand produces the most pleasing results. After rubbing the piece to a high sheen, wipe it clean with clear lemon oil and dry the piece. Put on a coat of clear paste wax, allow the wax to dry, and buff to a mellow shine.

Shelves, Chests, and Cupboards

The colonial joiner was a master at his trade, that of making tight, lasting joints. The joiner was responsible for making smooth, graceful moldings and finished millwork from rough planks. All he had with which to work were hand tools and his skill.

The village joiner often made furniture that above all else, was ingenious in design and construction. The pieces he made were simple and serviceable, and excelled in the quality of joinery, cutting, smoothing, turning, and finishing. The finished furniture was usually a local interpretation of classical form and function, and not a direct copy of European prototypes. The plans presented here are based upon some of the best examples of early colonial work made by local craftsmen. The "hand-made" appearance and native timber add to the warmth and style of these timeless pieces.

Fig. 2–1.   *Joiner at work, Colonial Williamsburg, Williamsburg, Virginia.*

Fig. 2–2. *Simple wall shelf, Index of American Design, Washington, D. C.*

Fig. 2–3. Wall shelf project.

Wall Shelf

The colonists did not have cabinets as we do today, and most of their kitchen tools and dishes were stored upon open shelves, much like the one in Figure 2–3. This wall unit was developed from such shelves, and may be adapted to the dimensions that meet your needs. For extra long shelves, it is suggested that three bracket supports be used.

Material List

Part	Number	Size	Material
Shelf	1	9″ x 36″ x 1½″	Pine
Shelf Support	2	6″ x 9″ x 1½″	

CONSTRUCTION

1. Cut the shelf stock to the length desired; round off both corners. A 1″ radius may be used. Using an "ogee" bit in an electric router, cut a molding on the two edges and front end, top and bottom. The rear edge is not routed.

2. Lay out and cut stock for the supports as suggested in Figure 2–4. Cut in the ogee-molded edge on the bracket fronts. Drill two ½″ diameter holes, 1″ deep, into the top of each support. Cut a ½″ wide by 2″ long by ¾″ deep dado into the rear top edge on the back of each support. (see detail). Glue ½″ hardwood dowels into the holes in the top of the shelf support, allowing ¾″ of doweling to extend beyond the top.

3. Cut two pieces of metal to fit over the dado cut into the back of the shelf support. Drill a hole a little larger than the size of the mounting screw head to be used. Cut a slot from this hole, up about 1″. The slot size should be slightly larger than the screw shank. Using four 1″ brads or flathead nails, secure the metal to the shelf support covering the pre-made dados.

4. Drill holes into the shelf to match the dowels extending into the supports. The back edges of the supports and the shelf should be flush. Glue the shelf to the supports with the dowels.

FINISH

Sand the shelf and supports smooth. Stain. Cover with several coats of lacquer or similar finish. Apply paste wax; buff.

MOUNTING

To mount the finished shelf to the wall, locate two studs in the wall, and mark them at the desired height. Screw two flathead wood screws into the studs allowing the heads to extend out ¼″. Place the large holes in the metal strips over the extended screw heads and let the supports slide down. The screw shanks will slide along the slots cut into the metal strips. If the shelf is too far out from the wall, remove shelf and adjust the screw heads until the correct position is attained. If a "between the studs" location is desired, use wall anchor bolts or plastic shields in the plaster or sheet rock walls (this type of mounting will not support heavy weights).

50

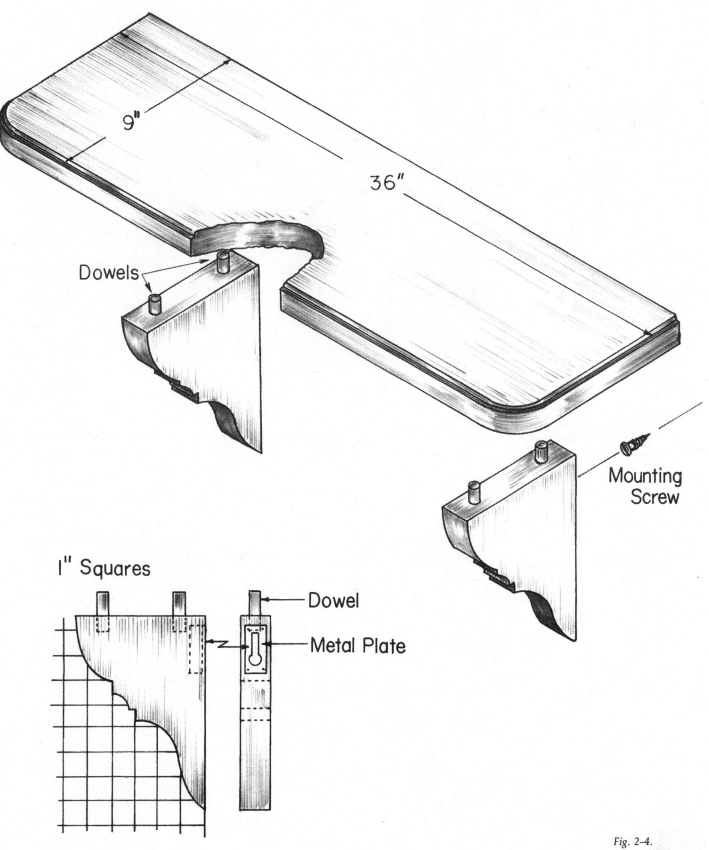

9"

36"

Dowels

Mounting
Screw

I" Squares

Dowel

Metal Plate

Fig. 2–4.

Bedside Wall Shelf

Fig. 2–5. Bedside wall shelf project.

Not a reproduction of an original, but more of a representation of various examples built by early settlers to serve their needs, this bedside shelf was developed from the one shown in Figure 2–3. It may be used beside a bed as a night stand and telephone shelf, or will serve as a small shelf in a hallway, for it does not require much space. Adjust the dimensions to your own requirements.

Material List

Part		Number	Size	Material
A		1	14″ x 32″ x ¾″	Pine
B		2	12″ x 21″ x ¾″	
C		1	13″ x 26″ x ¾″	
D	Drawer			
	Front	1	4″ x 26″ x ¾″	
	Sides	2	4″ x 11″ x ¾″	
	Back	1	4″ x 26″ x ¾″	
E		2	⅜″ x ⅜″ x 11″	
F		1	11¾″ x 25″ x ¼″	Plywood

CONSTRUCTION

1. Lay out and cut Part A. Round over the front and side edges or use an ogee bit in an electric router to create an edging. Mark and drill holes for screws and plugs.

2. Lay out and cut Parts B. Mark and drill holes for screws and plugs as shown in Figure 2–6.

3. Lay out and cut the stock for Part C (an ogee edge may be used on the outside if desired). Screw Part A into Parts B and screw Parts B into Part C. Glue in hardwood plugs over the screw heads.

4. Make a drawer unit 25⅞″ x 11″ x 4″ (or according to your needs), using the methods suggested in *Section One*. This drawer unit has a double raised panel front. Fit the finished drawer to the assembled wall shelf and mark the drawer guides. Nail Parts E to the sides of Parts B. Fill and set all nail holes.

FINISH

Distress if desired; sand all parts smooth. Stain or paint in the color of your choice. Cover with several coats of lacquer or similar finish.

Attach to the wall of the house with a ¾″ x 1¼″ stringer.

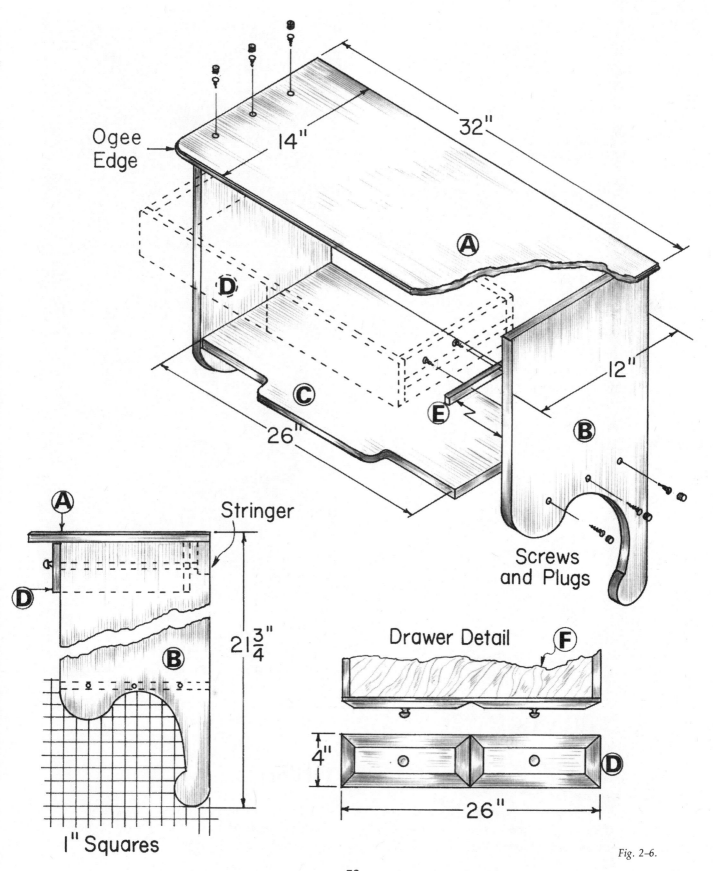

Ogee Edge

32"

14"

(A)

(D)

12"

(C)

(B)

26"

(E)

Screws and Plugs

(A)

Stringer

(D)

(B)

21 3/4"

1" Squares

Drawer Detail (F)

4"

(D)

26"

Fig. 2–6.

53

Shelburne Wall Shelf (Hutch)

This piece is more than just shelves—it is a compromise between a series of open shelves and a hutch-dresser type of construction. The cyma-curved sides and different depth shelves suggest the style often found in hutch tops. It is an unusual wall piece adapted from the original in the Shelburne Museum.

Note: Except for pieces B and C, all the shelves are different widths because of the shape of Parts A. The front edges of the shelves will follow the curve of Part A at that particular spot.

Material List

Part		Number	Size	Material
A	Sides	2	10½" x 36" x ¾"	Pine
B	Shelf	1	7" x 24" x ¾"	
C	Shelf	1	7" x 24" x ¾"	
D	Shelf	1	10" x 24" x ¾"	
E	Shelf	1	6⅞" x 24" x ¾"	
F	Shelf	1	5¾" x 24" x ¾"	
G	Shelf	1	8" x 24" x ¾"	
H	Back	1	24¾" x 35¼" x ¼"	Plywood
I	Spacer	1	4" x 6⅝" x ¾"	
J	Drawer	2	4" x 11⅝" x 6⅝"	

CONSTRUCTION

1. Lay out and cut stock for Parts A. (See detail, Fig. 2–8.) Cut a ⅜" x ⅜" rabbet on the back edges for Part H.

2. Lay out and cut the shelves, Parts B, C, D, E, F, and G to the required sizes, depending upon placement on Parts A. Nail Parts A into Parts B,

Fig. 2–7. Shelburne wall shelf (hutch), project.

C, D, E, F, and G, remembering to keep the back edges even with the pre-cut rabbets.

3. Nail Part H into the rabbets on Parts A and into the shelves. Cut a spacer and nail into the center opening between Parts B and C. Make two drawer units, Part J, to fit the openings. See *Section One* for drawer details.

FINISH

Set and fill all nail holes. Sand entire project smooth. Stain or paint. Cover with several coats of lacquer. Finish with paste wax.

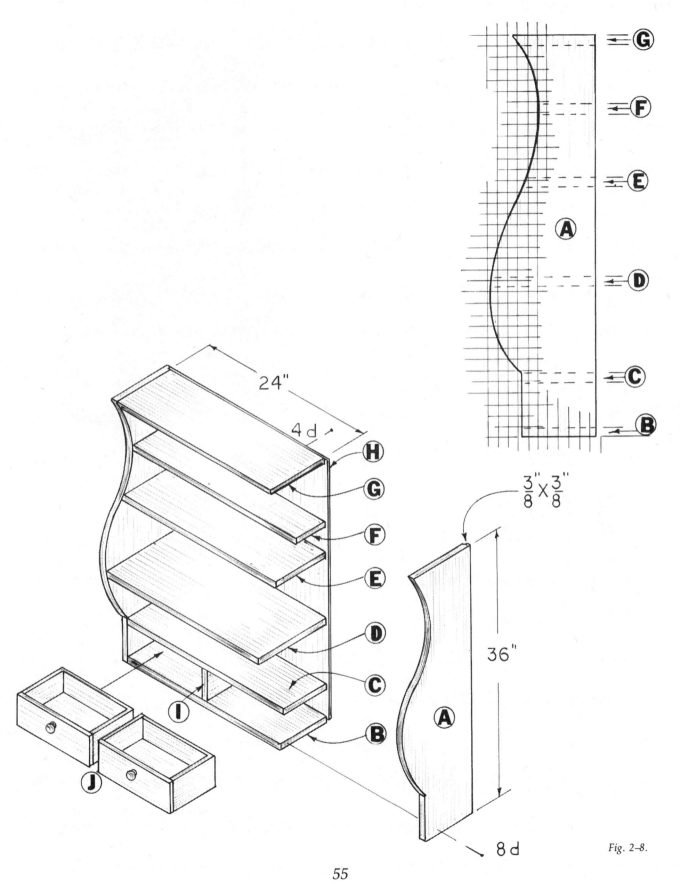

24"

4 d

$\frac{3"}{8} \times \frac{3"}{8}$

36"

8 d

H
G
F
E
D
C
B

I

J

A

G
F
E
A
D
C
B

Fig. 2–8.

55

Hutch Cupboard (Dresser)

Colonial kitchen "cabinets" consisted of a few boards pegged against a wall, for neither time nor economics afforded more. With the establishment of local cabinetmakers and joiners, the simple open shelving gave way to more refined and lasting work. Enclosed areas with doors and drawers were constructed for storage, but due to a longing for things of beauty and a natural pride of ownership, the best pewter and china was kept on display in open shelving for all to see. In time, the very simple cupboard developed into the "dresser" or what we now call the "hutch." The open shelves were retained, held by gracefully scalloped side boards. Often spice or herb drawers were placed between the open shelves. The doors and drawers were retained in the lower unit to provide additional storage.

The hutch dresser is made in two pieces; the lower dresser, and the top display area complete with spice drawers.

Note: Material lists and construction details are given in two separate sections: The lower unit, and the top display unit.

Fig. 2–9. Colonial hutch with open pewter shelves, Index of American Design, Washington, D. C.

Hardware (Typical)

Three pairs ⅜" offset or inset (dependent upon type of door construction), hinges.
Three catches, magnetic or friction.
Six ¾" diameter porcelain pulls.

Hutch Bottom Unit Material List

	Part	Number	Size	Material
A	Sides	2	18" x 28" x ¾"	Cherry,
B	Bottom	1	17⅝" x 46½" x ¾"	Pine,
C	Back	1	28" x 47" x ¼"	or Wood
D	Skirt	1	4" x 48" x ¾"	of Choice
E	Top Rail	1	3" x 48" x ¾"	
F	Center Rail	1	2" x 48" x ¾"	
G	Stiles	4	2" x 21" x ¾"	
H	Backer Rails	2	2½" x 46½" x ¾"	
I	Outer Drawer Guides	2	2½" x 17⅜" x ¾"	
J	Inner Drawer Guides	2	4" x 17⅜" x ¾"	
K	Top Drawer Guides	3	3½" x 17⅜" x ¾"	
L	Dentil Trim	2	1½" x 18¾" x ⅜"	
		1	1½" x 48¾" x ⅜"	
M	Top	1	20½" x 53" x 2"	
N	Doors	3	14¾" x 14⅛" x ¾"	
O	Drawers	3	5" x 13⅜" x 18"	

CONSTRUCTION

1. Lay out and cut the stock for parts A, B, and C. Cut a ⅜" x ⅜" rabbet on the rear inside edges of Parts A. Nail Parts A to Part B. Keep Part B up 4" from the bottom so that it will be flush with the top of the skirt, Part D. Keep Part B even with the front edges of Parts A. Nail Part C into the rabbets cut into Part A. Part C will run past the back edge of Part B even with the bottoms of Part A.

2. Lay out and cut the stock for Parts D, E, F, and G. (See details in Fig. 2–11.) Nail Part D into Parts A and B. Make a ⅜" deep ship-lap joint on

Parts E, F, and G where they cross one another. Glue and nail Parts E, F, and G together. Nail finished assembly into Parts A and D.

3. Lay out and cut the stock for Parts H. Glue and nail Parts H to Parts A and C. Lay out and cut the stock for the drawer guides (Parts I, J, and K). Install the outer drawer guides (Parts I), to Parts A, C, and H. Nail center guides (Part J), to Parts F, H, and C. Nail Parts K in center of drawer opening, square with the front.

4. Lay out and cut the stock for the dentil trim, Parts L. Miter the corner joints. Install the trim to Parts A and E flush with the top of the unit with small brads.

5. Glue up the stock for the top, Part M. Cut the top. With a router, cut a molded edge top and bottom, leaving the back edge plain. (See sectional drawing, Fig. 2–11.) If decorative butterfly dovetail locks are to be used, do the following: cut the dovetail pieces from ⅜″ stock, mark the cut pieces on the top of Part M where the joints of the glued-up stock occur, cut out the female dovetails with a router or chisel, glue in the pre-cut dovetail pieces and sand flush after the glue has dried.

6. Make three raised panel doors (Parts N), to fit the door openings with a ⅜″ overlap all around. (See *Section One* for door details.) Install the finished doors to the hutch unit with hinges.

7. Make three raised panel drawers, Parts O, to fit the openings with a ⅜″ overlap all around. (See *Section One*, drawer construction, for details.) Adjust the drawer guides, if necessary, for proper fit and action.

FINISH

Set and fill all nail holes. Sand the project smooth. Stain. Cover with several coats of lacquer or similar finish. Hand rub with pumice and lemon oil. Apply paste wax and buff.

Hutch Top Material List

Part		Number	Size	Material
A	Sides	2	8″ x 40″ x 1¾″	Same as lower unit
B	Top	1	10″ x 51″ x ¾″	
C	Back	1	40⅜″ x 45″ x ¼″	Plywood
D	Top Shelf	1	6″ x 45″ x ¾″	to match

Part		Number	Size	Material
E	Lower Shelves	2	6″ x 45″ x ¾″	
F	Shelf Skirts	2	2″ x 43½″ x ½″	
G	Top Skirt	1	2¾″ x 43½″ x ½″	
H	Dentils	1	1¼″ x 47¾″ x ⅜″	
		2	1¼″ x 8⅜″ x ⅜″	
I	Spice Drawers	3	3½″ x 15″ x 5½″	

Hardware

Six ½″ diameter porcelain pulls.

CONSTRUCTION

1. Study Figure 2–13 for the suggested shapes.

2. Lay out and cut Parts A. Cut in the design of the scrollwork. Cut a ⅜″ x 1″ rabbet on the rear inside edges for Part C. Cut a ¾″ x ¾″ dado where indicated for Parts D and E. Sand all scrollwork smooth. (Clamp both pieces of Parts A together when filing and sanding so that they will be identical.)

3. Lay out and cut the stock for Parts D and E. Cut a ¼″ x ⅜″ dado on the top of each board, 1″ in from the back edge to act as a dish rail or holder. Lay out and cut the stock for Part B. Cut the

Fig. 2–10. Hutch cupboard (dresser), project.

57

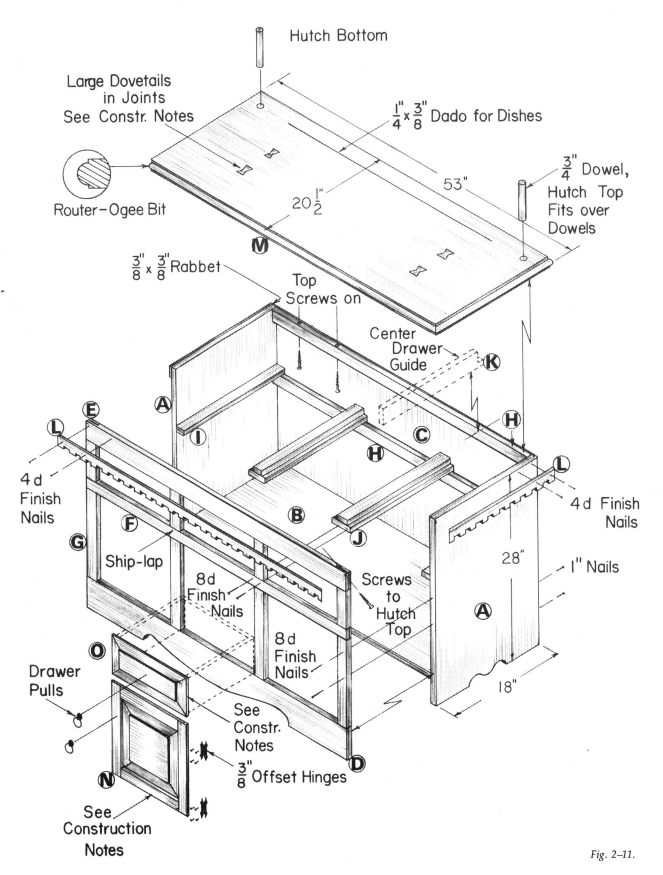

Hutch Bottom

Large Dovetails
in Joints
See Constr. Notes

$\frac{1}{4}" \times \frac{3}{8}"$ Dado for Dishes

Router—Ogee Bit

53"

$\frac{3}{4}"$ Dowel,
Hutch Top
Fits over
Dowels

$20\frac{1}{2}"$

$\frac{3}{8}" \times \frac{3}{8}"$ Rabbet

M

Top
Screws on

Center
Drawer
Guide

K

E

A

L

I

H

C

H

4 d
Finish
Nails

4 d Finish
Nails

G

F

B

J

Ship-lap

Screws
to
Hutch
Top

28"

A

1" Nails

8 d
Finish
Nails

8 d
Finish
Nails

O

Drawer
Pulls

See
Constr.
Notes

18"

N

$\frac{3}{8}"$ Offset Hinges

D

See
Construction
Notes

Fig. 2–11.

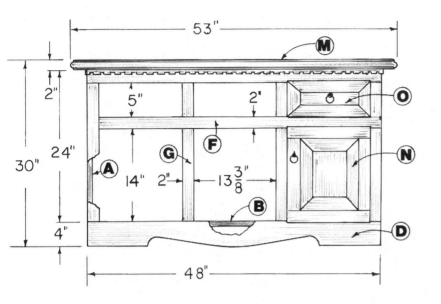

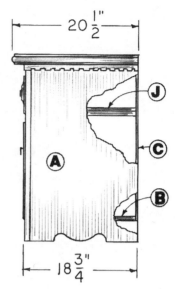

Fig. 2–12.

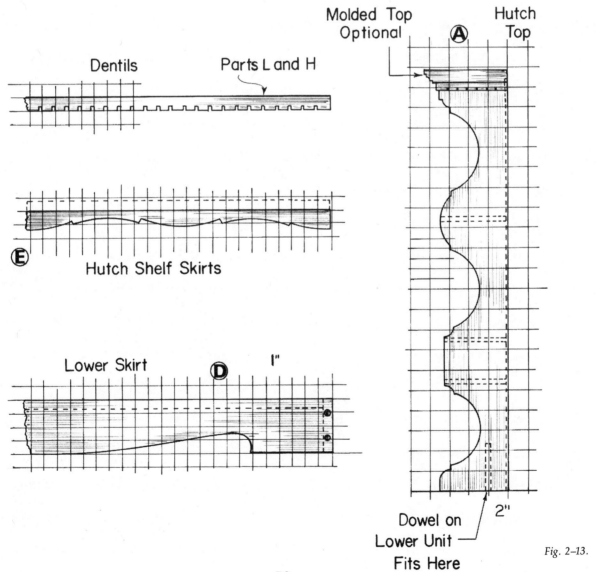

Dentils

Parts L and H

Hutch Shelf Skirts

E

Lower Skirt   D   1"

Molded Top
Optional   A   Hutch
                              Top

Dowel on
Lower Unit
Fits Here   2"

Fig. 2–13.

59

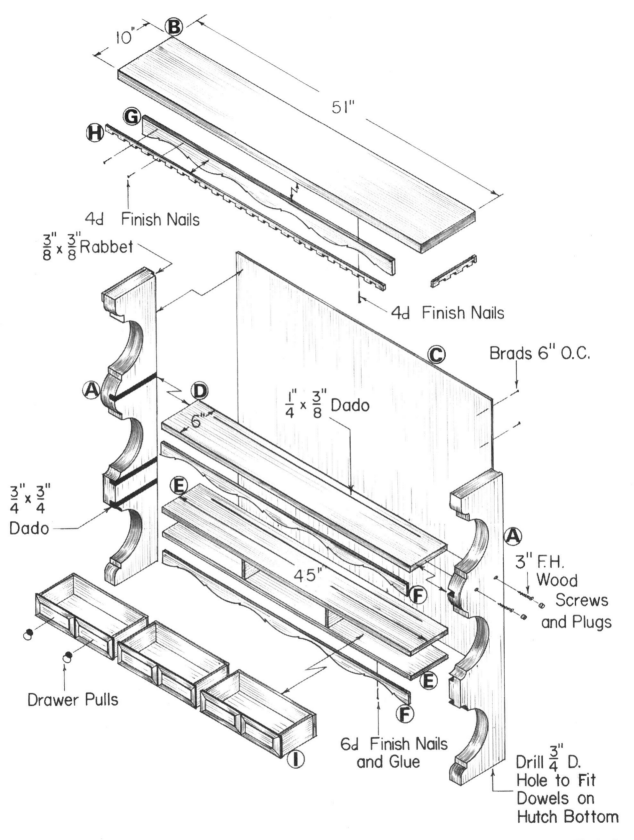

10"

B

51"

H **G**

4d Finish Nails

$\frac{3}{8}$" x $\frac{3}{8}$" Rabbet

4d Finish Nails

C

Brads 6" O.C.

A

D

$\frac{1}{4}$" x $\frac{3}{8}$" Dado

6"

$\frac{3}{4}$" x $\frac{3}{4}$"
Dado

E

45"

F

A

3" F.H.
Wood
Screws
and Plugs

E

Drawer Pulls

F

6d Finish Nails
and Glue

I

Drill $\frac{3}{4}$" D.
Hole to Fit
Dowels on
Hutch Bottom

Fig. 2–14.

60

molded edge (optional), on Part B with a router. Cut a ⅜″ x ⅜″ blind rabbet at the back edge so that Part C will fit into it.

4. Glue and nail Parts D and E into the dados precut on Part A, keeping the rear edges of Parts D and E flush with the rabbets cut into Parts A. Screw Part B down into Part A. Insert Part C into the precut rabbets and nail firmly into Parts A, B, D, and E.

5. Lay out and cut Parts F and G. Sand all scrollwork smooth. Secure Parts F to Parts D and E with small brads. Nail Part G under Part B.

6. Lay out and cut Part H. Nail the dentil, Parts H, to Parts A and G, under and tight to Part B. Make miter joints on outside edges.

7. Put small spacers between Parts E. Make these spacers from scrap ½″ stock. Make three double-face raised panel spice drawers. (See *Section One* for drawer construction details.) Spice drawers, Parts I, should have a ¼″ lap-over all around.

8. To secure the hutch top to the hutch bottom,

install a ¾″ diameter by 6″ long dowel into the *top surface* of the *hutch bottom* where Parts A of the hutch top fit when that unit is placed upon the bottom unit. Glue these dowels into Part M of the hutch bottom unit, leaving 4″ of the dowel extending. Carefully drill a ¾″ diameter hole, 4½″ deep into each Part A of the hutch top. (See detail drawing in Fig. 2–11.) Slip the hutch top over the dowels and let the top unit slide down the dowels until it sits perfectly upon the lower unit. A small ¼″ x ⅜″ molding may be placed around the bottoms of Parts A of the hutch top where they sit upon the lower unit.

FINISH

The beauty of this piece is in the finish work. After staining, apply lacquer or similar finish. Hand-rub the entire hutch with pumice and lemon oil until a satin sheen develops. Finish with paste wax.

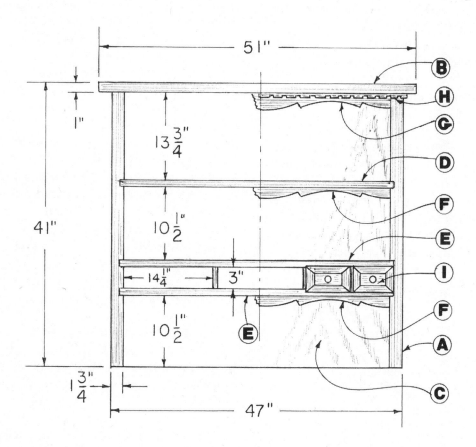

Fig. 2–15.

61

Fig. 2–16. Kitchen dry sink, Pennsylvania Farm Museum, Landis Valley, Lancaster, Pennsylvania.

Part	Number	Size	Material
K False Drawer	1	5″ x 18″ x ¾″	
L Top Door	1	20″ x 26″ x ¾″	
L-1 Slate	1	12″ x 12″ x ⅜″	Slate
M Doors*	3	13⅜″ x 24″ x ¾″	Raised Panel or Louvered Doors

*Note: Louvered doors may be purchased at local lumberyards. This type of door or shutter is best to use if speakers are to be placed in the lower section, so that sound can easily pass through them.

Hardware

One set flush (or appropriate) hinges for Part L.
Three sets of H or HL, ⅜″ off-set hinges.
Four door pulls, 1″ diameter, porcelain.
Three catches, magnetic.

Dry Sink

Because early homes did not have running water as we do today, water had to be carried in from a well, spring, or nearby brook. The dry sink was a kitchen piece that had a recessed area in the top to hold a metal tray or basin. Water was poured into the basin to wash the dishes, which were then stored underneath. The dry sink was the forerunner to the modern kitchen sink.

This once functional kitchen piece is now used proudly in any room in the home. The adaptation shown is designed to house a record player and speakers, however, the dry sink may be used for any purpose. It can house a TV, tape player, radio, or simply be used as a bar/planter or server. Some adjustments may be necessary to adapt for use with electronic equipment. Check the suggested measurements with your intended purpose and adjust the sizes as needed.

Material List

Part	Number	Size	Material
A Sides	2	18″ x 27″ x ¾″	Pine
B Base	1	17⅝″ x 44½″ x ¾″	
C Back	1	27″ x 45″ x ¼″	Plywood
D Skirt	1	4″ x 46″ x ¾″	Pine
E Top	1	18″ x 46″ x ¾″	
F Top Skirt	1	7½″ x 50″ x ¾″	
G Top Sides	2	7½″ x 19¼″ x ¾″	
H Top Back	1	7½″ x 50″ x ¾″	
I Center Divide	1	6¾″ x 18½″ x ¾″	
J Door Stiles	4	2″ x 23″ x ¾″	

CONSTRUCTION

1. Determine the proposed function of this piece. If it is to be used as a hi-fi or stereo cabinet, make sure the components will fit into the left-hand well. If speakers are to be placed in the lower section, be sure the depth is great enough. Adjust the measurements if needed.

2. Lay out and cut the stock for Parts A, B, C, D, and E. Cut the scrolled skirt design and a ⅜″ x ⅜″ rabbet on Parts A. Lay out and cut the scroll design on Part D. (See Fig. 2–18 for details.) Cut a blind ⅜″ x ⅜″ rabbet on the lower back edge of Part E. Nail Parts A into Part B. Part B is kept up 4″ from the bottom of Parts A, so that it will be flush with the top of Part D. Nail Part E down into Parts A. Nail Part D to Parts A and B. Insert Part C into the precut rabbets and nail to Parts A, B, and E. Part C will square up the entire cabinet.

3. Lay out and cut Part F. Cut a ⅜″ x ⅞″ rabbet on the lower inside edge. This rabbet fits over Part E. Lay out and cut Parts G. Cut a similar ⅜″ x ⅞″ rabbet on the lower edges. Drill ⅜″ countersunk holes on Parts F, G, and H for wood screws.

4. Screw Parts F and H to Part E. Screw Parts G into Parts E, F, and H. Lay out and cut Part I. Install Part I between Parts F and H, and nail in place. Fill screw holes with hardwood dowel plugs.

5. Lay out and cut Parts J. Nail Parts J into Parts D, F, and A. Lay out and cut Part K, the

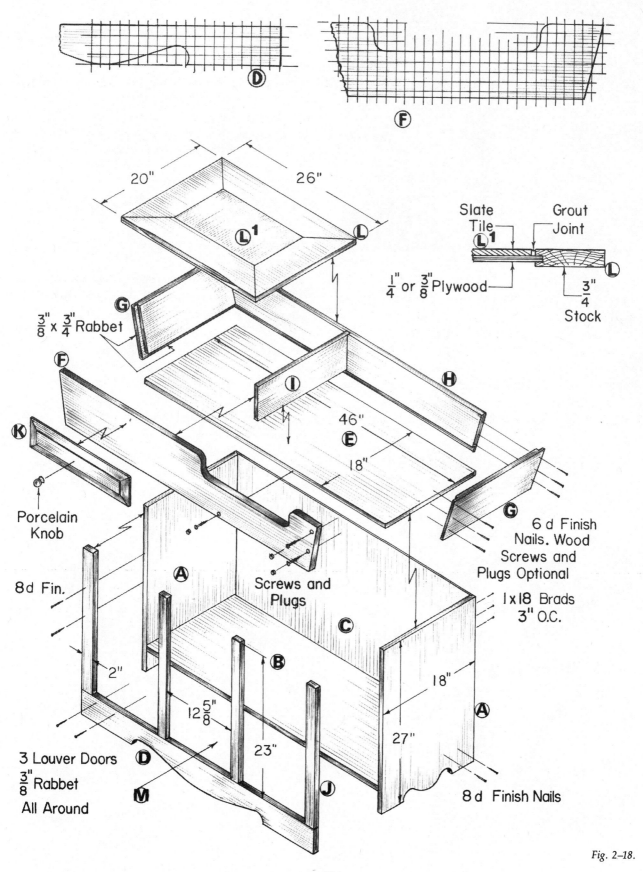

D

F

20"

26"

L¹ L

Slate
Tile   Grout
Joint

L¹   L

¼" or ⅜" Plywood

¾"
Stock

G

⅜" x ¾" Rabbet

F

I

H

K

46"

E

18"

Porcelain
Knob

A

Screws and
Plugs

C

6 d Finish
Nails. Wood
Screws and
Plugs Optional

G

8 d Fin.

2"

B

1 x 18 Brads
3" O.C.

18"

A

12 5/8"

23"

27"

3 Louver Doors
⅜" Rabbet
All Around

D

M

J

8 d Finish Nails

Fig. 2–18.

Fig. 2–17. Dry sink project.

false raised panel drawer front. Glue and screw Part K to Part F.

6. Lay out and cut the stock for the top door, Part L. (see sectional view in Fig. 2–18.) Part L is a door made of four pieces of ¾" stock with mitered joints. Cut a ¼" x ½" dado starting ⅜" down from the top in all of the pieces. Install a piece of ¼" plywood into the dado. Glue a piece of slate tile

to the plywood with tile adhesive. Fill the cracks with white or grey tile grout. Secure Part L to Part H with a set of appropriate hinges. *Note: Slate tile may be purchased at any ceramic tile outlet, or tile may be used in place of slate if so desired.*

7. Lay out and cut three doors (Parts M). Allow for a ⅜" x ⅜" overlap all around. Install the doors to the cabinet with hinges and catches.

FINISH

Several types of finish will work very well on this project. An oil stain under several coats of lacquer or similar finish is excellent, or antiqued color may be used if desired: Paint the entire project any color, using a water-based paint. Wipe on a black glaze and finish with several coats of lacquer. Hand rub the finished cabinet with pumice and oil. Finish with a coat of paste wax. A colonial method you may wish to use is to apply several coats of hot linseed oil, rubbed well into the wood. Finish with paste wax.

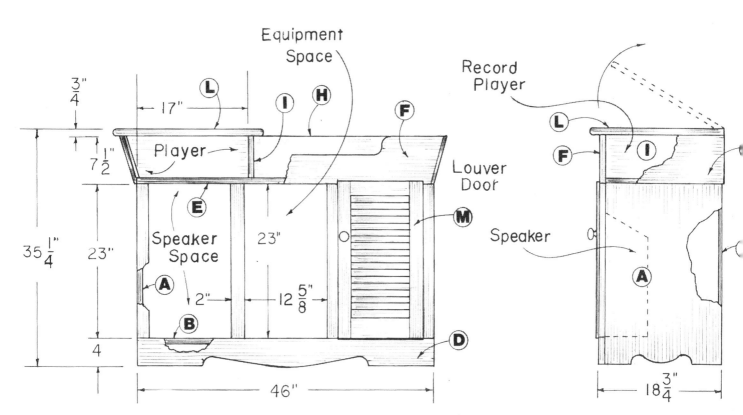

Fig. 2–19.

Fig. 2–20. Cabinet.
Pennsylvania Farm Museum, Landis Valley, Lancaster, Pennsylvania.

Kitchen Cabinets

The colonial housewife had little in the way of kitchen equipment. The food preparation area was most often the common table, and a dry sink or washtub completed her kitchen equipment. In time, hutch cupboards, cabinets with slate or soapstone sinks, and pantries were added.

In modern homes the average offerings of site-made or pre-made kitchen cabinets often do not meet the needs or desires of enthusiasts of early American styling. The plans shown here have been included to allow the modern craftsman to construct kitchen cabinets along typical early American lines.

The drawings represent adaptable sections of both upper and lower cabinets with the intention that any size or shape kitchen can be constructed, using the same basic methods. A straight wall, "L" shaped area, or "U" designed kitchen will all follow the same general directions and material usage.

Because the size and scope of each proposed series of kitchen cabinets will be different, a clear-cut material list cannot be given. However, the basic sizes of different parts are constant, and these are given to allow for planning. The number required of each part is determined by the layout.

Lower Unit Material List

Part	Size	Suggested Material
Toe board	1" x 6"	# 2 Pine
Base framing	1" x 6"	# 2 Pine
Base	⅝"	Plyscord, P.T.S. (Plug, touch-sanded)
Stiles	1" x 2"	# 1 Pine
Rails	1" x 2"	# 1 Pine
Glue blocks	1" x 2"	# 1 Pine scrap
Center shelf	⅝"	Plywood/scord, P.T.S.
Shelf supports	1" x 2"	# 1 Pine
Countertop supports	1" x 2"	# 1 Pine
Drawer guides		Commercial, metal
Countertop	⅝"	Plyscord, P.T.S.
Drawer material	1" x 6"	# 2 Pine
Door frames	1" x 2"	# 1 Pine
Door panels	1" x 12"	# 2 Pine
Backsplash Countertop		Any plastic laminate material
End panels	¼" to ⅜"	Plywood, A.C.

Fig. 2–21.   Kitchen Cabinets, Masasic House, Connecticut Valley.

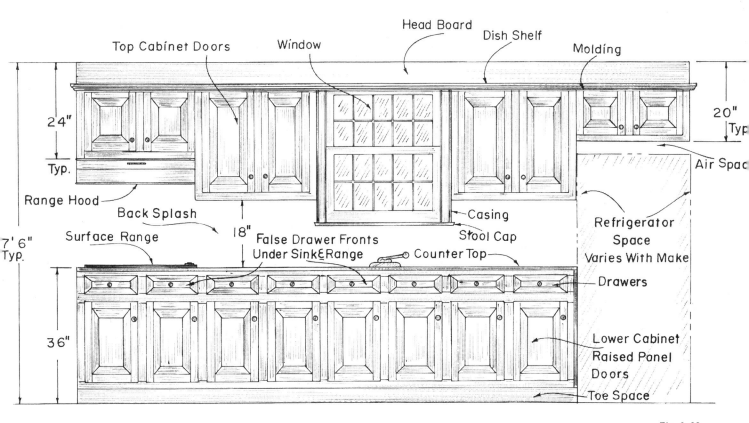

Head Board

Top Cabinet Doors

Window

Dish Shelf

Molding

24"

Typ.

Range Hood

Back Splash

20"
Typ

Air Spac

Casing

Stool Cap

18"

Surface Range

False Drawer Fronts
Under Sink & Range

Counter Top

Refrigerator
Space
Varies With Make

7' 6"
Typ.

Drawers

36"

Lower Cabinet
Raised Panel
Doors

Toe Space

Fig. 2–22.

66

CONSTRUCTION

1. Lay out the dimensions on the floor where the lower unit will be installed. Construct a box frame from 1″ x 6″ of # 2 pine as shown in Fig. 2–24. Install the base supports 24″ to 30″ on centers. Cut the plywood or plyscord sheets 23½″ wide and nail these sheets to the frame.

2. Door/drawer layout. Determine the number of doors and drawers you desire. Mark out the plywood of the base unit for the 2″ glue blocks. Glue and nail a small glue block for each stile to be used, flush with the front of the plywood base. Make a frame with the 1″ x 2″ # 1 pine for the door and drawer openings (see Fig. 2–25). Butt or half-lap joints will serve for this frame. Note in Figure 2–25 that the two top rails are secured to the short drawer stiles with reinforcement glue blocks. Normal size for the drawer openings is 5″ to 6″ in height. Secure the frame to the pre-made base unit and nail the lower rail into the exposed edge of the plywood base. Nail the stile bottoms into the pre-installed glue blocks.

3. Plumb and level the cabinet front and brace it in place. Cut the stock for the center shelf, if used, and nail a shelf support cleat into the house wall studs at the desired height. Nail the plywood (plyscord) shelf into the support and nail the upright stiles into the shelf.

4. Mark out the locations for the countertop supports. Nail the supports into the house wall studs, usually 16″ on centers. (See Fig. 2–25.) Cut support members to run from the top rail to the support cleat. Secure these members 24″ on centers and also on each side of a sink or surface unit range if either is to be installed. Cut the end panels and nail these panels into the base, the center shelf, the end stiles, and the top supports.

5. Drawers. Whenever a surface range or sink is used, false drawer fronts are used to preserve the continuity of design of the cabinet work. Mark and cut, and install the commercial drawer guides into the open drawer areas. It is recommended that a drawer cleat be installed into the house wall studs to support the rear end of the guides. Make the required drawer units to fit the openings. (See *Section One* for construction details.) Install the drawers into the openings.

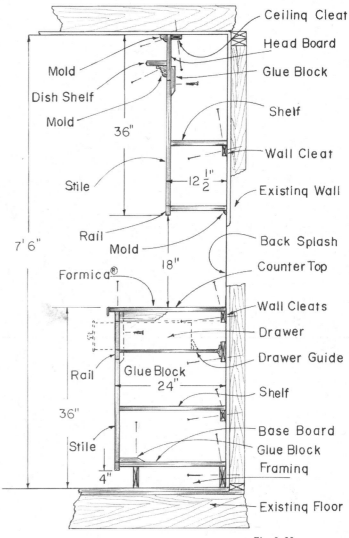

Fig. 2–23.

6. Make door frames with half-lap joints and raised center panels. (See *Section One* for construction details.) A ⅜″ x ⅜″ overlap type of door is recommended. Install the doors with appropriate hinges, and install the pulls and catches.

7. Cut and install the countertop plywood. If a plastic laminate type of full backsplash is to be used, install this backsplash first. Secure the countertop to the top rail and the supports with screws or screw-type nails. Install the plastic laminate top with a self- or molded edge. Follow manufacturer's instructions for installation of the top material.

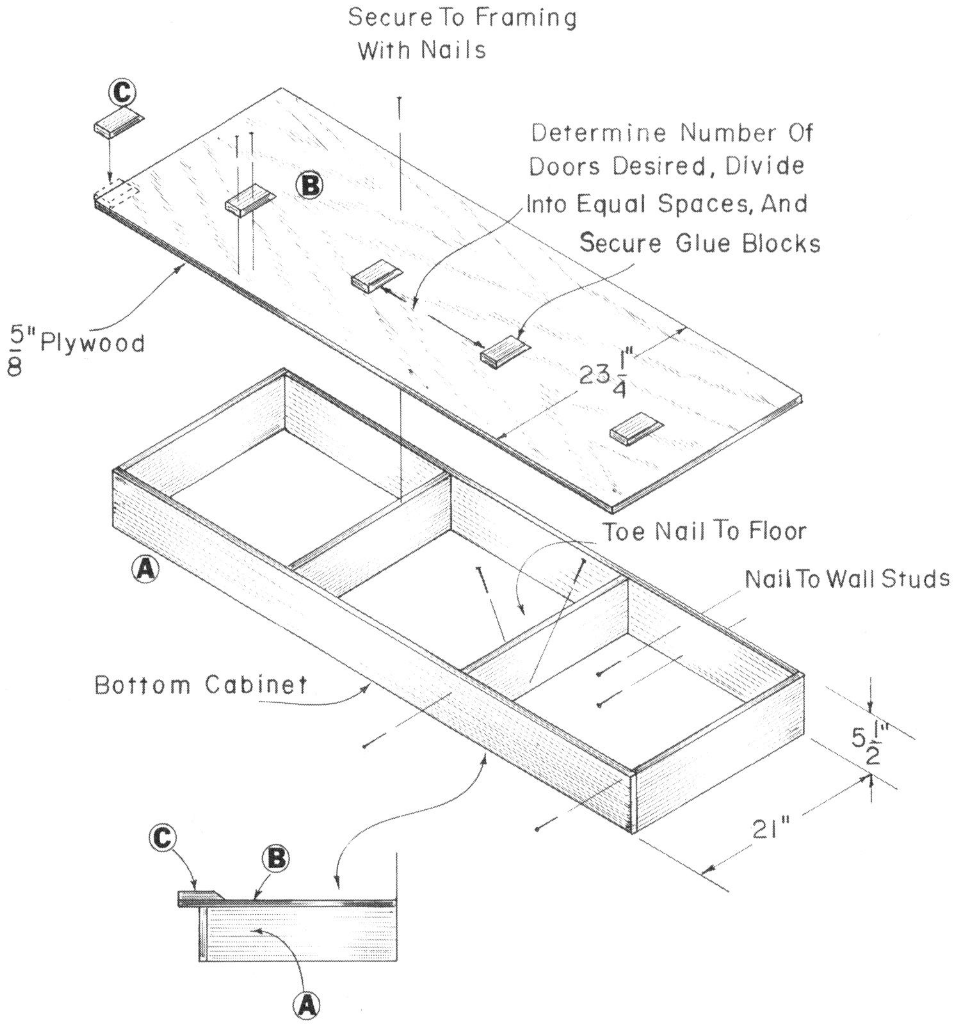

Secure To Framing
With Nails

Determine Number Of
Doors Desired, Divide
Into Equal Spaces, And
Secure Glue Blocks

$\frac{5}{8}$" Plywood

23$\frac{1}{4}$"

Toe Nail To Floor

Nail To Wall Studs

Bottom Cabinet

5$\frac{1}{2}$"

21"

Fig. 2–24.

8. Follow manufacturer's instructions for installation of sink, surface unit range, and wall oven. Dimensions of necessary openings will be included.

Top Unit Material List

Part	Size	Suggested Material
Shelves	1" x 12"	# 2 Pine
End panels	1" x 12"	# 2 Pine
Stiles	1" x 2"	# 1 Pine
Rails	1" x 2"	# 1 Pine
Head board	1" x 8"	# 2 Pine
Dish shelf	1" x 6"	# 2 Pine
Molding	2"	Crown, cove, or bed
Shelf cleats	1" x 2"	# 1 Pine
Ceiling cleats	1" x 2"	# 1 Pine
Glue blocks	1" x 2"	# 1 Pine
Door frames	1" x 2"	# 1 Pine
Door panels	1" x 12"	# 2 Pine

Hardware

$\frac{3}{8}$" offset hinges.
Magnetic or friction catches.
Door and drawer pulls of choice.
Metal drawer guides.

CONSTRUCTION

It is important to note the different heights suggested for the use of a range hood or over-the-refrigerator cabinets.

1. Cut the 1" x 12" stock for the shelves and end panels. Nail the end panels into the shelves. This can be done while the cabinets are flat on the floor or workbench.

2. Determine how many door units you desire

and divide the cabinet area into equal amounts. Construct a frame of 1″ x 2″ # 1 pine stiles and rails. See Fig. 2–26. The tops of the cabinet stiles are secured to the header board with screws and glue blocks. Nail the finished frame into the pre-made cabinet shelf assembly. The stiles and rails are nailed into the shelves and end panels. If a dish shelf is to be used, nail it in place at this time. The header-board is nailed to the dish shelf from the inside.

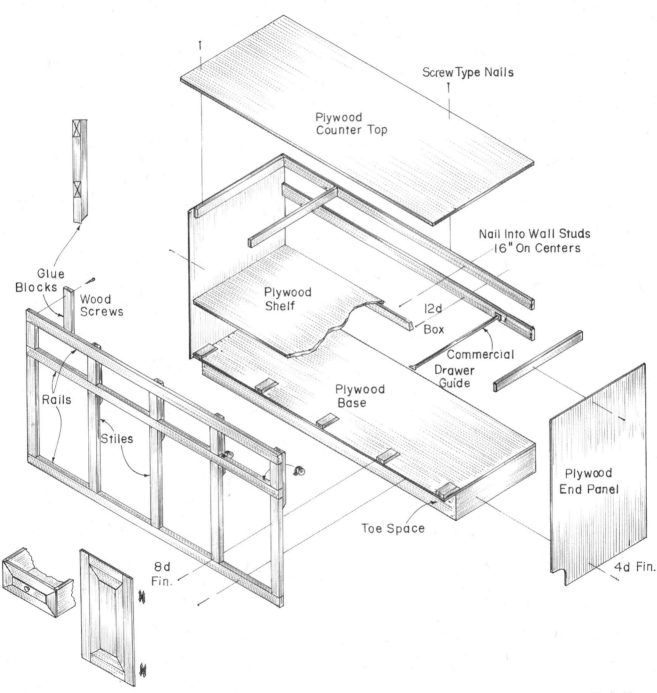

Screw Type Nails

Plywood Counter Top

Nail Into Wall Studs 16″ On Centers

Glue Blocks

Wood Screws

Plywood Shelf

12d Box

Commercial Drawer Guide

Rails

Stiles

Plywood Base

Plywood End Panel

Toe Space

8d Fin.

4d Fin.

Fig. 2–25.

3. Place the completed top unit frame against the proposed wall location, and level and mark for the shelf and ceiling support cleats. Remove the cabinet unit, and nail the shelf supports into the house wall studs, usually 16″ on centers. Nail the ceiling support cleat into the ceiling joists, usually 16″ on centers. Place the cabinet unit in its location and nail the top of the header board into the ceiling support cleat. Nail the shelves into the shelf wall supports.

4. Mark and install the cabinet moldings. Make the required number of raised panel doors to fit the openings. (See *Section One* for construction details.) A ⅜″ x ⅜″ overlap type of door frame is recommended. Install the doors with suitable hinges, and install the door catches and pulls.

FINISH

The kitchen cabinets are finished in the same manner that fine furniture is finished. Set and fill all nail heads. Sand all exposed parts smooth. Stain or paint. If stained, cover with several (6) coats of lacquer or varnish. Finish off with two coats of paste wax applied with steel wood. Thereafter, apply paste wax and buff, once or twice a year.

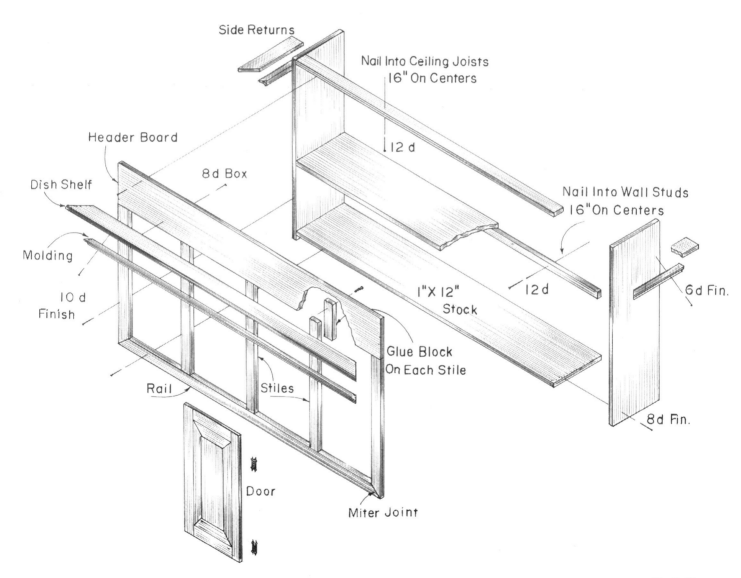

Fig. 2–26.

70

Fig. 2–27.   Wagon tool box, Pennsylvania Farm Museum, Landis Valley, Lancaster, Pennsylvania.

Spice Box

Several boxes of this type were used throughout early homes. Some were used to hold salt, some to hold freshly made candles, and some to hold spices. The box offered here is a cross between the wagon tool box and the apothecary chest. It retains the salt-box type of lid most common with these pieces. Either brass or leather hinges will do, for both were common.

Material List

Part		Number	Size	Material
A		1	10″ x 16″ x ½″	Pine
B		2	6″ x 9″ x ½″	
C		1	8″ x 12″ x ½″	
D		3	6″ x 10″ x ½″	
E		1	6½″ x 10″ x ½″	
F	Drawers	4	2″ x 4″ x 5½″	

Hardware

H	2	Brass or leather hinges
	4	Porcelain knobs, ½″ dia.

CONSTRUCTION

1. Lay out and cut the stock. (see Fig. 2–29).
2. On Part E, lay out and cut four rectangles into which the drawer units will fit. Nail Parts B to Part A from the back. Nail Parts D between Parts B. The center Part D acts as a drawer guide for the top drawers. Nail Part E into Parts B and Parts D. Fill all nail holes.
3. Make four small raised panel drawer units with butt joints and fit them into the holes cut into Part E. Some adjustment may be necessary to make the drawer units fit properly.
4. Attach Part C to Part A with the two hinges, Parts H. Screw the porcelain knobs, Parts I, to the drawer units.

FINISH

Sand all parts smooth. Distress if desired. Stain or paint. Cover with several coats of lacquer or similar finish.

71

Fig. 2–28.   Spice box project.

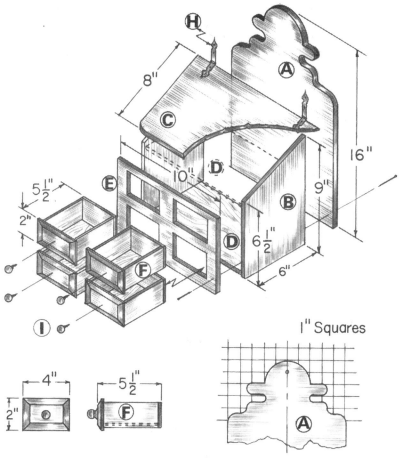

1" Squares

Fig. 2–29.

Apothecary Chest

Fig. 2–30. *Herb drawers in an apothecary shop, Shelburne Museum, Shelburne, Vermont.*

Old-world remedies involving herbs were passed on from generation to generation. Some of these remedies were worthless, but others were based upon sound medical theory. Both herbs and spices were valuable, primarily because of the cost to import them.

Most homes and all apothecary shops had special chests in which to store herbs and spices. The herbs were kept in individual drawers, the contents and their uses labeled on each. The typical early apothecary shop had a wall cabinet such as the one shown in Figure 2–30, and the home spice chest was much like the one shown in Figure 2–31.

This project evolved from those concepts. The multi-drawer unit with porcelain knobs adds the right touch to bring part of the old apothecary shop into the modern-day colonial setting. The size has been varied so that the chest may be used as an end table or lamp stand.

Material List

	Part	Number	Size	Material
A	Sides	2	13" x 24¼" x ¾"	Pine,
B	Top	1	13¾" x 24" x ¾"	Maple, Birch, Cherry
C	Back	1	24½" x 23¼" x ¼"	Plywood
D	Skirt	1	4" x 24" x ¾"	
E	Rails	2	1¾" x 20½" x ¾"	
E-1	Rail (Top)	1	1¾" x 24" x ¾"	
F	Stiles	2	1¾" x 18½" x ¾"	

	Part	Number	Size	Material
G	Top Front	1	3½" x 26" x ¾"	
H	Top Sides	2	4½" x 14½" x ¾"	
I	Top Back	1	4½" x 26" x ¾"	
J	Top Rounds	2	1⅜" dia x 8"	Dowel (closet rod)
K	Drawer Units	3	4⅞" x 20½" x 13"	
L	Raised Panels	9	5⅝" x 6½" x ¾"	
M	Drawer Guide	6	1½" x 12¾" x ¾"	

CONSTRUCTION

1. Lay out and cut the stock.

2. Cut a ¼" x ⅜" rabbet at the rear inside edges of Parts A. Cut a ¼" x ⅜" blind rabbet at the inside bottom edge of Part B. Nail Part B into Parts A. Insert Part C into the pre-cut rabbets and nail Part C into Parts A and B.

3. Lay out and cut the design into Part D. Nail Part D into Parts A. Cut Part E-1 to size and nail top rail into Parts A. Cut Parts F and nail into Parts A, D, and E-1. Cut Parts E and nail into pre-installed Parts F to make three equal drawer openings.

4. Cut the drawer guides, Parts M, glue and screw them into Parts F, C, and A. (See *Section One* for details.)

5. Lay out and cut Parts G, H, I, and J for the top assembly. Cut the design into Part G. Cut a ⅜" x 1" rabbet into the bottom inside edges of Parts G, H, and I. Keep in mind the suggested

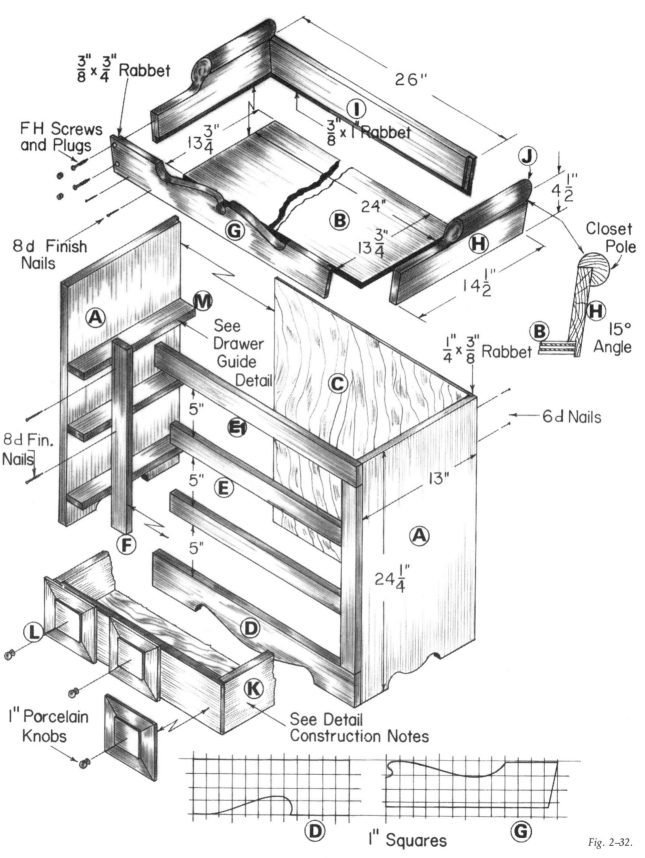

$\frac{3}{8}'' \times \frac{3}{4}''$ Rabbet

F H Screws
and Plugs

8d Finish
Nails

8d Fin.
Nails

1" Porcelain
Knobs

$13\frac{3}{4}''$

$\frac{3}{8}'' \times 1''$ Rabbet

26"

I

J

$4\frac{1}{2}''$

Closet
Pole

24"

$13\frac{3}{4}''$

B

H

$14\frac{1}{2}''$

15°
Angle

$\frac{1}{4}'' \times \frac{3}{8}''$ Rabbet

B

H

G

A

M

See
Drawer
Guide
Detail

5"

E

E

5"

F

5"

C

6d Nails

13"

A

$24\frac{1}{4}''$

L

D

K

See Detail
Construction Notes

D

1" Squares

G

Fig. 2–32.

74

angle for Parts H. Cut a ⅜" x ¾" rabbet on ends of Part G and on Part I so that they may receive Parts H. Check the suggested tilt angle in Figure 2–32.

6. Glue and nail Parts G and I to Part B. Install Part H into the rabbets in Parts G and I with wood screws covered with hardwood plugs. Cut the required rabbet on the rounds, Parts J. Glue and nail Parts J to the outside edges of Parts H. Sand these rounds to blend in at the front scroll break.

7. Make three drawer units, Parts K, to fit the openings on the chest. (See *Section One* for drawer details.) Make nine raised panels (Parts L). Glue and nail finished panels, three to each drawer unit. The raised panels have a ⅜" lap-over on the top, bottom, and sides.

FINISH

Set and fill all nail holes. Cover all screw heads with hardwood plugs. Sand the entire project smooth. Stain. Cover with several coats of lacquer or similar finish. Hand rub with pumice and lemon oil and finish with paste wax.

Fig. 2–31. Apothecary chest project.

Install a porcelain knob in the center of each raised panel.

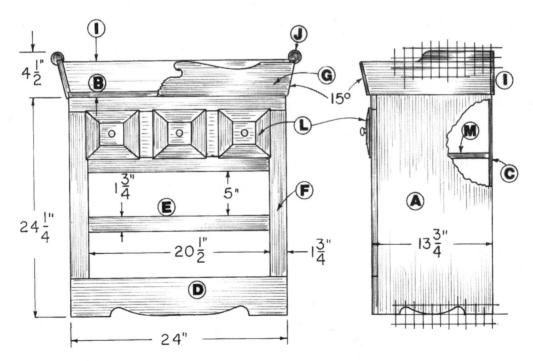

Fig. 2–33.

75

Colonial Styled Bookcase

Fig. 2–34. Corner cupboard,

Old Sturbridge Village, Sturbridge, Massachusetts.
Bookcase plan was adapted from this type of cupboard.

In most colonial homes there was little need for a bookcase. Most often the only book was the family Bible, kept on a Bible stand, a simple lap desk with a slanted top designed to hold only the one book, and possibly valuable legal papers. In the late 1700s the cost of books came nearer to the reach of the average family, and collections were accumulated; simple cases were designed and made to house these often expensive possessions. This bookcase was developed in part from a colonial styled hutch cupboard and some simple wall shelves that held the family's treasures. The primary purpose is to offer a bookcase that will blend well with antique furnishings.

Material List

	Part	Number	Size	Material
A	Sides	2	12″ x 80″ x ¾″	Pine
B	Shelves (Fixed)	3	11⅝″ x 34½″ x ¾″	
C	Back	1	35¼″ x 80⅜″ x ¼″	Plywood
D	Stiles	2	2″ x 80″ x ¾″	
E	Base	1	4″ x 32″ x ¾″	
E-1	Divider	1	2″ x 32″ x ¾″	
F	Top Skirt	1	6″ x 32″ x ¾″	
G	Stile	1	2″ x 24″ x ¾″	
H	Molding	1	1¾″ x 65″	Cove molding
I	Top	1	15″ x 40″ x ¾″	
J	Doors	2	15¾″ x 24¾″ x ¾″	Raised panel
K	Brackets	4	½″ x 60″	Metal
L	Shelves	3	11″ x 34″ x ¾″	

CONSTRUCTION

1. Cut Parts A, B, and C to suggested sizes and shapes. Cut a ⅜″ x ⅜″ rabbet on the rear edges of Part A to receive Part C. Nail Parts A into Parts B. Nail Part C into the rabbets on Parts A and into the fixed shelves, Parts B. (Part C will square up the whole bookcase.)

2. Cut Parts D, E, F, and G to suggested sizes. Cut Parts E and F to suggested shapes. Nail Parts D into Parts A and B. Glue and nail Part E into Parts A and B. Secure Part F between the tops of Parts A. Nail the divider, Part E-1, between Parts A and into the top fixed shelf, Part B. Secure Part G between Parts E and E-1.

3. Cut the molding, Part H, with mitered corners and nail it flush with the top of the unit into Parts A and F. Cut Part I and make a ⅜" x ⅜" rabbet on the rear edge. Nail Part I into Parts A, and nail Part C into the rabbet. Make two raised panel doors, Parts J. (See *Section One* for construction details.) Secure the doors to Parts D with hinges. Install catches and door pulls.

4. Cut Parts K, the metal adjustable shelf brackets to required size. Screw Parts K to Parts A.

Insert the shelf brackets into the slots. Cut the movable shelves, Parts L, to size. Recommended: three shelves.

FINISH

Set and fill all nail heads. Sand entire bookcase smooth. Stain or paint. Cover with several coats of varnish or lacquer. Finish off with paste wax.

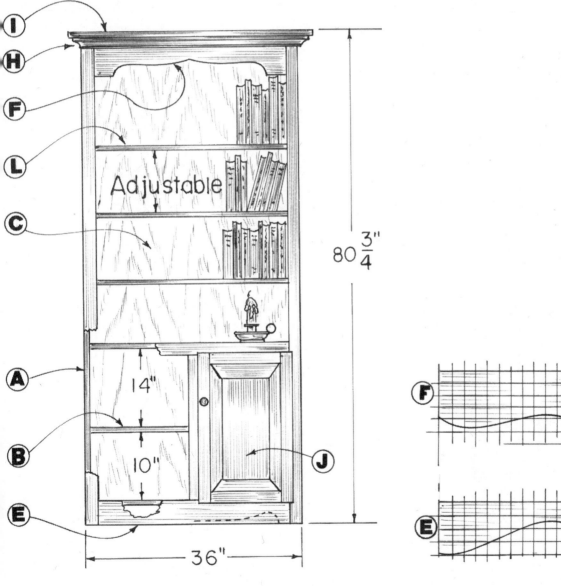

Fig. 2–35.

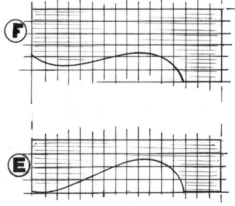

Fig. 2–36.

77

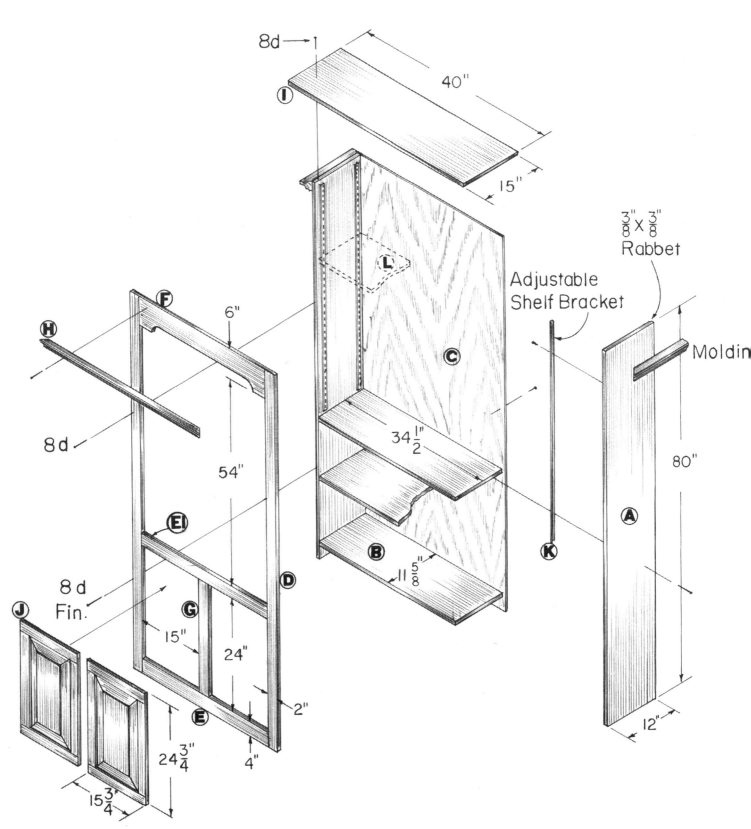

8d →

ⓘ

40"

15"

$\frac{3}{8}'' \times \frac{3}{8}''$
Rabbet

ⓛ

6"

Adjustable
Shelf Bracket

Moldin

ⓗ

ⓒ

54"

8d

$34\frac{1}{2}''$

80"

ⓔⓛ

ⓓ

ⓐ

8 d
Fin.

ⓖ

ⓑ

$11\frac{5}{8}''$

ⓚ

ⓙ

15"

24"

$24\frac{3}{4}''$

ⓔ

2"

4"

$15\frac{3}{4}''$

Fig. 2–37.

Salem Commode Table

This small bedroom commode once held all elements equivalent to a modern bathroom. Now it is likely to be used in a colonial-styled living room or family room as a small occasional table.

Material List

Part		Number	Size	Material
A	Sides	2	13" x 19" x ¾"	
B	Bottom	1	12⅝" x 20½" x ¾"	
C	Back	1	21¼" x 19⅜" x ¼"	Plywood
D	Skirt	1	3" x 22" x ¾"	
E	Stiles	2	1¾" x 16" x ¾"	
F	Rails	2	1" x 18½" x ¾"	
G	Scab	1	2" x 20½" x ¾"	
H	Scab	1	1½" x 20½" x ¾"	
I	Guides	2	2" x 12⅝" x ¾"	
		2	1" x 12⅝" x ¾"	
J	Top	1	15" x 24½" x 1"	
K	Drawer	1	3" x 18½" x 12"	
L	Doors	2	9¼" x 11" x ¾"	

Hardware

Two sets flush "H" hinges.
Four 1" diameter door pulls.
Two magnetic catches.

CONSTRUCTION

1. Lay out and cut stock for Parts A and B. Cut a ⅜" x ⅜" rabbet on the rear inside edges of Parts A to receive Part C. Nail Parts A into Part B.

Fig. 2–38. *Salem commode table project.*

2. Lay out and cut Part C. Insert Part C into the pre-made rabbets and nail into Parts A and B.

3. Lay out and cut Parts D, E, and F. Make ship-lap joints between Parts E and F. Assemble Parts D, E, and F into a frame. Nail the frame into Parts A and B.

4. Lay out and cut the reinforcement bars, Parts G and H. Secure Parts G and H as indicated in Figure 2–39. Part G reinforces the top Part F and Part H reinforces Part C.

5. Lay out and cut the drawer guides, Parts I. (See *Section One* for guide details.) Secure Parts I to Parts A flush with the top of the lower Part F.

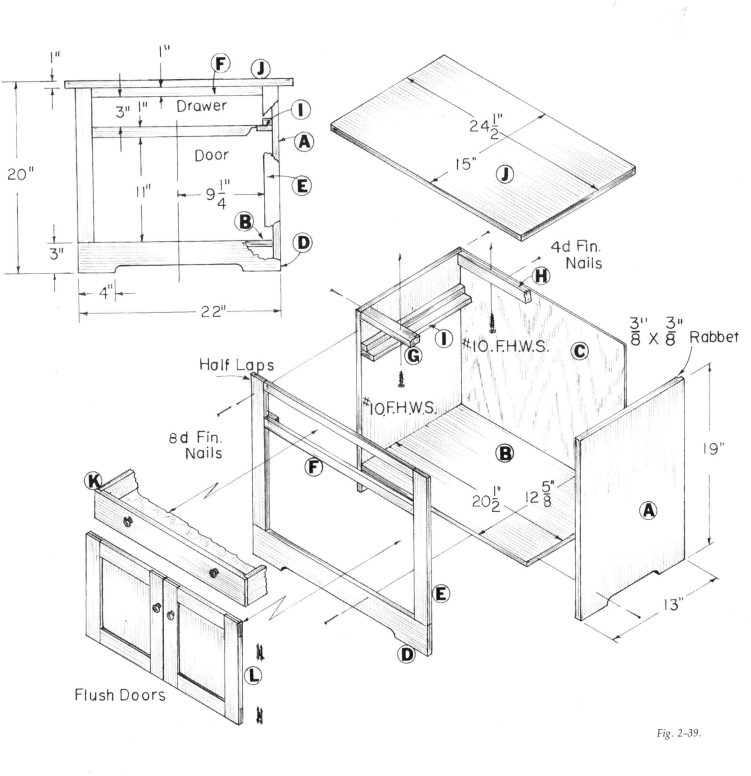

Fig. 2–39.

6. Make a drawer unit (Part K) to fit flush in the opening. (See *Section One* for details.) Make two flush doors to fit openings. (See *Section One* for details.) Secure the doors to the openings with flush "H" hinges. Install the catches and pulls.

FINISH

Set and fill all nail heads. Sand entire project smooth. Stain or paint. Cover with several coats of lacquer. Finish with paste wax.

Fig. 2–40. *Small commode table, Mr. and Mrs. Frank Okarmus, Springfield, Massachusetts.*

Side Server

Designed as a small side server, this piece may be used in a dining room group or in any room of an early American-styled home. It could be used to house a radio or stereo equipment.

Material List

	Part	Number	Size	Material
A	Sides	2	11″ x 28″ x ¾″	Pine or wood of choice
B	Bottom	1	10¾″ x 32½″ x ¾″	
C	Top	1	11¾″ x 34″ x ¾″	
D	Back	1	28⅜″ x 33″ x ¼″	Plywood
E	Skirt	1	4″ x 34″ x ¾″	
F	Stiles	2	2″ x 24″ x ¾″	

	Part	Number	Size	Material
G	Rails	2	2″ x 30″ x ¾″	
H	Center Stile	1	2″ x 16″ x ¾″	
H-1	Center Stile (Top)	1	2″ x 4″ x ¾″	
I	Top Skirt	1	3¾″ x 35½″ x ¾″	
J	Top Sides	2	3¾″ x 13½″ x ¾″	
K	Top Back	1	3¾″ x 34¾″ x ¾″	
L	Drawers	2	3⅞″ x 14″ x 11″	
	Drawer Fronts	2	4⅝″ x 14¾″ x ¾″	
M	Doors*	2	14¾″ x 16¾″ x ¾″	
N	Drawer Guides	2	3″ x 10⅝″ x ¾″	
O	Center Guide	1	4″ x 10⅝″ x ¾″	

* Note: Parts M, the doors, may be made from solid ¾″ stock glued up or made of 3″ x ¾″ frames with ¼″ plywood center panels. Another method would be to use the raised panel inserted into a door frame as suggested in Section One.

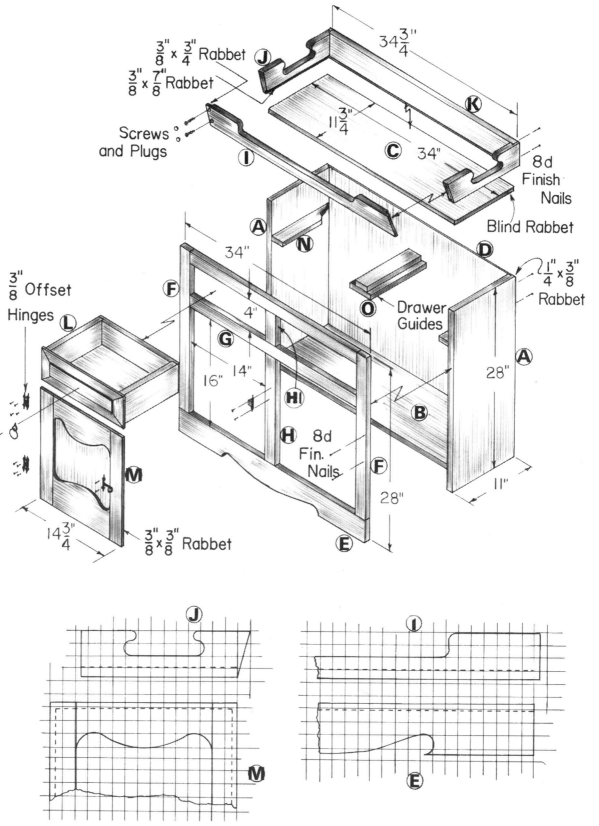

$\frac{3}{8}$" x $\frac{3}{4}$" Rabbet

$\frac{3}{8}$" x $\frac{7}{8}$" Rabbet

J

$34\frac{3}{4}$"

Screws and Plugs

K

I

$11\frac{3}{4}$"

C   34"

8 d Finish Nails

A

N

Blind Rabbet

D

$\frac{1}{4}$" x $\frac{3}{8}$" Rabbet

$\frac{3}{8}$" Offset Hinges

L

34"

F

4"

G

O   Drawer Guides

A

28"

16"   14"

HI

B

28"

H   8d Fin. Nails

M

F

$14\frac{3}{4}$"

$\frac{3}{8}$" x $\frac{3}{8}$" Rabbet

E

11"

J

I

M

E

Fig. 2–41.

82

CONSTRUCTION

1. Lay out and rough-cut the stock to size. A ¾" piece of plywood may be used for the sides and top if desired, because the end grains will be covered.

2. Lay out Parts A, B, C, and D. Cut a ¼" x ⅜" rabbet at the inside rear edges of Parts A. Cut a blind ¼" x ⅜" rabbet on Part C.

3. Nail Parts A to Part B. Nail Part C into Parts A. Insert Part D into rabbets and nail into Parts A, B and C.

4. Lay out and cut the design suggested for Parts E and F. Nail Part E into Parts A and B. Cut and nail Part F into Parts A. Install Parts G and nail them into Parts F. Install Parts H and nail them into Parts G and E. (Ship-lap joints may be used here if desired; however, butt joints will serve the purpose.)

5. Lay out and cut Parts I, J, and K to the suggested shape and size. Cut a ⅜" x ⅞" rabbet on the bottom of each piece. Cut a ⅜" x ¾" rabbet on both ends of Parts J. (See suggested angle cut in Fig. 2–41.) Nail Part I to Part C. Nail Part K to Part C. Nail Parts J to Part C. Screw Part I into Parts J and cover the screw heads with hardwood plugs. Nail Part K into Parts J.

6. Lay out and cut the drawer guides, Parts N and O. Install these guides flush with the drawer rails. Make two drawer units to fit the openings. (See *Section One* for drawer details.) Install raised panel drawer fronts (Part L), with a ⅜" lap-over all around.

7. Make two paneled doors of your choice. (See *Section One* for door construction details.) Install the pre-made doors to the unit with H, or H and L off-set hinges. Install the drawer and door pulls. Install the catches.

Note: If an extra center shelf is desired, install the shelf at this time.

FINISH

Set and fill all nail holes. Sand the entire project smooth. Stain and cover with several coats of varnish or lacquer. Rub to a high sheen with pumice and lemon oil. Finish with paste wax.

Fig. 2–42. *Hand-painted chest of drawers, Index of American Design, Washington, D. C.*

Chest Of Drawers With Wall Mirror

Storage furniture for the colonists consisted of either a plain chest, a trunk, or a sea locker. These pieces were designed for travel or cartage. As the chest developed into a more permanent piece, drawers were added at the bottom. Instead of resting on the floor, short legs, or skirts, were added. In time, as local cabinetmakers developed the skills to work with native wood, the chest with drawers became more drawers than chest. Yankee ingenuity had then developed what we now think of as "a chest of drawers."

This chest is offered as a colonial bedroom piece. The basic lines have been retained; a mirror has been added to serve in a modern-day bedroom.

Material List

	Part	Number	Size	Material
A	Sides	2	18″ x 28″ x ¾″	Pine
B	Back	1	28¾″ x 43½″ x ¼″	Plywood
C	Skirt	1	4″ x 44″ x ¾″	
D	Stiles	2	2″ x 24″ x ¾″	
E	Rails	3	2″ x 40″ x ¾″	
F	Outer Guides	4	2¾″ x 17⅝″ x ¾″	
G	Center Guide	4	2″ x 17⅝″ x ¾″	
H	Top	1	21″ x 50″ x 1¾″	
I	Top Drawers	2	6″ x 19¾″ x 17″	
J	Lower Drawers	2	6″ x 40¾″ x 17″	

Hardware

Six 1″ diameter pulls, porcelain; or six maple leaf pulls.

CONSTRUCTION

1. Lay out and cut the stock for Parts A, B, C, D, and E. Cut a ⅜" x ⅜" rabbet on the rear inside edges of Parts A. Cut the suggested shape and design into Part C. Nail Part C to Parts A. Nail Part D to Parts A, and nail Parts E into Parts D. A ship-lap joint may be used where Parts D and E join, if desired.

Nail Part B into rabbets precut in Parts A.

2. Lay out and cut the stock for Parts F and G. Screw Parts F to Parts A flush with the tops of Parts E. The center guides, Parts G, are installed dead center of the drawer openings. Insert a 2" divider between the top two sections of Parts E to make two drawer openings.

3. Glue up the 1¾" stock to required thickness for Part H. Cut a heavy chamfer on the top front edge to simulate years of wear. Cut a ⅜" x ⅜" blind rabbet on the back lower edge to receive Part B. Nail Part H to the center guides and Parts A. Nail Part B into the blind rabbet.

4. Make two raised panel drawers, Parts I, with a ⅜" lap-over all around to fit the top two openings. Make two large raised panel drawers, Parts J, to fit the large drawer (lower) openings. (See *Section One* for drawer construction hints.) Install one drawer pull on the small drawers and two drawer pulls on the large drawer.

FINISH

Set and fill all nail holes. Sand the entire project smooth. Stain and cover with several coats of varnish or lacquer. Rub with pumice and lemon oil. Apply paste wax and buff.

Mirror Material List

Part		Number	Size	Material
A	Top	1	6" x 24" x 1¾"	The same
B	Side Pieces	2	3¼" x 30" x 1¾"	as the
C	Bottom	1	3¼" x 24" x 1¾"	chest
D	Pediment	2	2" x 11" x ¾"	
E	Finial	1	2" diameter x 6"	
F	Mirror	1	20" x 24" x ¼"	Plate

CONSTRUCTION

1. Lay out and cut the stock. Make 45° miter joints as shown in Figure 2–45. Cut in the design

Fig. 2–43.   *Chest of drawers project.*

on Parts A, B, and C, using a table saw and finishing with a router. (See sectional view, Fig. 2–45.) Cut a ⅜" x ⅝" rabbet on the rear inside edges in order to insert the mirror, Part F. Glue and dowel the mitered joints together.

2. Cut Part D. Using a router, cut a molded edge on three sides, leaving the rear edge plain. (See circled detail view, Fig. 2–45.) Nail Parts D to Part A.

3. Lathe-turn a finial, leaving a ⅜" x ¾" dowel-like tenon on the bottom. Drill a ⅜" hole 1" deep in the center of Part A, the broken pediment, and glue Part E into the hole.

FINISH

The mirror frame is finished in the same manner as the chest of drawers. When the frame is finished, insert the mirror, Part F, into the precut rabbets and lock it in with small wood strips. Install two screw-eyes three-quarters of the way up the frame, and string a heavy picture wire between the screw-eyes.

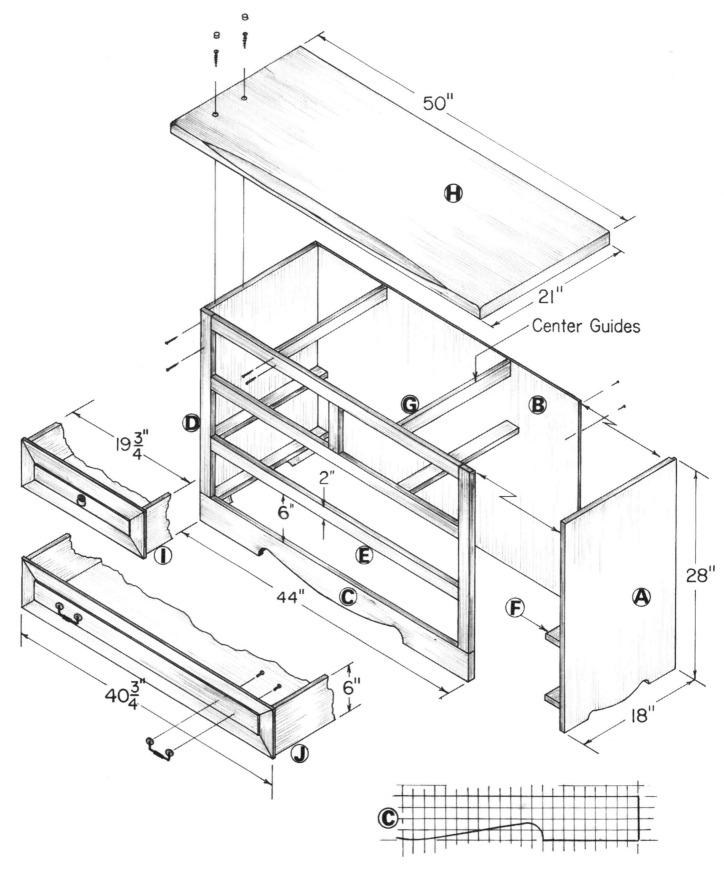

50"

21"

Center Guides

H

B

G

D

19¾"

2"

6"

E

44"

C

I

F

A

28"

18"

40¾"

6"

J

C

Fig. 2–44.

86

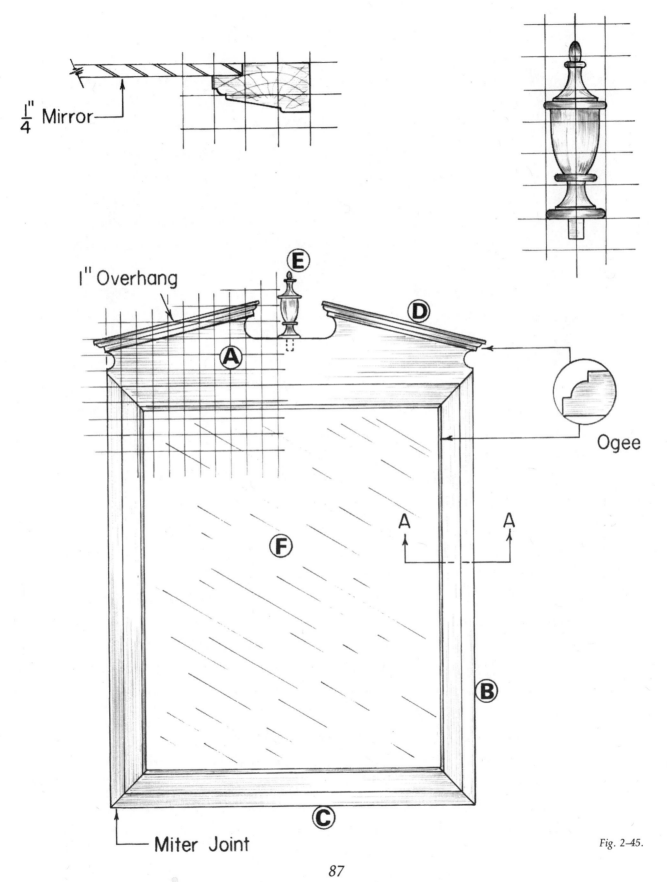

$\frac{1}{4}"$ Mirror

1" Overhang

Ⓔ

Ⓐ

Ⓓ

Ogee

A   A

Ⓕ

Ⓑ

Ⓒ

Miter Joint

87

Fig. 2–45.

Sea or Blanket Chest

The sea chest, a piece usually adorned with carving, was a product of the seamen of New England. These chests made many trips around the world on-board ships while their owners sought whales for oil or traveled to foreign lands for trade.

The chests shown may be made in either of two ways: as a sea chest or as a colonial bedroom chest. The sea chest has a carved or painted eagle, and the colonial chest has the floral design common to Pennsylvania. A cedar lining will make it more practical.

Material List

Part		Number	Size	Material
A	Sides	2	17″ x 18½″ x ¾″	Pine
B	Front and back	2	17″ x 34½″ x ¾″	
C	Bottom	1	17″ x 33″ x ¾″	
D	Top	1	19¼″ x 36½″ x ¾″	
E	Trim (top)	1	1½″ x 38″ x ¾″	
		2	1½″ x 20″ x ¾″	
F	Lining		24 square feet cedar closet lining	

Hardware

1 pair 2″ butt hinges or hand-wrought strap hinges.

CONSTRUCTION

1. Purchase pre-glued ¾″ thick boards or glue up pine stock for the required widths.

2. Lay out and cut the stock for Parts A, B, and C. Cut dovetails on Parts A. Transfer the dovetails to Parts B and cut matching members so that Parts A and B fit together tightly to form a box. Glue and nail Parts A and B together. Insert Part C into the bottom of the assembly ½″ up from the bottom and nail securely in place. (Part C will serve to square up the whole box assembly.)

3. Lay out and cut the stock for Parts D and E. Make 45° mitered joints on Parts E. Nail Parts E to the edges of Part D. Attach Part D to the chest

Fig. 2–47. *Blanket chest with colonial design, Index of American Design, Washington, D. C.*

Fig. 2-48. *Sea or blanket chest project.*

89

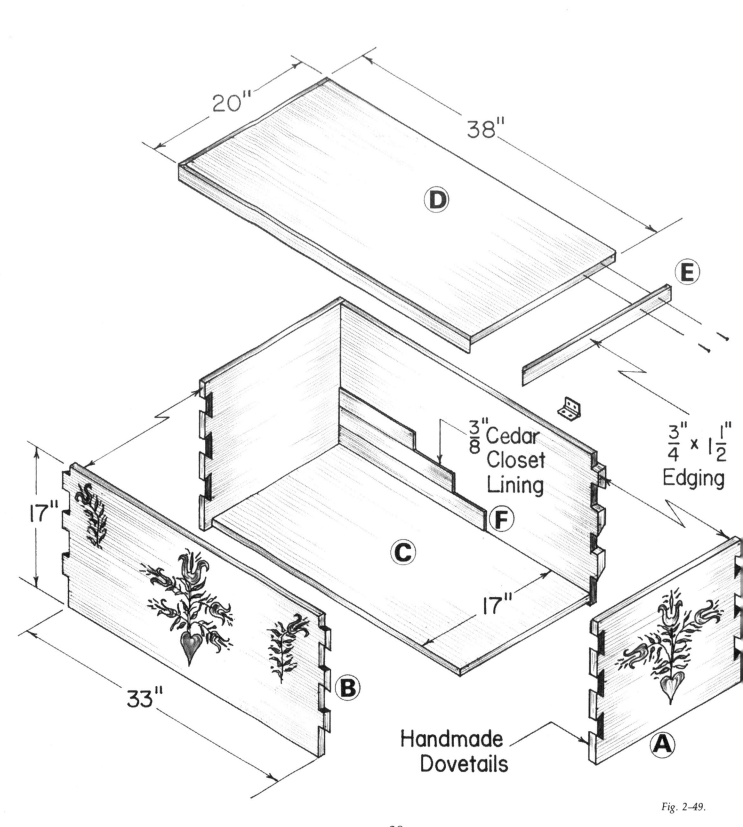

20"

38"

D

E

3/8" Cedar Closet Lining

3/4" × 1 1/2" Edging

17"

F

C

17"

B

33"

Handmade Dovetails

A

Fig. 2–49.

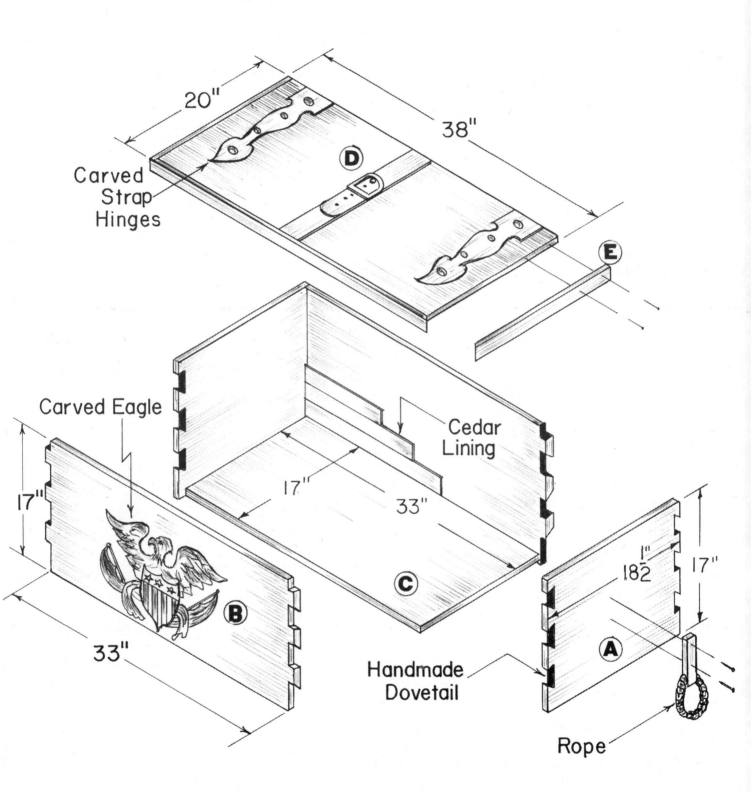

20"

38"

Carved
Strap
Hinges

D

E

Carved Eagle

Cedar
Lining

17"

17"

33"

$18\frac{1}{2}$"

17"

B

C

A

33"

Handmade
Dovetail

Rope

Fig. 2–50.

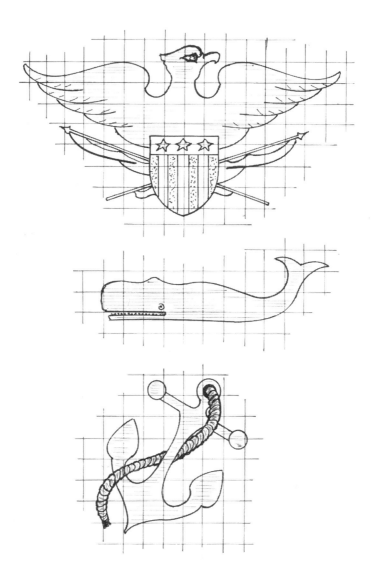

Fig. 2–51.

assembly with 2″ butt hinges or hand-wrought strap hinges.

4. Cut and fit the cedar lining to the box sides, bottom, and top. Nail the lining with small brads through the tongue. *Do not* paint or stain the cedar lining, or it will be ineffective.

FINISH

Colonial. Set and fill all nail holes. Sand the chest smooth. Paint. Transfer Pennsylvania Dutch motifs—birds, tulips, or flowers—where desired and paint these motifs in bright colors. Wipe on a glaze over the chest when the paint has dried. Cover with several coats of lacquer or similar finish. Apply paste wax; buff. (See *Section Eight* for suppliers of Pennsylvania Dutch motifs.)

Sea Chest. Lay out the desired design—an eagle, anchor, or ship—on the chest. Cut the background material away so that the design appears in relief. A router is the best tool to use, or a hand chisel may be used. Paint the chest in several bright colors. When the paint has dried, wipe on a black glaze to give the chest an aged look. Cover with several coats of lacquer or similar finish. Apply paste wax; buff.

SECTION THREE

Tables

Fig. 3–1.   Dining room, Raleigh Tavern; Colonial Williamsburg, Williamsburg, Virginia.

The table represents the spirit of mutual concern the early settlers had for one another, for a place was always set at the table when travelers and new settlers arrived.

Some tables were designed for specific uses and they took on a variety of shapes and sizes.

Fig. 3–2.   *Interior of Cobbler's Shop, Colonial Williamsburg, Williamsburg, Virginia.*

Cobbler's Bench

The original cobbler's bench was constructed in many shapes, styles, and designs, depending upon the cobbler's own skill in woodworking. Basically, the bench is a work station or table, a place where the cobbler could sit with his tools and materials close at hand to make shoes and boots for his clientele.

This coffee table follows the general design of a cobbler's bench including a parts drawer (or drawers), and a leather tool-holder nailed to the side of the table.

Material List

	Part	Number	Size	Material
A	Top	1	15″ x 48″ x 1¾″	Pine
B	Sides	2	8″ x 15″ x ¾″	
C	Shelf Top	1	11″ x 15¾″ x ¾″	
D	Shelf Back	1	8″ x 15″ x ¾″	
E	Rear Leg Cleat	1	4″ x 13″ x 1¾″	
F	Drawer Guide	1	1½″ x 13″ x 1½″	
G	Front Leg Cleat	1	4″ x 13″ x 1½″	
H	Legs	4	2″ dia. x 13″	Fir
I	Drawer Sides	2	10″ x 13″ x ¾″	Pine
J	Drawer Front	2	10″ x 10″ x ¾″	
K	Upper Drawer	1	4″ x 15″ x 8″	
L	Small Drawer	1	2″ x 3″ x 3″	Optional

Fig. 3–3. Cobbler's bench, Index of American Design, Washington, D. C.

Hardware

18″ of ⅝″ leather strap or belt.
6 Porcelain drawer pulls.

CONSTRUCTION

1. Glue up bench-top stock to size, being careful that the glue dowels do not appear on the radius-cut for the seat area.

2. Lay out and cut the bench-top to shape. Cut in the seat radius with a router, ¼″ to ⅜″ deep at the center.

3. Cut the stock for the leg cleats and drawer guide. Cut a ½″ x ¾″ rabbet into the rear cleat and drawer guide as suggested in Figure 3–5. Drill a 2″ diameter hole in the end of each leg cleat so that the legs will be splayed 2″ out and forward. Secure the legs to the cleats. (See *Section One* for leg fastening details.) Secure the leg cleats and drawer guide to the bottom of the bench top with five 2½″ #10 flat head wood screws.

4. Lay out and cut the stock for the shelf sides, top, and back, Parts B, C, and D. Cut a ⅜″ x ¾″ rabbet on each side of the back, Part D. Cut a ⅜″ x ¾″ dado into Parts B and D in order to receive the top, Part C. Secure the sides to the bench top with #8 wood screws. Cover the screw heads with hardwood plugs. Insert the shelf back, Part D, into the rabbets and nail into the side pieces. Insert Part C into the precut dados and nail in place.

5. Make a drawer unit, Parts I and J, as outlined in *Section One*. Nail a ⁷⁄₁₆″ x ¹³⁄₁₆″ cleat to the top sides of the drawer unit. These cleats should work freely into the precut rabbets in the rear leg cleat and the drawer guide.

6. Construct an upper drawer unit to fit into the shelf assembly, Part L. (See *Section One* for details on drawer construction.) The multi-front panel is optional.

7. The very small drawer, Part L, is optional. If this drawer is used, an adjustment must be made on the top drawer, Part K.

96

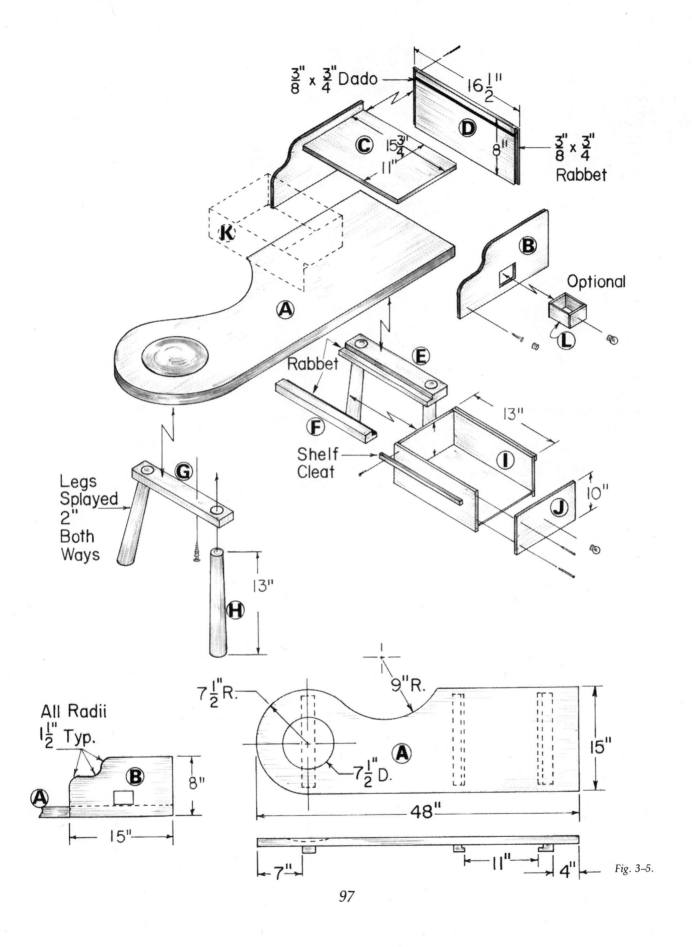

$\frac{3}{8}"$ x $\frac{3}{4}"$ Dado

16$\frac{1}{2}"$

D

$\frac{3}{8}"$ x $\frac{3}{4}"$ Rabbet

C

15$\frac{3}{4}"$

11"

8"

K

B

Optional

A

L

E

Rabbet

F

Shelf Cleat

13"

I

Legs Splayed 2" Both Ways

G

J

10"

13"

H

All Radii 1$\frac{1}{2}"$ Typ.

B

A

8"

15"

7$\frac{1}{2}"$ R.

9" R.

A

7$\frac{1}{2}"$ D.

15"

48"

7"

11"

4"

Fig. 3–5.

97

Fig. 3-4 Cobbler's bench project.

FINISH

Sand the entire bench smooth. Fill all nail holes. Stain. Cover with 6 to 8 coats of lacquer or similar finish. Apply paste wax; buff.

For effect, a ¾" wide strip of leather may be nailed to one side of the bench-top. This leather is nailed so as to make several small loops to act as tool holders. The leather can be obtained by salvaging an old belt and sanding off the finish. Oiling the leather will make it appear old. An authentic touch can be given to the bench by seeking out old tools and putting them into the leather loops.

Fig. 3–6. Trestle table, Index of American Design, Washington, D. C.

Trestle Coffee Table

The original trestle table top is about twelve feet long and over two feet wide and made from one single plank. The plank top is supported on three T-shaped legs. The Metropolitan Museum of Art in New York has an exceedingly rare 17th-century table of that type.

The table in this project has been reduced in size in order to make it as a coffee table. The trestle legs have been widened in order to give the table balanced proportions. By increasing the size of the working drawings, a functional dining or kitchen table may be adapted from the same basic design.

Material List

Part	Number	Size	Material
A Top	1	18″ x 43″ x 1¾″	Pine
B Legs	2	12″ x 8″ x 1¾″	
C Leg Support	4	4″ x 12″ x 1¾″	
D Spreader	1	4″ x 33″ x 1¾″	

CONSTRUCTION

1. Rough-cut the stock. Glue up the lumber to the widths for the table top and legs.

2. Lay out and cut the legs, Parts B, according to the design suggested in Figure 3–8. Cut a 1¼″ x 1¾″ mortise in the trestle legs to receive the stretcher, Part D. Cut the leg supports, Part C. Screw the leg supports into the trestle legs with five 2¼″ #12 flat head wood screws.

3. Cut the spreader, Part D. (See detail in Fig. 3–8.) Cut a 1¼″ x 1¾″ x 1¾″ tenon on the ends. This tenon fits into the mortise holes cut into the trestle legs. If necessary, adjust the tenon for a tight fit; drill a ⅜″ diameter hole where the tenon clears the outside of the trestle leg. (See details in Fig. 3–8.) Secure the stretcher to the legs by means of a 3″ piece of ⅜″ diameter doweling through the hole in the tenon.

4. Cut out the table top. Cut the outside top edges down with a block plane to give the top a worn appearance; cut deeper in the center than at the edges. Screw the top of the leg supports into the bottom of the table top with five 2¼″ #12 wood screws.

FINISH

Disassemble the table parts. Sand all parts smooth. Stain. Cover with several coats of varnish or lacquer. Polish with pumice and lemon oil. Finish with a coat of paste wax. Reassemble table.

Fig. 3–7. Trestle coffee table project.

100

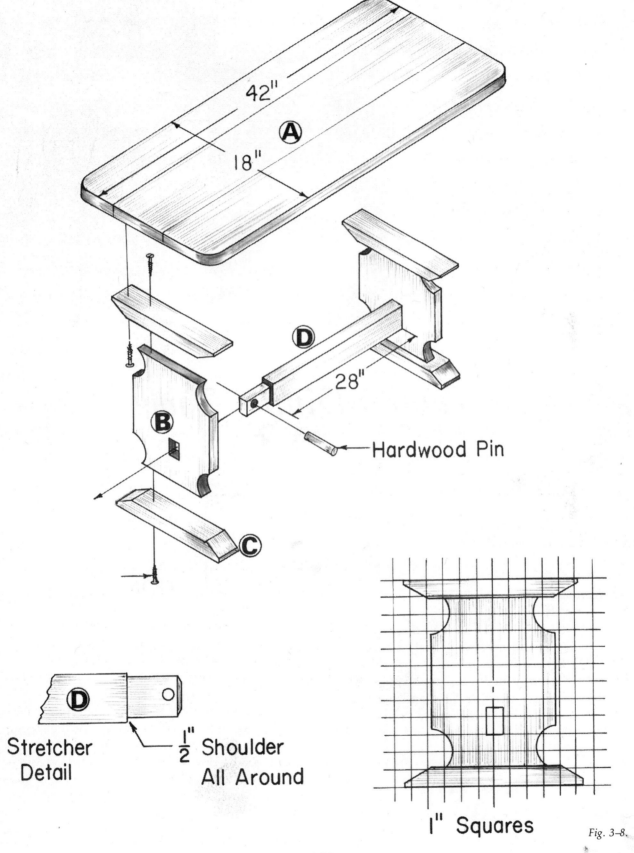

42"

18"

Ⓐ

Ⓓ

Ⓑ

Ⓒ

28"

Hardwood Pin

Ⓓ

Stretcher Detail

$\frac{1}{2}$" Shoulder All Around

1" Squares

Fig. 3–8.

Fig. 3–9. Oval table, Index of American Design, Washington, D. C.

Family Dining Table

The trestle or "sawbuck" tables were the standard dining tables of the colonies. Many early tables consisted of only one plank supported on two or three legs.

As the colonies developed, the trestle legs became more ornate and the tops were made with drop-leaves to conserve space when the table was not in use. The earliest tables were developed by cabinetmakers who drew on their memories of old-world styles.

The table plan shown retains the trestle legs and center spreader found in early sawbuck tables. The top is made in an oval shape rather than the round or rectangular design, to show originality. This table is rather large and may be reduced in the basic dimensions to accommodate individual needs.

Material List

Part		Number	Size	Material
A	Top	1	54" x 74" x 1¾"	Pine
B	Legs	2	18" x 24" x 1¾"	
C	Leg Tops	2	4" x 28" x 1¾"	
D-1	Leg Bottoms	2	4" x 28" x 1¾"	
D-2	Leg Bottoms	2	4" x 22" x 1¾"	
E	Spreader	1	4" x 52" x 1¾"	
F	Leaf Support	2	4" x 23" x 1¾"	

Hardware

3 pairs strap hinges.

CONSTRUCTION

1. Rough cut the stock to size. Glue up the stock to the required widths for the top and legs.

2. Lay out and cut the legs (see Fig. 3–12). Cut a 3" x 1¼" mortise in each leg to receive the spreader, Part E. Cut in the heart design.

3. Lay out and cut the top leg supports, Parts C, and leg bottoms, Parts D. Secure the leg top pieces to the trestle legs with five 2½" #12 flat head wood screws. Secure the double leg bottoms to the trestle legs with five 4½" #14 flat head wood screws, countersunk so that at least one-half of the screw is in the trestle leg.

4. Lay out and cut the spreader, Part E. Cut a

3″ x 1¼″ x 2½″ tenon on each end. Fit the tenon into the leg mortise holes and drill two ⅜″ diameter holes where the tenon clears the leg. Cut four ⅜″ x 3″ dowel pins and fit them into the holes drilled in the ends of the spreader.

5. Lay out the table top and mark out a large oval. Drop-leaves should *not* occur on *glue joints*. Cut out desired oval. Cut down the outside top edges of the table with a block plane to produce a worn effect. Secure each trestle leg to the top center section with six 2¼″ #14 flat head wood screws. Secure leaf-supports to the table top by means of a countersunk carriage bolt. Drill a countersunk hole into the table top. Drop in the carriage bolt so that it extends below the bottom of the table top. Cover the counterbore with a hardwood plug. Drill out the leaf support and counterbore the bottom for the carriage bolt nut. Use a washer between the leaf-support and the table top for easy operation. Secure the drop-leaf sections to the center table top with three large strap hinges.

FINISH

Disassemble all table parts. Sand all parts smooth. Stain. Cover with several coats of lacquer or similar finish. Rub down with pumice and lemon oil. Finish with paste wax.

Reassemble all the table parts. Lock on the leaf supports and peen over the carriage bolt threads to prevent loosening. Re-wax the piece.

Fig. 3–10.   Family dining table project.

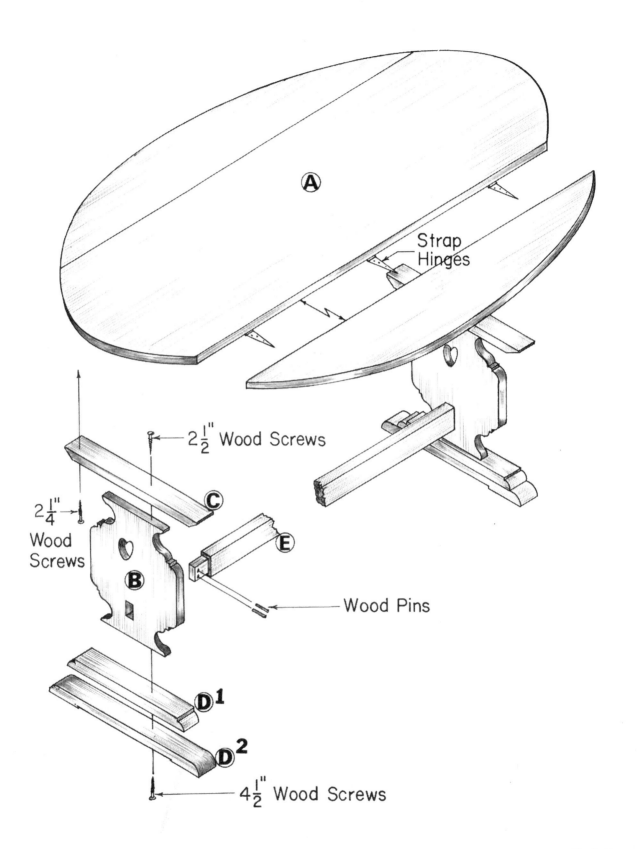

Strap
Hinges

Ⓐ

$2\frac{1}{2}$" Wood Screws

Ⓒ

$2\frac{1}{4}$" →
Wood
Screws

Ⓑ

Ⓔ

Wood Pins

Ⓓ¹

Ⓓ²

$4\frac{1}{2}$" Wood Screws

Fig. 3–11.

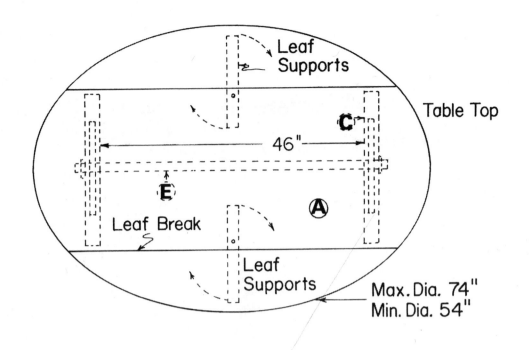

Leaf
Supports

Table Top

46"

Ⓒ

Ⓔ

Leaf Break

Ⓐ

Leaf
Supports

Max. Dia. 74"
Min. Dia. 54"

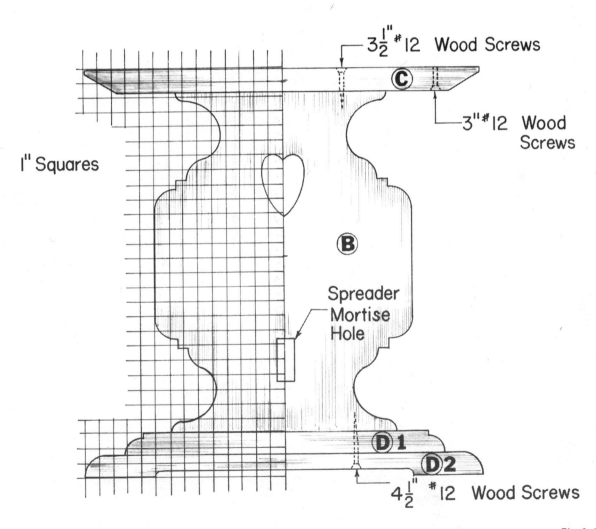

$3\frac{1}{2}$"#12 Wood Screws

Ⓒ

3"#12 Wood
Screws

1" Squares

Ⓑ

Spreader
Mortise
Hole

Ⓓ1
Ⓓ2

$4\frac{1}{2}$"#12 Wood Screws

Fig. 3–12.

Fig. 3–13. *Colonial table and candle stand, Index of American Design, Washington, D. C.*

Tilt-Top Table

Tilt-top tables come in all sizes, shapes, and designs. Some have ornate carvings, scalloped tops called piecrust tops, and claw and ball feet. Basically, this type of table has three legs supporting a central column, which in turn supports the table top. Some authorities claim the three legs had a religious symbolism standing for the Holy Trinity. Some tables have fixed tops and others have an arrangement whereby the top can turn or tilt to lie flat against a wall. The mechanism that tilts and turns the top is called a "birdcage." With the top in the tilt position, the top of the birdcage becomes a small candle stand.

The table plan offered here is designed along the simple lines associated with early colonial pieces.

Material List

	Part	Number	Size	Material
A	Top	1	20″ dia. x ¾″	Pine, Birch
B	Main Stem	1	4½″ dia. x 20″	Maple or Cherry
C	Legs	3	10″ x 15″ x ¾″	
D	Cage Top	1	6″ x 6″ x ¾″	
	Cage Bottom	1	6″ x 6″ x ¾″	
E	Straps	2	2″ x 8″ x ¾″	
F	Turnings	4	1½″ dia. x 5½″	

106

CONSTRUCTION

1. Rough cut the stock to size. Glue up the main stem stock and table top.

2. Lathe-turn Part B to the suggested shape. Cut a ¾" diameter tenon on the top of the main stem to go into the birdcage. Drill a ⅜" diameter hole through the tenon to receive the wedge pin shown in Figure 3–15. Cut in three dovetails (or square mortises), in the bottom section to receive the three legs. (A mortising chisel, a router, or a shaper may be used for this operation.)

3. Lay out and cut the legs, Parts C. Cut matching dovetails (or square tenons), in the leg tops. Fit the leg tenons to the stem mortises. An ogee molded edge may be used on the legs if desired.

4. Glue and pin the finished legs into the main stem. Cut the material for the birdcage, Part D. Drill a ¾" hole in the center of the bottom piece and partway through the top piece. This will enable the birdcage to fit over the round tenon on the top of Part B. Drill a ⅜" diameter hole in all four corners of the top and bottom pieces, three-fourths of the way through. These holes will receive Parts F. Drill a ⅜" hole in the edge of the top piece to take the dowel pins from the straps, Part E.

5. Cut the stock for the turnings, Part F. Lathe-turn the pieces to the suggested shape, leaving a ⅜" diameter x ⅜" tenon on each end. Glue the finished turnings into the pre-drilled holes in Parts D.

6. Lay out and cut stock for the top, Part A. Cut the top out in a circle. (An oval or square top may be used if you prefer). Cut an ogee-molded edge on the top piece.

7. Lay out and cut stock for the straps, Part E. Drill holes for five 2" #10 wood screws in each piece. Drill a ⅜" hole for the dowel pin coming from the top of the birdcage. Screw the straps into the table top. Line up the birdcage and glue in the dowel pins to the birdcage. *Do not allow glue to touch the pin as it goes into the straps.* It must swing free at this point. An elbow catch may be used to lock the table top in a down position.

Fig. 3–14.   Tilt-top table project.

FINISH

Sand all parts smooth. Stain in the desired color. Cover with several coats of lacquer or similar finish. Polish with pumice and lemon oil.

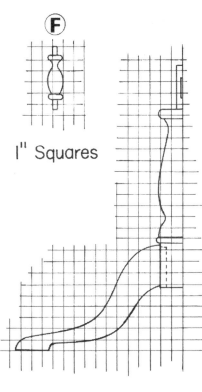

F

I" Squares

120°

Leg Placement

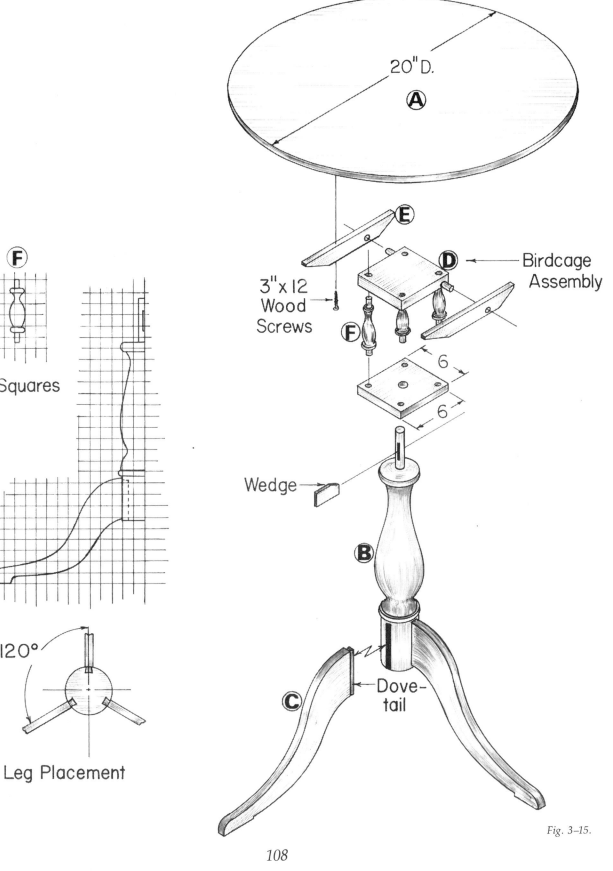

20"D.

A

E

3"x I2
Wood
Screws

F

D ← Birdcage
Assembly

6

6

Wedge

B

C

Dove-
tail

Fig. 3–15.

Fig. 3–16. Dough box, Old Sturbridge Village, Sturbridge, Massachusetts.

Dough Box End Table

The dough box was a plain box in which bread dough was placed before baking, to allow it to rise. In colonial times, the box was very often crudely made. When time allowed, the dough box was constructed with legs or placed on top of a small table so that the housewife could use the top as a cutting board or work surface.

The dough box plan is designed to be used as an end table. The interior may hold magazines or the box can be adjusted to hold a stereo system. Either way, the piece makes a pleasant addition to colonial styled interiors.

Material List

Part		Number	Size	Material
A	Bottom	1	18″ x 24″ x 1¾″	Pine
B	Sides	2	10″ x 24″ x ¾″	
C	Ends	2	10″ x 18″ x ¾″	
D	Box Top(s)	1	19½″ x 25½″ x ¾″	
E	Leg Cleats	2	3″ x 16″ x 1¾″	
F	Legs	4	2″ dia. x 11″	Fir

Note: Part D is assembled in one unit, then split into two pieces. See paragraph #3, Construction.

CONSTRUCTION

1. Glue up the stock for Parts A and D; lay out and cut. Lay out and cut the stock for Parts E and F. Drill a 2″ diameter hole in each end of Part E, splayed 2″ out and forward (about a 15° angle). Glue in the precut legs and pin to the leg cleats with a cross-dowel pin. (See *Section One* for details.) Fasten the assembly to the bottom of Part A with five 2¼″ #12 flat head wood screws.

2. Lay out and cut the stock for the box proper, Parts B and C. Cut the bottom and top edges of these boards at a 15° angle. (See detail, Fig. 3–18, lower right-hand corner.) The box tapers outward at the top. Cut a ⅜″ x ¾″ rabbet on each side of Parts C to receive Parts B. Glue and nail the box together. (Hand-forged or horseshoe nails may be used to nail the box together. leaving the large nail heads exposed.) If you prefer, use 8d finishing nails. Drill ³/₁₆″ diameter countersunk holes on the inside of the assembled box. (See detail in Fig. 3–18.) Secure the box assembly to the table bottom with wood screws through these holes.

3. Lay out and cut the stock for Part D. Cut the finished piece in half. Nail one half of Part D to the box assembly. Exposed nails may be used for effect. Install butterfly flush hinges to the remaining half of the top and secure this section to the fixed portion. Insert a dowel in the box front and insert a leather thong through a hole drilled in the movable section of Part D. The leather thong acts as a lock when looped over the dowel.

FINISH

Sand the entire dough box smooth. Stain in the desired color. Cover with several coats of lacquer or similar finish. Finish with paste wax.

Fig. 3–17. Dough box end table project.

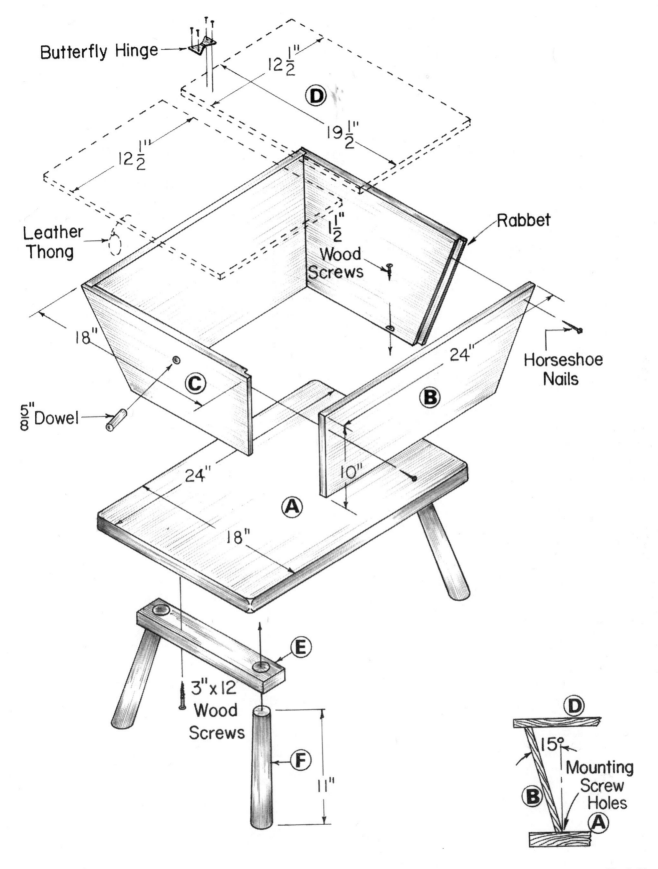

Butterfly Hinge

12 ½"

D

19 ½"

Rabbet

12 ½"

1 ½"

Leather
Thong

Wood
Screws

18"

24"

Horseshoe
Nails

C

B

⅝" Dowel

24"

10"

A

18"

E

3"x12
Wood
Screws

F

11"

D

15°

B

Mounting
Screw
Holes

A

Fig. 3–18.

Fig. 3–19. Sketch of a frontier-styled table, from the original in Plimoth Plantation, Plymouth, Massachusetts.

Step End Table

Most end tables are designed to be used beside a sofa or a chair, luxuries unheard of in colonial times. The step end table is a composite of ideas and designs rather than a copy of any one prototype. This plan is the result of combining parts of a utility stool or table with a later period lamp stand.

This end table has four plain legs, no stretchers, and follows the general lines of colonial furniture. The cyma-curve end pieces holding up the top tier, or drawer unit, are common with the style of furniture in that period. This piece maintains the early principles, yet is functional for modern colonial-styled living rooms.

Material List

	Part	Number	Size	Material
A	Top	1	18″ x 36″ x 1¾″	Pine
B	Sides	2	10″ x 14″ x ¾″	
C	Step Top	1	14″ x 18¾″ x ¾″	
D	Drawer Front and Back	2	3″ x 17⅞″ x ¾″	
E	Drawer Sides	2	3″ x 12¼″ x ¾″	
F	Bottom	1	12¼″ x 17⅛″ x ¼″	Plywood
G	Leg Cleats	2	4″ x 16″ x 1¾″	
H	Legs	4	2″ dia. x 12″	Fir

CONSTRUCTION

1. Rough cut stock to size and glue up to the suggested widths.

2. Lay out and cut table top, Part A. Round over the front edges only. Lay out and cut the table sides, Parts B. Cut a ⅜" x ¾" blind dado into the inside tops to receive Part C. Drill countersunk screw holes into the dado and where Parts B will be secured to Part A.

3. Screw Parts B to Part A. Cover the screw heads with hardwood plugs. Lay out and cut Part C. Insert Part C into the precut dados and secure with wood screws. Cover the screw heads with plugs.

4. Lay out and cut Parts G and H. Drill a 2" diameter hole in each end of Part G so that the legs will splay 2" out and forward. Insert the precut legs into the holes. (See *Section One* for leg fastening details.) *Note: Turned legs may be used if you desire. Secure the leg assembly to the bottom of Part A with five 3" #10 wood screws.*

5. Construct a drawer unit as suggested in *Section One*, Drawer Construction, Parts D, E, and F. Attach ⅜" x ⅜" strips to the inside of Parts B to act as drawer guides. Adjust the drawer unit to insure a free, easy sliding action if needed.

FINISH

Sand all parts smooth. Cover all remaining screw holes with hardwood plugs. Set and fill all nail holes. Stain. Cover with several coats of varnish or lacquer. Rub with pumice and lemon oil. Finish with paste wax.

Fig. 3–20. Step end table project.

113

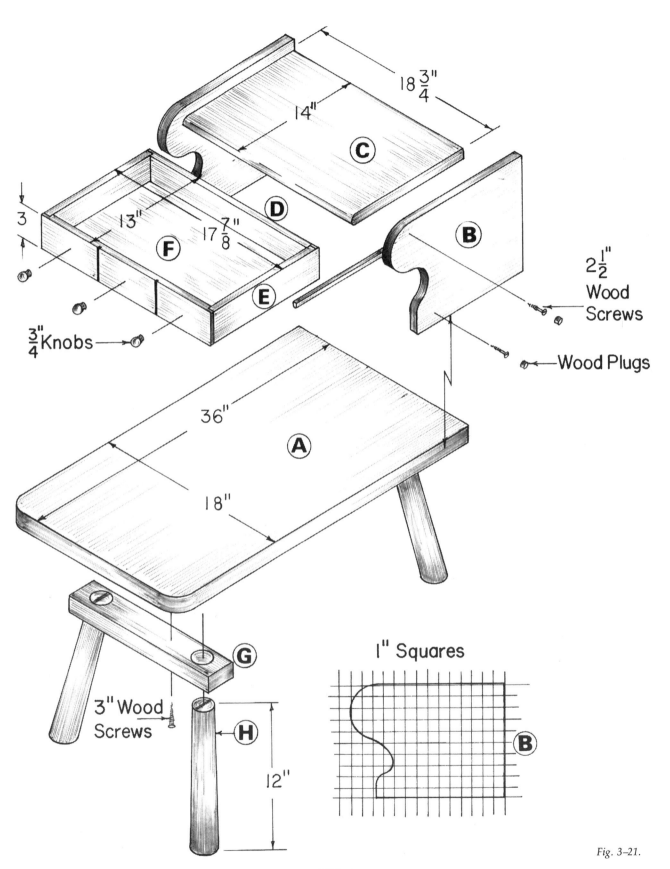

$18\frac{3}{4}''$

$14''$

C

D

B

3

$13''$

$17\frac{7}{8}''$

F

E

$2\frac{1}{2}''$ Wood Screws

Wood Plugs

$\frac{3}{4}''$ Knobs

$36''$

A

$18''$

G

3" Wood Screws

H

$12''$

1" Squares

B

Fig. 3–21.

Trestle Rudder Table

Few items of furniture display the advancement in craftsmanship or the use of complex machines as does the table. As soon as conditions permitted, settlers progressed from the plank table to more appealing designs. Turned legs, carved stretchers, and different shaped tops appeared. A logical development was the use of drop-leaves so that tables could be increased or decreased in size, depending upon need.

The table shown here has been known by many different names: drop-leaf, butterfly, rudder, gateleg, or side-wing table. Developed from the early trestle plank and the gate-leg styled table, the size was reduced in order to make it an occasional or end table. If a full-sized dining table is desired, the basic dimensions can easily be increased. The overall construction and trestle or rudder shapes will remain the same.

Material List

Part		Number	Size	Material
A	Leg	2	12" x 19½" x ¾"	Pine,
B	Shoe	2	2" x 15" x ¾"	Cherry,
C	Top Stretcher	2	4" x 22" x ¾"	or Wood
D	Bottom			of Choice
	Stretcher	2	2" x 22" x ¾"	
E	Pivot Seats	2	1¾" x 11" x ¾"	
F	Rudders	2	8" x 14¼" x ¾"	
G	Top	1	26" x 36" x ¾" Oval	

CONSTRUCTION

1. Glue up the stock to widths needed for Parts A and G.

2. After glue has dried, lay out and cut Parts A. Lay out and cut the shoes, Parts B. Secure Parts B to Parts A with 2½" #10 flat head wood screws.

3. Lay out and cut the stretchers, Parts C and D. Cut a ¾" x 1¾" notch in the center tops of each piece. Parts E will fit into these notches. Secure Parts C and D to Parts A with 2" #10 flat head wood screws in countersunk holes.

4. Lay out and cut Parts E, the rudder pivot seats. Cut a single round on the ends. Drill a ⅜" diameter hole in the center of these rounds to receive the dowels from Parts F. Secure Parts E into the notches in Parts C and D with wood screws. Note the top Part E is drilled so that screws can be fastened into the top, Part G. (See detail, Fig. 3–24.)

5. Lay out and cut the rudders, Parts F. Cut a ⅞" x 3" relief on the top part of the rudder so that it will swing around the top Part E. Drill a ⅜" diameter hole in the top and bottom of Part F for the dowel pin. Install the rudder between Parts E with ⅜" diameter dowel.

6. Lay out and cut the table top, Part G. Note that the overall oval is 26" x 36" with a fixed section 16" x 26" and drop-leaves of 10" x 21". Secure the drop-leaves to the center section with butt hinges. Secure the top to the table with wood screws through the top, Part E, and through the inside top edges of Parts A. Check the action of the rudder swings, and check to see that they hold the drop-leaves level. Small buttons or a wedge should be installed on the underside of the leaf, if needed.

FINISH

Cover all screw heads with hardwood plugs. (Hardwood buttons may be used if preferred.) Sand entire table smooth. Stain or paint. Apply six to eight coats of lacquer. Buff with lemon oil and pumice, and finish with paste wax.

Note: If a full-size table is desired, increase the total height to 30". Increase the width of the trestle legs to 20" and the stretchers to 30". A base of this size will support a fixed table-top of 30" x 36" with 12" drop-leaf sections.

Fig. 3–22. Trestle rudder table project.

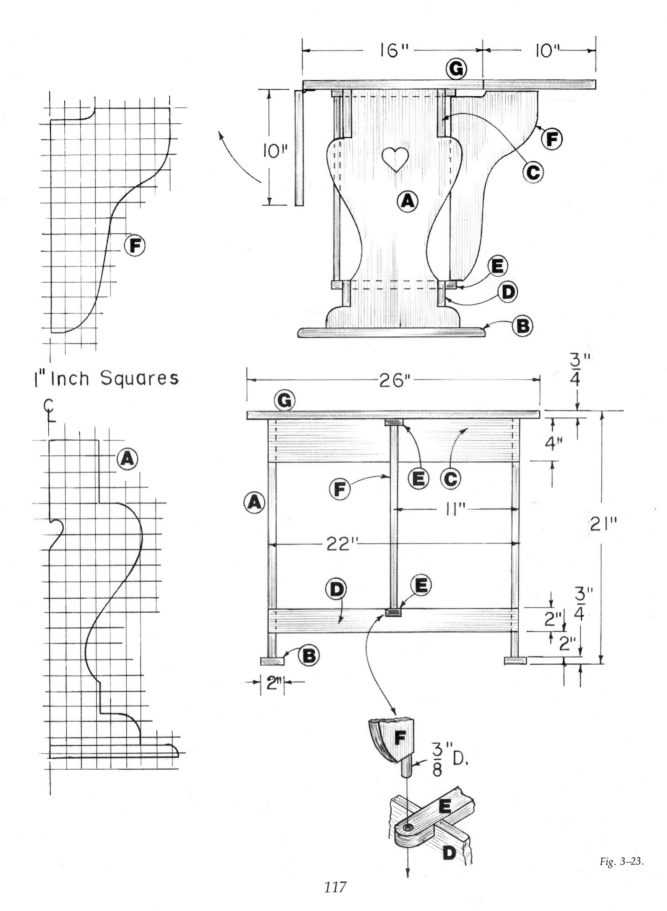

1" Inch Squares

16"   10"

10"

G

F

C

A

E

D

B

3/4"

26"

G

4"

E   C

F

A

11"

22"

D   E

21"

B

2"

3/4"

2"

2"

F

3/8" D.

E

D

117

Fig. 3–23.

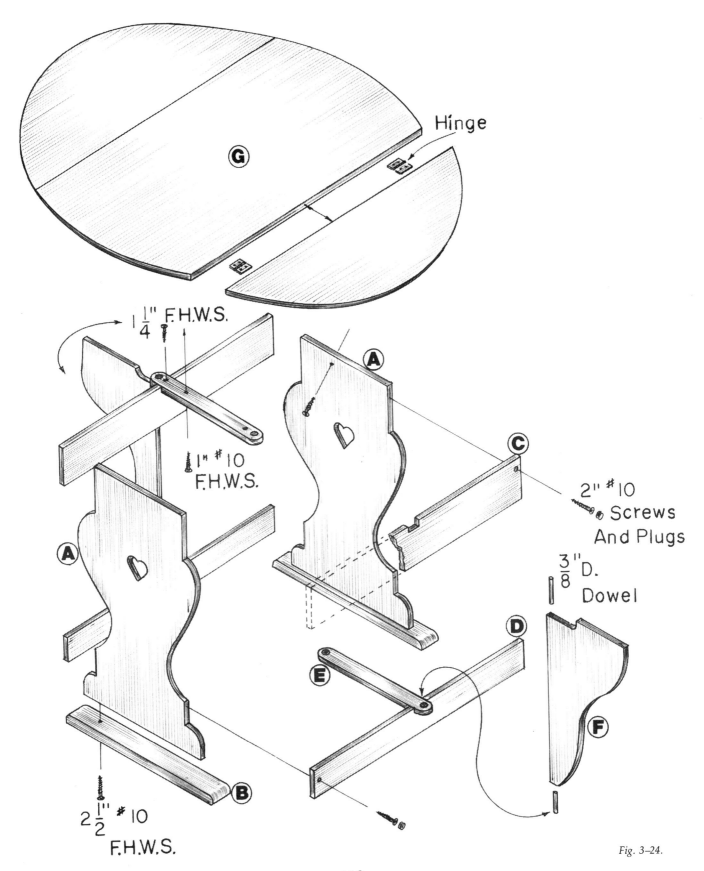

Hinge

G

1 $\frac{1}{4}$" F.H.W.S.

A

1" #10
F.H.W.S.

C

2" #10
Screws
And Plugs

A

$\frac{3}{8}$" D.
Dowel

E

D

F

B

2 $\frac{1}{2}$" #10
F.H.W.S.

Fig. 3–24.

118

SECTION FOUR

Clocks

The meeting house, one of the first buildings erected by settlers, was more than a place of religious worship. The colonial meetinghouse also served as a general gathering place, a defense in some areas against possible Indian attack, a public center for common issues, and a leading factor in the development of our local and state forms of government.

Colonial meetinghouses were often devoid of any religious symbols, but many had one common element, the tower clock. All handmade, it was the town's symbol of civic pride. Most early settlers could not afford to own timepieces, and the tower clock served the entire population. Recorded accounts in Boston show funds granted for the care of its tower clock as early as 1650.

The following section is devoted to colonial types of timepieces. The clockworks may be powered by any means desired; key wind, electricity, battery, or weight-driven. It would be wise to have the clock works and face (dial), on hand before starting work, as the clock movements and dials can vary in size from one manufacturer to another. (See *Section Eight* for list of suppliers.)

Fig. 4–1. Tower clock, Longmeadow, Massachusetts.

120

Steeple Clock

The steeple clock, whose design is credited to Elias Ingraham, has a Gothic styled case that ranges in height from 10″ up to 30″. It usually has a hand-painted dial, and many times a painted decorative panel is in the lower-door section.

This basic clock design was copied by many rural craftsmen, thus numerous variants are still to be found. Basically, the steeple clock has a pointed top or "roof," and conical turned projections on the corners. Many clocks are very plain and simple, but others are very ornate, complete with fancy scrolls and twisting spires.

The clock case plan offered here carries a simplicity found in early pieces.

Fig. 4–2. Steeple clock, Old Sturbridge Village, Sturbridge, Massachusetts.

Material List

	Part	Number	Size	Material
A	Base	1	5″ x 7″ x ¾″	Pine,
B	Sides	2	4″ x 7½″ x ¾″	Cherry,
C	Roof	2	4″ x 7¾″ x ¾″	Maple,
D	Finials	2	¾″ x 3¾″	or Birch
E	Door Side Pieces	2	1″ x 6¾″ x ¾″	
F	Door Roof Pieces	2	1″ x 8″ x ¾″	
G	Door Base	1	2½″ x 5″ x ¾″	

Hardware and Clock Works

	Number	Size	Material
Pair small butt hinges	1	1″ x 1″	Brass
Door pull	1	¼″ dia.	Brass
Door catch	1	Any type	
Glass	1	5½″ x 10″	Single strength
Clock face (dial)*	1	5″ x 12″ (typical)	
Clock movement*			

* See *Section Eight* for suppliers.

CONSTRUCTION

1. Lay out and rough-cut Parts A, B, and C. Cut a ¾″ notch in Part A as suggested in Figure 4–4 so that Part B will fit flush. Nail Parts A and B together with 6d finishing nails.

2. Cut the required angles on Part C to fit on top of Part B so they will form a tight joint at the top center, much like a steeply pitched roof. Nail and glue Parts C to Parts B.

3. Lathe-turn Parts D to the suggested shape. Cut an angle on the lower edge so the finials fit on Part C's steep pitch; Parts D must be perfectly plumb. Glue and brad Parts D to Parts C.

4. Cut the stock for the door (Parts E, F, and G). Cut a ¼″ x ⅜″ rabbet for the door glass in the back inside edges of these parts. Nail Parts E to

Fig. 4–3. Steeple clock project.

Part G at the bottom. Cut the required angles on Part F to match the angles on the main case. Glue and nail Parts F to Parts E. Some adjustments may be needed to make the completed door fit the clock case perfectly.

5. Cut in the small butt hinges and secure the finished door to the assembled clock case. Secure the door pull and catch.

FINISH

Set and fill all nail holes. Sand the entire clock case smooth. Stain. Cover with several coats of lacquer. Hand-rub with pumice and lemon oil. Finish with paste wax.

INSTALLING THE MOVEMENT

Attach the clock face to the clock case with glue blocks and brass screws. The clock face may be purchased, made from cardboard, or copper enameled, as in the case of the original. You may make the face yourself, and hand-paint or decorate it to your choice. Install the clock movement. (See *Section Eight* for suppliers.)

Install the door glass into the precut rabbets with glazier's points or wood strips.

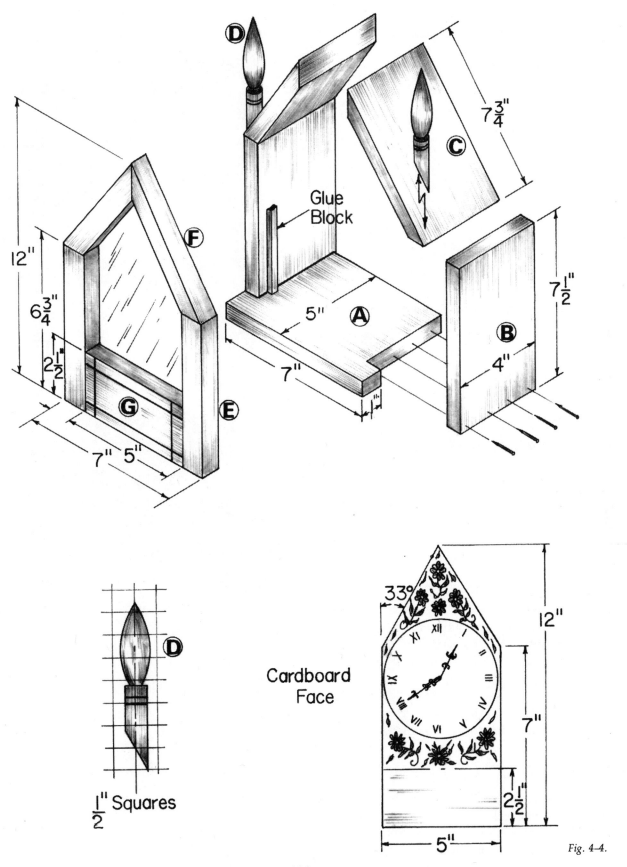

D

Glue
Block

7¾"

C

12"

F

6¾"

2½"

G

E

A

5"

7"

¼"

B

7½"

4"

7" 5"

D

½" Squares

Cardboard
Face

33°

12"

XII XI X IX VIII VII VI V IV III II I

7"

2½"

5"

Fig. 4-4.

Wall Clock

Fig. 4–5. Early American wall clock, Index of American Design, Washington, D, C.

Many variations of hanging wall clocks were made in young America. The "wag-on-the-wall" and the "tea-pot" clocks are two of the most famous examples. Designs may range from a highly decorative case such as the one in Figure 4–5 to a very simple box-like affair. Some wall clocks have only a face enclosed by a square box with an exposed pendulum, while other types contain the pendulum in a long case, complete with turned finials.

The project offered here is a composite of several different styles. The top of the case is designed as a "hood" and the lower box may be used to house or enclose a pendulum. In essence, this clock has authentic colonial styling, but is not a reproduction of any specific timepiece.

Material List

	Part	Number	Size	Material
A	Top	1	6½″ x 12¾″ x ¾″	Pine,
B	Upper Sides	2	4½″ x 10½″ x ¾″	Cherry,
C	Lower Sides	2	4″ x 6¾″ x ¾″	Maple,
D	Base	1	6½″ x 11″ x ¾″	or Wood
E	Middle	1	6½″ x 12¾″ x ¾″	of Choice
F	Back	1	10½″ x 18½″ x ¼″	Plywood
G	Skirt	1	3″ x 10″ x ¾″	
H	Dentil	1	1″ x 11″ x 5/16″	
		2	1″ x 4½″ x 5/16″	
I	Clock Front	1	10¾″ x 10½″ x ¾″	
J	Door	1	9″ x 6¾″ x ¾″	

124

Hardware and Movements

K	Movement*	1	3¼" diameter (typical)
	Face*	1	6½" dia. with bezel
	Hinge	1	Pair, 1" x 1" butts
	Pull	1	½" diameter porcelain
	Catch	1	Magnetic

* See *Section Eight* for list of suppliers.

CONSTRUCTION

1. Lay out and cut all the stock. Cut a ¼" x ¼" rabbet on the back inside edges of Parts A, B, C, and D. (Parts A and D have blind rabbets; the plywood back, Part F, fits into these rabbets.) Cut a ¼" dado across the back of Part E so that Part F will pass flush. The back (Part F) is the member that secures and squares up the whole clock case.

2. Nail Parts C to Parts D and E. Nail Parts B to Parts A. Nail Part F into the precut rabbets. Set all nail heads.

3. Check the actual size of the movement before cutting the required hole; mark opening and cut. (Movement sizes vary depending upon manufacturers.) After cutting the hole, nail Part I to Parts A, B, and E. Set the nail heads.

4. Cut Part G into the suggested cyma curve and nail Part G under Part D. Cut the dentil, Parts H, and secure with brads to Part I and Parts B. Set all nail and brad heads.

5. Construct a raised panel door. (See *Section One* for details.) Using the 1" brass hinges, attach the finished door to one side of Part C. Install the catch and pull.

FINISH

Fill all nail holes and sand the entire project smooth. Stain the case. Cover with several coats of lacquer or similar finish. Rub with pumice and lemon oil, and finish with paste wax.

Fig. 4–6. *Wall clock project.*

INSTALLING THE MOVEMENT

This will depend upon what type of movement you have chosen. For typical installation use a round, self-contained movement. This movement is attached by means of four small screws that go through the outside ring of the bezel.

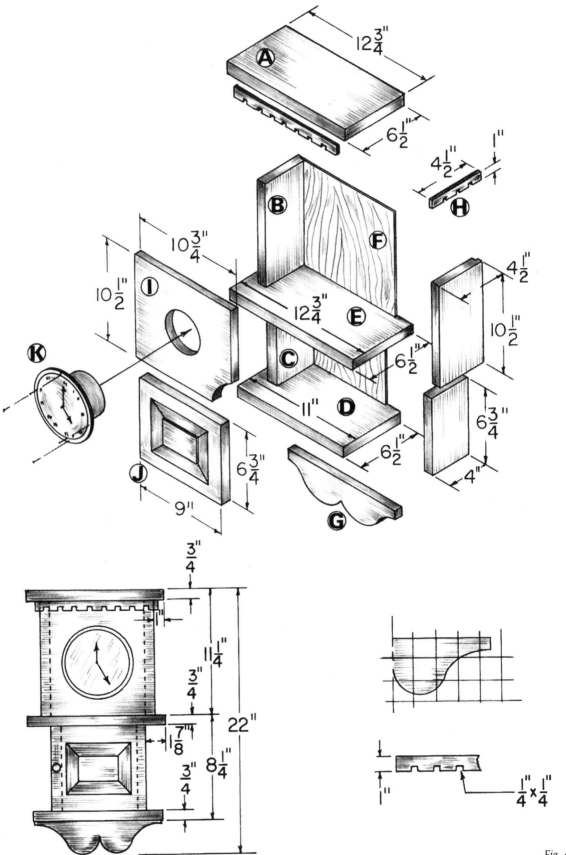

12 3/4"

6 1/2"

Ⓐ

Ⓑ

Ⓕ

4 1/2"

1"

Ⓗ

10 3/4"

10 1/2"

Ⓘ

Ⓔ

12 3/4"

4 1/2"

10 1/2"

Ⓚ

Ⓒ

6 1/2"

Ⓓ

11"

6 3/4"

Ⓙ

6 3/4"

6 1/2"

4"

9"

Ⓖ

3/4"

1"

11 1/4"

3/4"

1 7/8"

3/4"

22"

8 1/4"

1/4" x 1/4"

1"

Fig. 4–7.

Fig. 4–8. *Carriage or bracket clock, Colonial Williamsburg, Williamsburg, Virginia.*

English Carriage Clock

Accurate time-keeping is important on land, but it is even more important at sea, in order to determine an exact position. England, as a seafaring nation, contributed greatly to the science of measuring time. The colonies also depended upon the sea, and therefore needed accurate timepieces. All clock movements were imported in the early years of the settlements until skilled workers in Connecticut started making their own timepieces. The clock movements needed cases and it is here that the Yankee feeling for functional design fully emerged as an art.

The clock shown here goes under several names: the English mantel, bracket, or carriage clock. Some of the original cases were very ornate, complete with moon dials, while others were fairly simple. The simple case with clean sharp lines is the one that typifies the style of locally made colonial furniture.

CONSTRUCTION

1. Lay out and cut all stock. (See Fig. 4–10.) Cut a ⅜″ x ⅜″ rabbet at the rear of Parts A and B. Nail Parts A to Parts B. Insert Part C into the precut rabbets and nail into Parts A and B.

2. With an ogee router bit, cut an edge on Parts D, except the back edge. Glue and nail the four feet (⅜″ x 1″ x 1″), to one of the pieces. This then becomes the bottom piece. Screw Parts D to Parts B from the inside of the case.

3. Cut miter-joints on the crown molding so that the molding starts (bottom edge), ¾″ back from the outer edge of Part D. Nail the cut molding to Part D. Cut Part F to fit into the space between the tops of the molding. (See Fig. 4–10 for details.) Attach a ½″ door pull to Part F, and glue and nail Part F into the slot between the molding tops.

4. Miter-cut the door parts, Part G. Cut a ¼″ x ⅜″ rabbet into the back inside edges to allow for the door glass. Glue and nail Parts G together to form a frame. Install the brass hinges and attach the door frame to the clock case.

Fig. 4–9. *English carriage clock project.*

Material List

Part		Number	Size	Material
A	Sides	2	5″ x 9½″ x ¾″	Pine
B	Top and Bottom	2	5″ x 8″ x ¾″	or Wood
C	Back	1	8¾″ x 8½″ x ¼″	of Choice
D	Top and Bottom Facings	2	6½″ x 12″ x ¾″	
E	Molding	1	36″ of 3″ Crown mold	Pine
F	Spacer	1	2½″ x 6″ x ¾″	
G	Door	4	1″ x 9½″ x ¾″	

Hardware and Movements

Glass	1	7½″ x 7½″	Single strength
Hinge	1 pr.	1″ x 1″	Brass butt
Top handle	1	2½″ drawer pull (bail type)	
Door pull	1	½″ diameter	
Clock face (dial)*	1	7⅞″ x 7⅞″	Brass
Clock movement*	1	Of choice	

* See *Section Eight* for suppliers.

FINISH

Set and fill all nail holes. Sand entire clock case smooth. Stain. Cover with several coats of lacquer or similar finish. Rub with pumice and lemon oil. Finish with paste wax.

Install the glass in the door frame with glazier's points. Install the pull and catch.

INSTALLING THE MOVEMENT

Install the clock face with screws into small glue blocks. Install the clock movement behind the face.

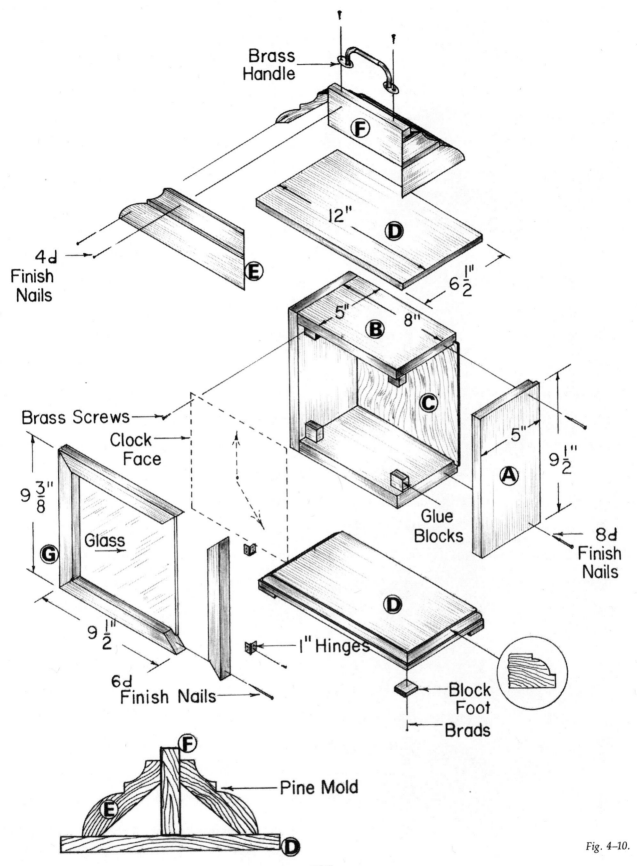

Brass
Handle

F

4d
Finish
Nails

E

12"

D

6½"

Brass Screws

Clock
Face

5"

B

8"

C

9⅜"

Glass

G

9½"

9½"

A

5"

Glue
Blocks

8d
Finish
Nails

1" Hinges

D

6d
Finish Nails

Block
Foot

Brads

F

Pine Mold

E

D

129

Fig. 4–10.

New England Wall Clock

Fig. 4–11. New England wall clock project.

A Colonial settler could seldom purchase a complete house clock. Most often he would buy the clock movement and dial and then find a local joiner or cabinetmaker to build a case.

There is an eighteenth-century story concerning clockfaces that still has influence on modern clocks. The Roman numeral four is written as "IV," meaning one less than five. However, most clockfaces have the number four written as "IIII." Legend says that an English king in the seventeenth century wrote the numeral four as four ones. Several surrounding noblemen thought this error was very funny and made the mistake of laughing. They were "rewarded" with a week or two in the Tower of London for their indiscretion, and the king declared from that day forward all fours would be written as four ones. Even in modern America a major percentage of clockfaces have fours of this type.

Material List

	Part	Number	Size	Material
A	Sides	2	4¼" x 23¼" x ¾"	Pine or Material of Choice
B	Back	1	8" x 22⅞" x ¼"	Plywood
C	Bottom	1	4¼" x 7¼" x ¾"	
D	Top	1	6½" x 11¾" x ¾"	
E	Plate	1	1" x 8¾" x ¾"	
F	Molding	1	¾" x 10¼" x ¾"	Cove
		2	¾" x 5¾" x ¾"	Cove
G	Door	1	8¾" x 22¼" x ¾"	

Movement

H	Clock*	1	* 6" diameter self-contained unit with bezel, dial, hands and movement, with or without pendulum.

* See *Section Eight* for suppliers.

CONSTRUCTION

1. Lay out and cut the stock for Parts A and B. Cut a ⅜" x ⅜" rabbet on the rear inside edges of

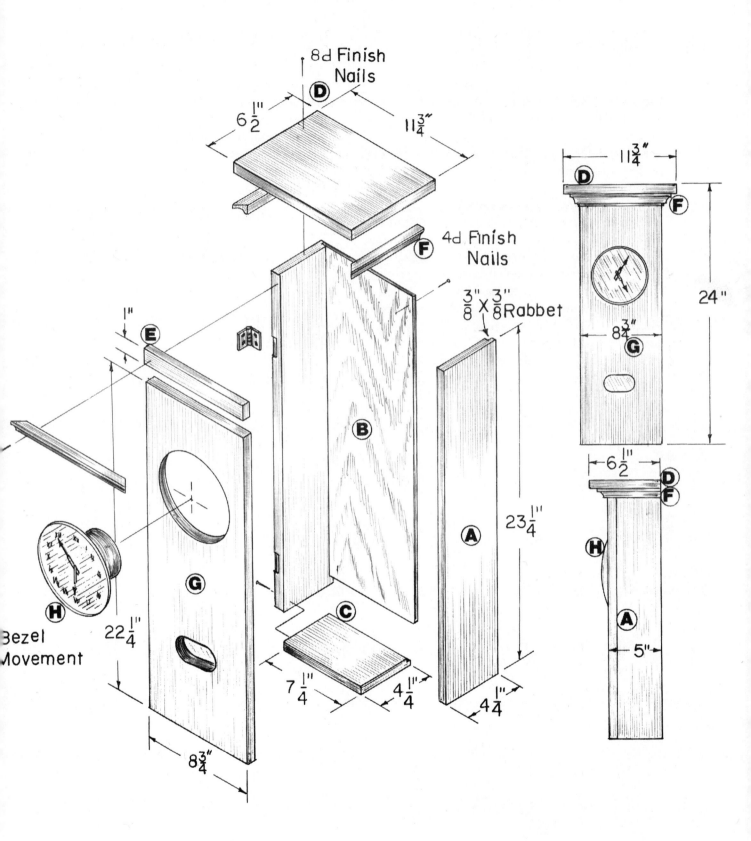

8d Finish
Nails

6 ½"

D

11 ¾"

4d Finish
Nails

F

⅜" X ⅜" Rabbet

11 ¾"

D   **F**

24"

8 ¾"

G

6 ½"

D
F

H

A

5"

1"

E

Bezel
Movement

H

22 ¼"

G

8 ¾"

B

23 ¼"

A

C

7 ¼"   4 ¼"   4 ¼"

Fig. 4–12.

131

Parts A to receive Part B. Nail Part B into the rabbets with large head brads.

2. Lay out and cut stock for Part C. Cut a ⅜″ x ⅜″ rabbet into the back edge to receive Part B. Cut Parts D and E to size. Nail Part D into Parts A. Nail Part E to Parts A and Part D down into Part E.

3. Cut the molding, Parts F, with mitered joints on the outside edges. Nail Parts F into Parts A, D, and E.

4. Lay out and cut stock for the door, Part G. Decide what type of movement you want to use. The bezel self-contained movement will not need the pendulum view shown in the drawing. If this type of movement is used, it is surface mounted and there is no need for the door, Part G, to open and close because the glass bezel is operable. Therefore Part G may be nailed to Parts A if desired. If a pendulum movement is used, it will be mounted inside the case between Parts A. If this type of movement is used, a piece of glass is installed behind the door for both the face and the pendulum view.

To install the glass, cut the glass to cover the openings and secure to the rear of Part G with small wooden strips. Secure the door to the case with butt hinges and a door catch.

Install a wall-hang bracket on the rear of Part B.

FINISH

Set and fill all nail heads. Sand entire project smooth. Stain or paint to a color of your choice. Cover with several coats of lacquer and finish with paste wax.

INSTALLING THE MOVEMENT

Follow manufacturer's directions.

Grandmother's Clock

The grandfather's or tall case clock was made in colonial America as early as 1682 by Abel Cottey in Philadelphia. All the gears were handmade from sheet brass and the gear teeth were cut in individually with a file. Because the movements were handmade and took weeks to complete, the selling price in 1770 was about $40.00, a fairly high price. Once the movement was purchased, the owner then sought out a cabinetmaker or joiner to make a case for the works.

This type of clock is known by several names: Grandfather's, tall, hall, floor, or long case are just a few. Smaller versions were called grandmother's or granddaughter's clocks. The difference is in the overall height and the moon dial. Several hundred variations are still around today, with many clocks being passed from generation to generation. Here is an opportunity for you to make your own heirloom.

This clock is not overly difficult to make, but it will require time and thought. (Study Figs. 4–15 and 4–16 carefully before starting.) It would be wise to have both the movement and the dial (face), on hand before starting work.

Fig. 4–13.   *Tall case clock, bequest of Helena D. Swift, Metropolitan Museum of Art, New York, N. Y.*

Material List

Part		Number	Size	Material
A	Sides	2	6½" x 39" x ¾"	Pine,
B	Bottom Sides	2	9¼" x 15" x ¾"	Cherry,
C	Top Sides	2	9" x 14" x ¾"	Maple,
				or Birch
D	Back	1	15½" x 66" x ¼"	Plywood
E	Bottom	1	9" x 14" x ¾"	
F	Top	1	9" x 14½" x ¾"	
G	Skirt	1	3" x 18" x ¾"	
		2	3" x 10" x ¾"	
H	Pediment	1	5½" x 16½" x ¾"	
I	Moldings	1	¾" x ¾" x 16"	Scotia
		2	¾" x ¾" x 11"	
J	Edging (Top)	2	4" x 12" x ¾"	
		1	4" x 18" x ¾"	
K	Edging (Bottom)	2	4" x 11½" x ¾"	
		1	4" x 20" x ¾"	
L	Molding for Edging	1	3 Lin. Ft. ¾" x ¾"	Scotia
M	Top Door Rails	2	1" x 14½" x ¾"	
	Stiles	2	1" x 12" x ¾"	
N	Middle Door			
	Rails	2	1¾" x 10" x ¾"	
	Stiles	2	1¾" x 29" x ¾"	
	Grill	6	⅝" x 12" x ½"	

Part	Number	Size	Material
O Lower Door			
Rails	2	1¾″ x 16″ x ¾″	
Stiles	2	1¾″ x 13″ x ¾″	
Door Panel	1	10″ x 13″ x ¾″	

Hardware and Clock Works

P Clock Face	1	12″ x 12″	Brass
Q Movement	1	Of Choice	Brass

1 Piece of 11″ x 13″ Single strength glass (top door).
1 Piece of 7½″ x 26″ Single strength glass (center door).
1 Finial, 2″ diameter x 7″ (See Fig. 4–16).
3 Pairs, 1½″ 1½″ brass butt hinges.
3 Magnetic door catches.
3 Door pulls, ½″ diameter brass or porcelain.

CONSTRUCTION

1. Study the drawings in Figures 4–15 and 4–16 carefully before starting work. Note that the clock case is made or assembled by securing Parts A, B, and C together with "spacer" blocks and screws. Extra care must be taken when assembling these parts together so that they will be in line and straight. The back (Part D) locks the two side assemblies together as a complete unit (see Fig. 4–16).

2. Lay out and cut the stock for Parts A, B, C, and D. It is important to keep all end-cuts perfectly square. Cut a ⅜″ x ⅜″ rabbet into the inside back edges of Parts A, B, and C in order to receive Part D.

3. Glue and screw Parts B and C to the main side piece (Part A) using spacer blocks between the parts. Notice that Part A extends inside both Parts B, and C (see Fig. 4–16). Take special care to see that the back edges are in a straight line. With a backsaw or chisel adjust the rabbets where Parts B and C overlap Part A. Nail Part D into the rabbet. Part D ties the whole unit together; therefore, these cuts must be plumb and square.

4. Lay out and cut Parts E and F. Cut a ⅜″ x ⅜″ blind rabbet into the bottom back edge of Part E in order to receive Part D. Nail Parts E and F into place.

5. Lay out and cut stock for Parts J and K. These are the edge molding pieces that cover the spacer blocks. Make 45° miter joints on the outside corners of these pieces. Nail Part J to Part C as noted in Figure 4–16. Nail Parts K into Parts B.

6. Cut the rail pieces, which are made from

Fig. 4–14. Grandmother's clock project.

scrap 1″ x ¾″ stock. One rail piece goes on top of Part K in the front; the other rail piece is nailed into Part J at the top.

7. Cut strips of stock ¾″ square and make scotia molding from them by using a router bit. Nail the scotia molding in the places noted in Figure 4–15. The molding goes on the top and bot-

134

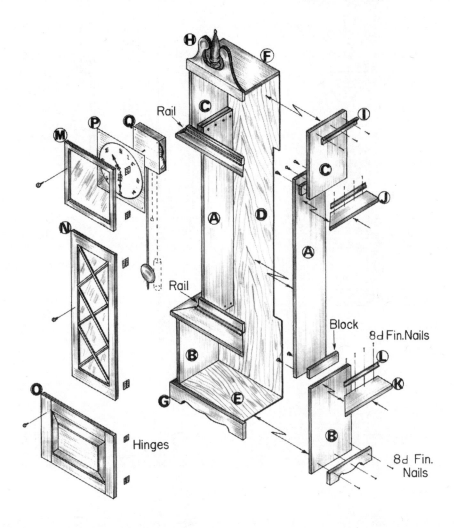

Rail

Rail

Hinges

Block

8d Fin.Nails

8d Fin.
Nails

Fig. 4–15.

tom of Part J. It is also nailed to the top of Parts K. Scotia molding is also nailed to the extreme top on Parts C. (If pine is used to make the clock case, pre-made scotia molding may be purchased. If any other wood is used it is best to make the molding, for in this way a perfect match may be had in the wood stock.)

8. Lay out and cut stock for Part H. Nail Part H to Parts F and C.

9. Lay out and cut stock for Parts G. Nail Parts G to Parts B and E as noted in Figure 4–15.

10. Lathe-turn stock for the finial. Leave a ³⁄₈" dowel-like extension on the bottom of the turning. Drill a ³⁄₈" hole in the center of the broken pediment (Part H) and secure the finial in this hole with glue.

11. Lay out and cut stock for Parts M. Make miter-joints on these parts and construct a door

frame to fit the top hood opening. Cut a ¼" x ¼" rabbet into the back inside edges to receive the glass. Nail and glue the miter joints together. Secure this door to Part C with one pair of small brass butt hinges.

12. Lay out and cut stock for Parts N, the center door. Use ship-lap joints on this door for added strength. Cut a ¼" x ³⁄₈" rabbet on the back inside edges to receive the glass. Nail and glue the parts together to form a frame. *Note: If you use the diamond-shaped cross-members as shown in Figure 4–16, do the following: cut the required grid stock to size, fit the stock together at a 45° angle to form diamonds, using a ship-lap joint in the center and butt joints on each end. The end cuts will have to be 45°. A miter box will help a great deal in making these cuts. Glue and nail the cross-grids in between the door frame, keeping the back flush with the precut rabbet.*

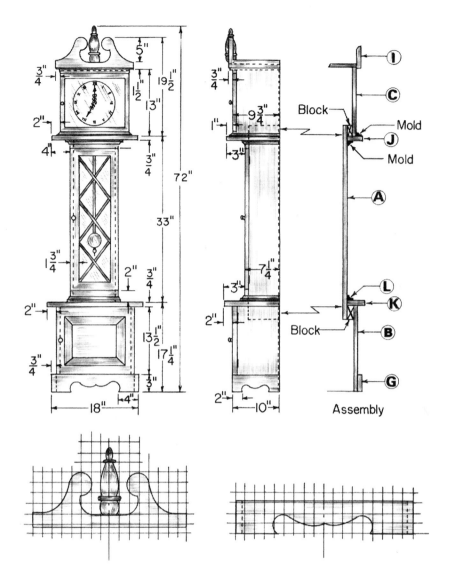

Fig. 4–16.

After the glue has dried 24 hours, use a router with a scotia bit to mold all the edges of the grid and door frame.

13. Secure the finished door to Part A with small brass butt hinges.

14. Lay out and cut the stock for Parts O. (See *Section One* for details on making a raised panel door and frame.) Secure the finished door to Parts B with another pair of brass butt hinges. *Note: This panel and door may be "fixed" to the opening by nailing it into Part B instead of using hinges.*

FINISH

Remove all the doors. Set and fill all nail holes. Sand the entire project smooth. Stain. Cover with several coats of lacquer. Rub with pumice and lemon oil, and finish with paste wax.

INSTALLING THE MOVEMENT

Blocks may be needed for the movement to sit upon. This depends upon the type of movement used. The blocks are glued and screwed in place on the inside of the top hood. Chimes, if used, are secured to Part D, which acts as a tone box. After the movement and chimes are set, line up and secure the clock face. Small glue blocks may be needed. Install these on the sides of Part C. Pre-drill the screw holes so the blocks will not split.

Install the glass in both doors with small glazier's points or wood strips. Re-install the doors on the clock case.

SECTION FIVE

Colonial Reflections

Fig. 5–1. Colonial weights and measures collection, Shelburne Museum, Shelburne, Vermont.

This section was developed in order to supply information and drawings of several items that do not fit into a particular category, yet are pieces that were very important in colonial times. They add greatly to the totality of design in colonial settings.

All of the plans are based upon museum pieces. With a little effort, you may reap a double harvest: that of owning the finished piece, and the pleasure of knowing that you, like your forefathers, made it yourself.

Barometer

The barometer offered here is designed along early American lines. The early barometers were long, tube affairs, cumbersome, and very expensive; only the wealthy could afford to import them from England.

Because foreknowledge of the weather was very important to early New Englanders, some type of forecasting equipment was acquired as soon as funds permitted. A 100-mile trip could take over three days to complete even in good weather, making the forecasting of weather almost a necessity.

This barometer is adapted from models of a later period, and adds a fine touch to modern colonial decor in addition to providing the function of weather prediction. The dimensions given are for the size of the weather forecasting equipment used, mainly, the barometer, hygrometer, and thermometer. Smaller units may be used, but the wood members should be reduced proportionately so that a pleasing relationship between wood and accessories is maintained.

Material List

Part	Number	Size	Material
A Wood Plaque	1	11″ x 33″ x 1¼″	Pine,
B Pediment Trim	2	2″ x 3″ x ¾″	Cherry,
C Barometer			Maple,
Ring	1	10¾″ dia. x ¾″	Oak or
			Birch

Hardware and Accessories

Finial	1	1½″ x 3″	Wood or
			Brass
Mirror	1	2½″ dia. convex	
Thermometer	1	2″ x 10″ to 12″ (typ.)	
Hygrometer	1	2½″ dia. (typ.)	
Barometer	1	10″ dia. (typ.)	
Eagle	1	3″ Cabinetmaker's	Brass

See *Section Eight* for a list of suppliers.

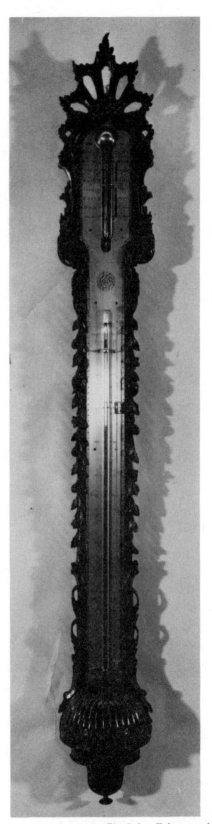

Fig. 5–2. *Tube type of barometer,*
Colonial Williamsburg, Williamsburg, Virginia.

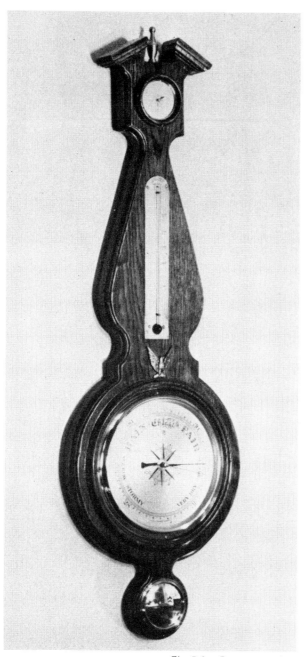

Fig. 5–3.   *Barometer project.*

CONSTRUCTION

1. Lay out and cut the stock to the suggested shape and size for Part A. Sand the edges smooth. With an ogee (or similar) router bit, cut a beaded edge all around Part A, except the extreme top, (See Fig. 5–4).

2. Lay out and cut the stock for the broken pediment, Part B. Cut in the ogee bead edge on three sides, leaving the back plain. Nail the pediment pieces to the top of Part A. Lathe-turn a finial of either brass or wood. (See Fig. 5–4 for typical shape.) If preferred, this finial may be purchased readymade. Center and secure the finial.

3. The barometer unit will come with a brass ring ready for mounting (the wood ring is optional). To make the wooden barometer ring which is an ornament rather than a functional part, lathe-turn a 10¾" diameter x ¾" circle made from the same type of wood as the plaque, Part A. Cut a bead on the outside of this ring to match the ogee bead cut into Part A. The inside clearance of the wooden ring should be ¹/₁₆" larger than the metal ring on the barometer. (See Section AA in Fig. 5–4 for details.) Sand the wood ring smooth while it is still on the lathe and cut it free from the stock. Drill the completed ring for brads, and nail the ring to Part A. Similar rings may be made for the mirror and hygrometer if desired.

FINISH

Sand all parts smooth. Stain. Cover with several coats of lacquer. Rub to a mirror-finish with lemon oil and pumice.

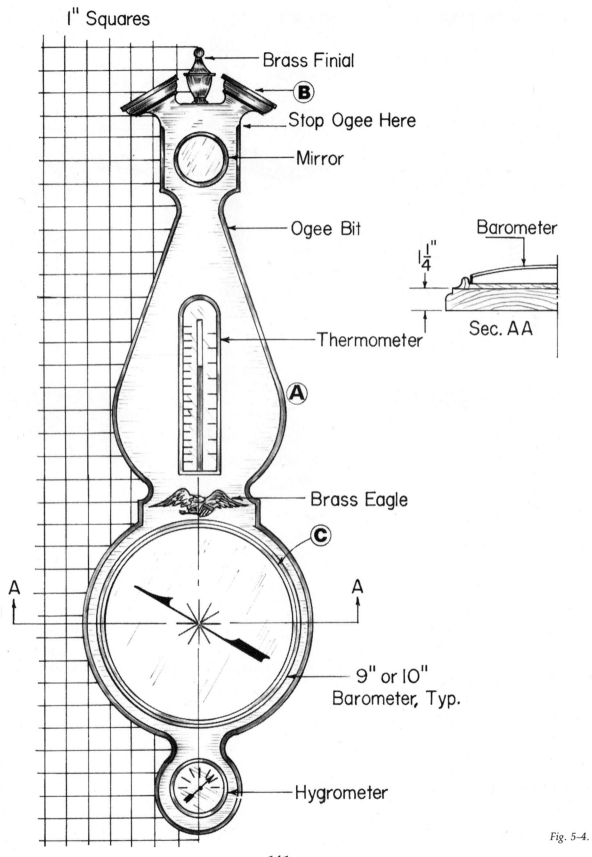

1" Squares

Brass Finial

Ⓑ

Stop Ogee Here

Mirror

Ogee Bit

Thermometer

Ⓐ

Brass Eagle

Ⓒ

A   A

9" or 10"
Barometer, Typ.

Hygrometer

Barometer

1¼"

Sec. AA

Fig. 5–4.

141

Colonial Scale

Some colonial housewives used scales to measure ingredients for cooking, but the most important use of scales was by the merchants, who measured everything from nails to milled flour. Even today the term for the size of a nail is derived from the colonial measuring system and the cost per pound.

The scale works on a very simple principle: that of having a known weight on one side to balance the amount of material to be weighed on the other side. When the two pans were evenly balanced, the material being weighed was the same as the known weight.

This project offers an ideal way for the woodturner to express his own individuality. The working drawings are meant to be used primarily as a guide.

Material List

	Part	Number	Size	Material
A	Main Stem	1	2¼″ dia. x 18½″	Any Wood of Choice
B	Base	1	7⅜″ dia. x 2¾″	
C	Balance Arm	1	1¾″ x 20¾″ x ½″	
D	Dish	2	6″ dia. x 1¾″	
E	Finial	1	1″ x 1¾″ dia.	Brass

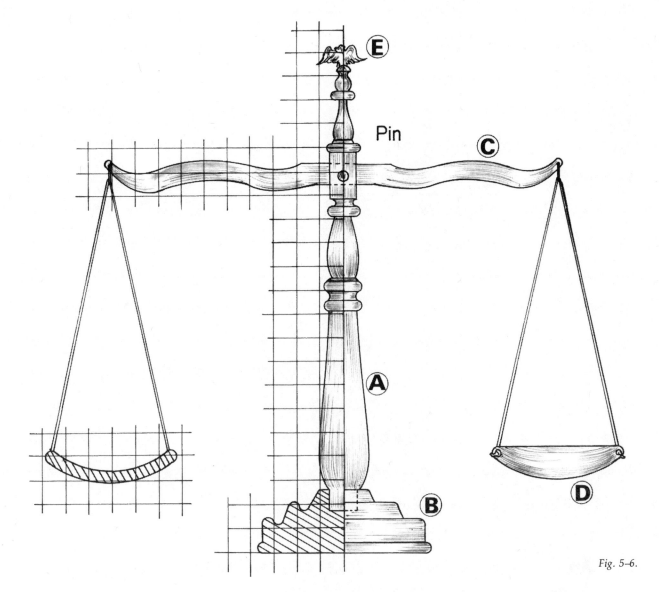

Fig. 5–6.

CONSTRUCTION

1. Glue up the stock for the required thickness. Lathe-turn Parts A and B to the suggested shape. Leave a 1½″ x 1″ diameter dowel-like tenon on the bottom of Part A. Drill a 1″ diameter hole through the center of Part B. Cut a ⅝″ x 1″ square mortise on Part A where indicated in Figure 5–6. Drill a ¼″ hole at a right angle to the square mortise for the balance arm lock pin.

2. Lay out and cut the stock for Part C. Cut Part C to shape. Drill a ³/₁₆″ diameter hole on each end. Insert Part C into the square mortise cut into Part A, and mark and drill a matching ¼″ diameter hole through Part C.

3. Lathe-turn Parts D to shape. Drill three equally spaced ¼″ diameter holes on the outer rim, 120° apart.

FINISH

Sand all parts smooth. Stain. Cover with several coats of lacquer. Finish with paste wax.

ASSEMBLY

Glue Part A into Part B. Insert Part C into the square mortise cut into Part A and insert the pin. The pin may be a brass bolt, hardwood dowel or thumbscrew. Part C must swing freely in the mortise. Attach three rawhide cords to Part D through the pre-drilled holes and secure the tops of these cords together. Fasten the tops of the rawhide cords to the holes drilled in Part C with a small brass ring or rawhide ring. Attach an eagle or turned brass finial to the top center of Part A.

Fig. 5–7.   Multi-arm chandelier, Shelburne Museum, Shelburne, Vermont.

144

Chandelier

In colonial days, houses were lighted very poorly; candles and firelight were the main source of light. Single candle holders (sconces), were very often made from odds and ends or made by local whitesmiths. The larger chandeliers or "light branches" as they were often called, were made by local or itinerant artisans who added touches of their own to the forms and designs.

The chandelier is designed as a central light branch for modern colonial styled homes. It contains the central wooden turning and multi-candle arms found in the original pieces. The only major change has been to electrify the chandelier.

Material List

Part		Number	Size	Material
A	Main Stem	1	4" dia. x 14"	Pine
B	Candle Dish	5	3" dia. x 1¾"	Pine
C	Finial (top)	1	1¼" dia. x 2½"	Brass
D	Pendant (bottom)	1	1¾" dia. x 2"	Brass

Hardware

6	⅛" I.P.S. x 18" brass pipes
5 Sockets	40 W. electrical sockets
5 Covers	40 W. plastic candle covers
5 Bulbs	40 W. candelabra type
15 Nuts	⅛" I.P.S. lock nuts
18 Feet	110 V. lamp cord
1 Foot	chandelier chain
One 4" dia.	ceiling outlet cover with hook

Note: the electrical hardware may be purchased from lighting specialty shops and many other outlets, including hardware stores. The 18" long ⅛" I.P.S. may be purchased straight or in gooseneck form.

CONSTRUCTION

1. Glue up the stock for the main stem and the candle dishes (Parts A and B).

2. Lathe-turn Part A to shape. Remove from the lathe and cut Part A in two where indicated in Fig. 5–9. Drill a ⅜" hole through the top half. Replace the lower part back on the lathe and hollow out the interior much like a bowl. Drill a ⅜" hole dead center through the lower part. Drill five ⅜" entrance holes in the bowl section for the candle arms. (See Fig. 5–9.)

3. Lathe-turn the candle dishes, Parts B. Cut in a ⅞" diameter hole in the top center, ¾" deep to take the plastic candle covers (¾" diameter, typical). Drill a ⅜" hole through the center of the finished candle dish for the candle arm.

4. Bend five of the ⅛" I.P.S. candle arms to shape. Feed a piece of lamp cord through each candle arm leaving 6" excess on both ends. Place a threaded I.P.S. nut on each end of the arm. Place a candle dish over the I.P.S. pipe and thread down an adjustable candelabra electrical socket. (Part B is held between the bolt-like action of the threaded nut and adjustable candelabra socket.) Secure both ends of the lamp cord to the terminals on the electrical candelabra socket.

5. Feed the other end of the I.P.S. candle arm into the lower section of Part A. Lock the arm to this section by securing another I.P.S. lock nut from the inside of the hollowed out section of Part A. Do this for all of the five candle arms.

6. Insert a straight piece of ⅛" I.P.S. pipe through the pre-drilled hole in the top portion of Part A. Mark this pipe where it clears into the hollowed-out section and drill a ¼" hole through the pipe. Feed a piece of lamp cord down through the pipe and exit the cord through the ¼" holes. (This is the main electrical feed for all of the arms.)

7. Lathe-turn the brass pendant and finial, Parts C and D. (These parts may be purchased pre-made if you so desire, or if a lathe is not available.) Drill and tap a blind ⅛" I.P.S. hole in Part D. Drill and tap a ⅛" I.P.S. hole through Part

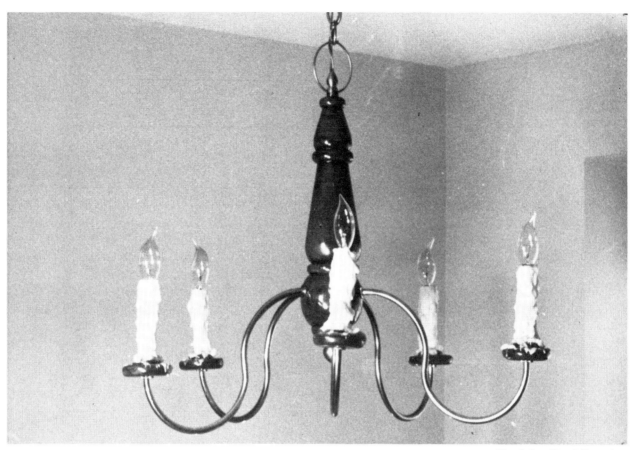

Fig. 5–8. Chandelier project.

C. Drill a ¼″ cross-hole in the top of Part C. (This hole will take the first link of the chandelier chain.) Secure Part D to the lower end of the central ⅛″ I.P.S. pipe. Put the lower section of Part A over the pipe and down to the finial. Allow the lamp cord wires to exit into the hollowed-out section.

8. Take one wire from each candle arm and solder-join it to one of the feed wires. Take the remaining candle feed wires and solder-join them to the other main feed wire. Use solderless nuts and also tape each joint very securely. Tuck the wires and joints into the hollowed out section of Part A. Push the top half of Part A down over the central I.P.S. pipe and screw down the top finial, Part C. The central pipe acts as a large bolt with both sections of Part A held together by means of the threaded finial and pendant, Parts C and D.

9. Secure the chandelier chain to the finial through the pre-drilled holes. Lace the lamp cord up through the chain. Put a two-prong A.C. plug on the free end of the lamp cord.

FINISH

Parts A and B may be stained or painted. Sand both parts smooth. Stain or paint. Wipe on a black glaze after distressing. Cover with several coats of lacquer. Finish with paste wax. The brass parts should be bright. Apply paste wax; buff. Place a plastic candle cover over each adjustable socket. Candle covers may have melted wax dripped over them for a realistic effect. Place a 40-watt candelabra bulb in each socket.

MOUNTING

Cover the existing ceiling outlet box with a chandelier outlet cover, complete with hook and A.C. feed outlet; hook up the electrical connections inside the electrical box, screw on the cover, insert the chandelier chain over the provided hook, and plug the two-prong A.C. cap plug into the female outlet. The chain, outlet cover, and box act as a ground.

146

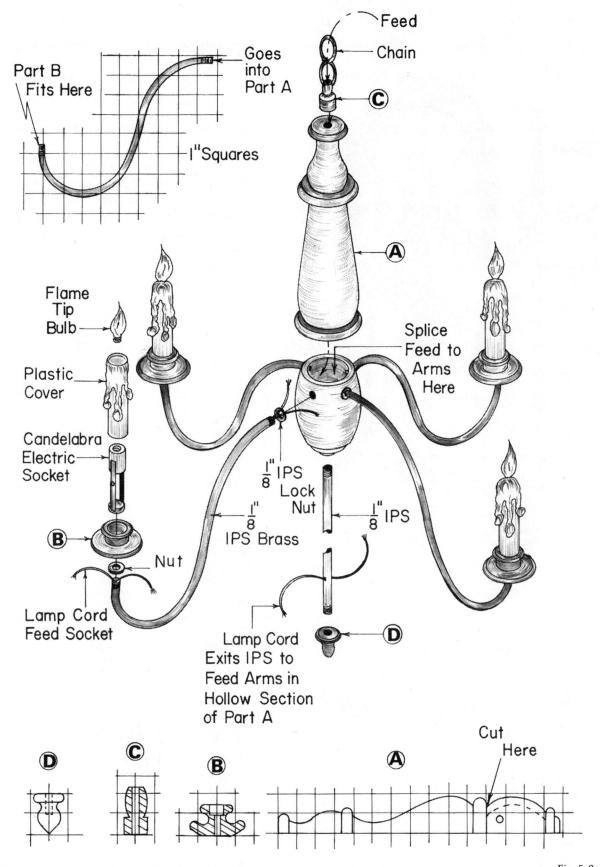

Part B
Fits Here

Goes
into
Part A

1"Squares

Feed

Chain

Ⓒ

Ⓐ

Flame
Tip
Bulb

Plastic
Cover

Candelabra
Electric
Socket

Splice
Feed to
Arms
Here

Ⓑ

$\frac{1}{8}$" IPS
Lock
Nut

$\frac{1}{8}$" IPS

$\frac{1}{8}$"
IPS Brass

Nut

Lamp Cord
Feed Socket

Lamp Cord
Exits IPS to
Feed Arms in
Hollow Section
of Part A

Ⓓ

Ⓓ   Ⓒ   Ⓑ   Ⓐ   Cut
Here

Fig. 5–9.

147

Fig. 5–10. Flax wheel, Metropolitan Museum of Art, New York, N. Y.

Spinning Wheel

No other colonial piece lends itself so well to artistic expression as the spinning wheel. All the arms and legs could very well be plain rounds, but the early craftsmen made spinning wheels for aesthetic appeal as well as for household function.

The wheel was a woman's tool, used by ladies of nobility as much as by housewives, and this quite likely is the reason that most of the parts have feminine names. The bobbin assembly is called the "mother of all," and the bobbin holders are called the "sisters."

The art of spinning was passed on from mother to daughter as were the valuable wheels themselves.

The spinning wheel requires careful planning, for it is the most difficult piece to make that is included in this book. Study the drawings and make it in steps, such as the base, the bobbin and adjustment assembly, the wheel and wheel holders, and lastly the "rock," or flax holder. The many turnings allow for your individual expression, and the finished project is one in which any craftsman may take justifiable pride.

Material List

	Part	Number	Size	Material
A	Base	1	6" x 18" x 2½"	Maple,
B	Front Leg	1	1¾" dia. x 17"	Birch,
C	Rear Legs	2	1¾" dia. x 13"	Cherry,
D	Treadle	1	4" x 12" x ¾"	or Pine
		2	1¾" x 19" x ¾"	
E	Turn Handle	1	1¾" dia. x 5"	
F	"The Mother"	1	2½" dia. x 10¼"	
G	"Sisters"	2	1½" dia. x 11"	
H	Sister Hold	1	1⅞" dia. x 14½"	
I-1	Bobbin	1	4" x 4¾" x 1"	
I-2		1	2" dia. x 1¼"	
I-3		1	2" dia. x 3"	
J	Wheel Base	2	1¾" dia. x 15"	
K	Wheel Rim	1	25½" dia. x 4½" x 1"	
L	Wheel Spokes	8	1" dia. x 4"	
M	Wheel Hub	1	6½" dia. x 1¼"	
N	Wheel Strap	1	¾" x 17" x ½"	
O	Wheel Axle	1	⅜" dia. x 11"	Steel
P	Bobbin Hold	2	1" x 3" x ¼"	Leather
Q	"The Rock"	1	1½" dia. x 20"	
R	Cross Rock	1	1½" dia. x 11"	
S	Flax Cage	1	2" dia. x 6"	
		4	¼" dia. x 8"	Dowels

CONSTRUCTION

1. *The base.* Lay out and cut the stock for Parts A, B, C, and D. Cut the required taper on Part A. Cut a 45° wedge away from the lower rear edges of Part A where the rear legs, Parts C, will enter. Drill a 1" diameter hole in the rear ends at the suggested splay angle. (See Fig. 5–12.) Drill a 1"

diameter hole near the front of Part A for the front leg, Part B. Again see Figure 5–12 for location and splay angle. Make a 1¾″ by 3½″ slot in the forward end of Part A. "The mother," Part F, rides in this slot. Drill a ⅝″ diameter hole from the front end of Part A to the center of the slot (Part E will fit here). Drill two ⅞″ diameter holes 3½″ up from the rear of Part A in order to receive Parts J. (See Fig. 5–12 for suggested angles.) Drill a ⅞″ diameter hole in the forward end of Part A to receive "The rock," Part Q.

2. Lathe-turn Parts B and C to the suggested shape leaving a 1″ diameter dowel on the top ends. These dowel-like tenons will fit the predrilled holes on Part A. Glue Part B into the forward hole on Part A. Glue Parts C into the predrilled holes at the rear of Part A. Drill a ⅜″ diameter blind hole in the lower end of Part B to receive the forward pin for Part D. (See Fig. 5–15) Drill a matching hole in Part C. Make the required triangle treadle suggested for Part D. (See Fig. 5–13.) Drill a ⅜″ diameter hole in one leg of the triangle and insert Part D between Parts B and C with steel pins. Part D must be able to swing up and down freely.

3. *The "mother of all."* Lathe-turn Parts E, F, G, and H. Force-fit Part E onto a threaded ⅝″ diameter rod. Drill and tap Part F so that the threaded rod will feed this part back and forth within the slot cut in Part A. Drill a ¼″ diameter hole through Part F where it clears the bottom of Part A. Push a ¼″ diameter pin through this hole. Drill a hole in Part H as suggested in Figure 5–13. With a round file, enlarge and shape this hole to match the taper turned on the top of Part F. Fit Part H to Part F. Put the whole assembly on Part A and mark plumb line holes to be drilled for "the sisters," Parts G.

4. Lathe-turn Parts G, I-1, I-2 and I-3. (The ideal shape for Part I-1 is to turn out a bowl and cut out a 1″ section from the center.) Cut ¼″ x 1″ mortises on Parts G. Drill two ½″ diameter holes along the plumb line on Part H. With a file, enlarge the holes to match the tapers cut on the bottoms of Parts G. Force-fit Parts G into Part H. Cut the leather for Part P. Drill a ¼″ diameter hole in the rounded ends of each piece. Insert the leather into the precut mortise on Parts G and glue them

Fig. 5–11. *Spinning wheel project.*

in place. Cut a ¼″ diameter brass or steel rod (A section of ⅛″ I.P.S. pipe may be used if desired), to run between Parts G allowing the rod to extend 1″ beyond both ends of the leather, Parts P. Drill ¼″ diameter holes in Parts I-1, I-2 and I-3. Install these parts on the rod. String the rod between the two leather loops.

5. *The wheel.* Lathe-turn Parts J to the suggested shape. Cut a ⅜″ by 1″ slot in the tops to receive the wheel axle, Part O. Insert Parts J into the pre-drilled holes on Part A.

6. Lay out four boards and draw the wheel diameter on the boards. (See Fig. 5–13 for suggested joints and construction.) Cut the boards to shape. Cut a ⅜″ x ½″ rabbet on each edge of the meeting joints. Cut a ⅜″ x 1″ spline piece to fit into the rabbet joints. Insert the splines dry and drill two

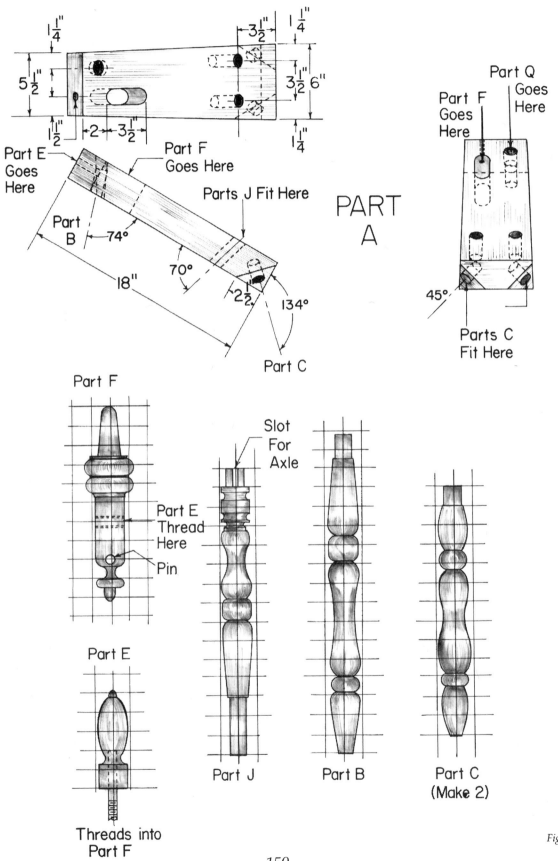

1¼"

5½"

1½"

2

3½"

3½"

1¼"

3½"

3½"

6"

1¼"

Part E Goes Here

Part F Goes Here

Parts J Fit Here

PART A

Part B

74°

70°

18"

2½"

134°

Part C

Part F Goes Here

Part Q Goes Here

45°

Parts C Fit Here

Part F

Part E Thread Here

Pin

Slot For Axle

Part E

Threads into Part F

Part J

Part B

Part C (Make 2)

Fig. 5–12.

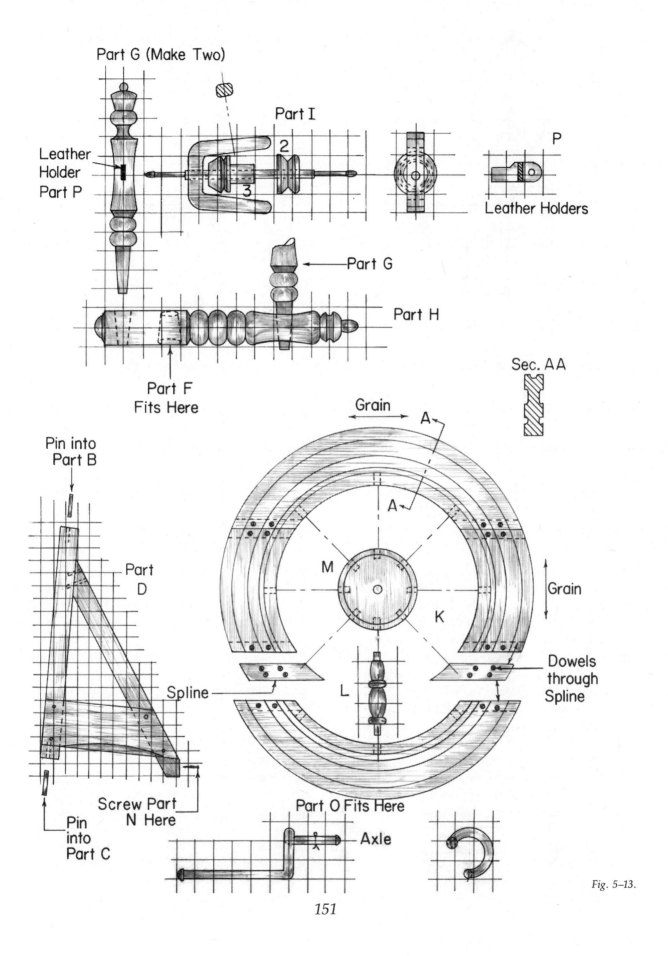

Part G (Make Two)

Leather Holder Part P

Part I

2

3

P

Leather Holders

Part G

Part H

Part F Fits Here

Sec. AA

Grain

A

A

M

K

Grain

Pin into Part B

Part D

Spline

L

Dowels through Spline

Pin into Part C

Screw Part N Here

Part O Fits Here

Axle

Fig. 5–13.

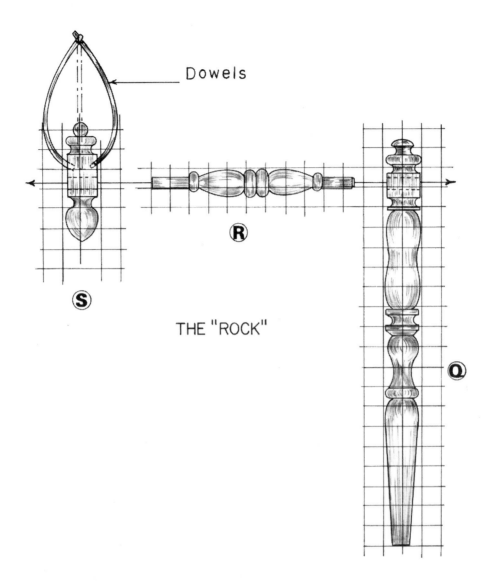

Dowels

THE "ROCK"

Fig. 5–14.

¼" diameter holes for dowel pins on each side of the joint. Drill eight evenly spaced ⅜" diameter holes on the inside of the wheel rim. Lathe turn the wheel hub, Part M. Drill a ⅜" diameter hole dead-center for the axle. Drill eight ⅜" diameter holes evenly spaced around the outer edge (rim). Lathe-turn eight spokes, Parts L, leaving a ⅜" diameter dowel on each end. Glue the bottom of the spokes into the holes in the hub, Part M. Glue the top of the spokes into Part K as you assemble the wheel rim around the hub. Glue and pin the splines as you assemble the wheel.

7. Make Part O to the suggested shape. Force-fit the axle into the pre-drilled hole on Part M. Drill a ⅛" diameter hole on the extreme end of the axle for a cotter pin. Drop the finished wheel and axle into the slots cut into Part J. Cut the stock for Part N. Drill a ⅛" diameter hole on the bottom

end and a ⅜" diameter hole on the top end. Put the top of Part N on the axle and hold it in place with a cotter pin in the pre-drilled ⅛" hole on Part O. Screw Part N (bottom) loosely to Part D with a flat head wood screw. The low point of the loop on Part O should match the low arc of the treadle and still clear the floor by two inches or more.

8. *The rock.* Lathe-turn Parts Q, R, and S to the suggested shape. Drill a ½" diameter hole through Part Q. Insert one end of Part R into this hole. Drill a ½" diameter hole in the bottom of Part S and insert the other end of Part R into this hole. Drill four equally spaced ¼" diameter holes in the top round of Part S and insert the four ¼" diameter dowels into these holes. Tie the tops of these dowels together to form a cage. Insert "the rock" assembly into the hole drilled on the forward end of Part A.

152

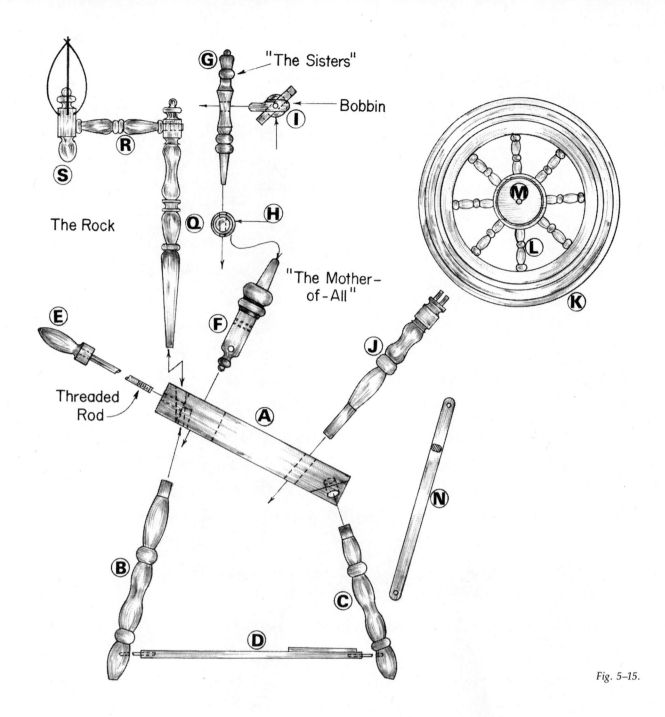

"The Sisters"

Bobbin

"The Mother-of-All"

The Rock

Threaded Rod

Fig. 5–15.

FINISH

Sand all parts smooth. Stain. Cover with several coats of lacquer. Rub with pumice and lemon oil. Finish with paste wax.

SPINNING

This spinning wheel will operate. Tie a heavy cord around the wheel, Part K, and to the bobbin, Part I-2. Take the slack out of this cord by turning the turn handle, Part E, and bringing the "mother" forward. Turning the wheel will now turn the bobbin at high speed. A 3/16 diameter hole must be drilled in the end of the axle, Part O, to exit in front of the bobbin.

To spin, start the wheel turning by hand and use the foot treadle, Part D, to keep the wheel spinning. Feed the flax fibers from the flax cage through the hole drilled in the axle end Part O, and onto the bobbin, Part I-1. The twisting action of the turning bobbin twists the flax fibers into a thread.

Fig. 5–16. *Tote chair, Index of American Design, Washington, D. C.*

154

Tote or Child's Chair

It is not hard to see how this child's chair evolved from the early rough three-legged stool. The major change is the shape. The high back is a perfect medium for individual artistic expression. It is a type of chair that farmers or householders made in their spare time for their children.

This plan was developed from the chair in Figure 5–16, with one change: The entire chair back is one piece, and the seat and front legs were attached to it.

Material List

Part	Number	Size	Material
A Back	1	9" x 36" x 1¾"	Pine
B Seat	1	12" x 13" x 1¾"	
C Legs	2	2" x 2" x 14½"	Fir

CONSTRUCTION

1. Glue up the stock for Parts A, B, and C. Cut out the suggested design on Part A. Cut a 1¾" x ¾" dado where indicated for the seat, Part B. (See Fig. 5–18).

2. Lay out and cut the stock for Part B. Cut Part B to the suggested shape, leaving a 1¾" x ¾" tenon on the rear edge to fit into the dado on Part A. Drill two 1¼" diameter splayed holes in the bottom of Part B where indicated to receive Part C.

3. Lay out and cut the stock for Parts C. Lathe-turn or cut with a sharp knife, a 1¼" x 1¾" round, dowel-like tenon on the tops. Cut a "wedge" slot across each tenon. (See *Section One* for details.)

4. Glue Parts C into the pre-drilled holes on Part B and drive a hardwood wedge into the pre-cut slots. Trim off the excess wedge flush with the top of Part B. Glue and screw Part B into the dado on Part A.

Fig. 5–17. Tote or child's chair project.

FINISH

Sand the entire chair smooth. Paint or stain. If desired, decorate with Pennsylvania Dutch design. Cover with several coats of lacquer or similar finish. Apply paste wax.

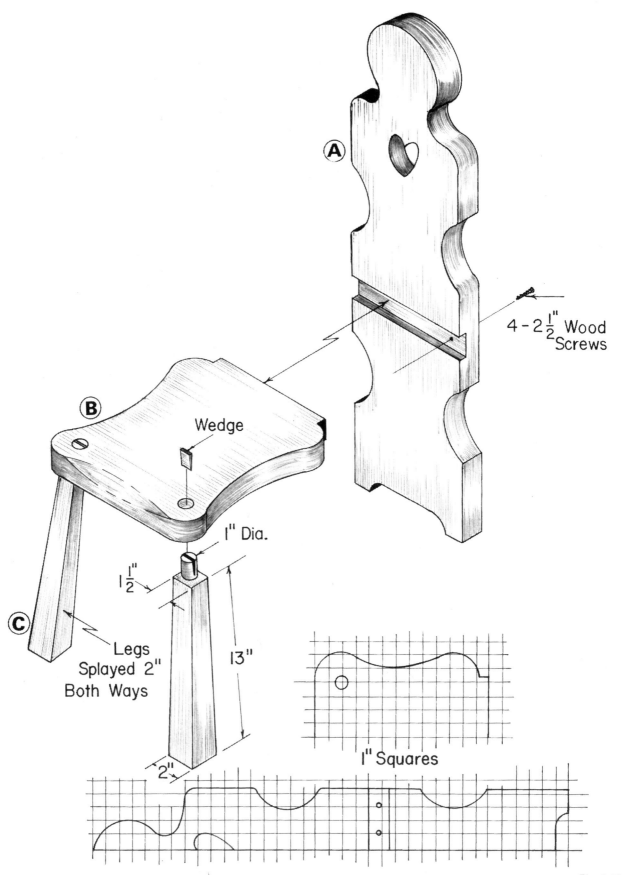

Ⓐ

Ⓑ

Wedge

Ⓒ

$4 - 2\frac{1}{2}$" Wood Screws

1" Dia.

$1\frac{1}{2}$"

13"

2"

Legs Splayed 2" Both Ways

1" Squares

Fig. 5–18.

Fig. 5–19. Excellent example of trestle-type of construction, Index of American Design, Washington, D. C.

Trestle Desk

While the early colonists were primarily farmers, and concerned with survival, the established settlements became the centers for artisans of all types. Craftsmen needed appropriate work areas, thus developed the sailmaker's bench, the tinker's pig, and the cobbler's bench. The old lap desk no longer served the needs of the merchants, and table-like desks soon developed.

This desk is designed along colonial lines. The legs are much like those found on early tables. Small drawers take the place of the open pigeonholes for invoices or orders, and the large center drawer may be utilized for ledgers or bookkeeping journals. The important factor is the top, which makes a large work area. This desk

adds a touch of authentic styling to colonial rooms.

Material List

	Part	Number	Size	Material
A	Sides	2	12″ x 24″ x 1¾″	Pine
B	Shoes	2	4″ x 19″ x 1¾″	
C	Plates	2	4″ x 19″ x 1¾″	
D	Spreader	1	4″ x 38″ x 1¾″	
E	Top	1	24″ x 48″ x 1¾″	
F	Drawer Riser	1	5″ x 48″ x ½″	
G	Top Shelf	1	6″ x 48″ x ¾″	
H	Back	1	7″ x 48″ x ¾″	
I	Drawer Sides	2	7″ x 10″ x ¾″	
J	Drawers (top)	4	3″ x 11⅞″ x 4¾″	
K	Drawers (lower)	1	5″ x 32″ x 20″	
L	Drawer Guides	2	½″ x ½″ x 20″	

Fig. 5–20. Trestle desk project.

Hardware

Four ½" diameter porcelain drawer pulls.
Two 1" diameter porcelain drawer pulls.

CONSTRUCTION

1. Glue the 1¾" stock together for the required widths for Parts A and E.

2. Lay out and cut the stock for Parts A, B, C, and D. Cut the design on Parts A. (See Fig. 5–21.) Cut a "relief" on the lower edge of Part B. Cut a ½" x ½" rabbet on Part C for drawer guides. Using six 3½" #10 flat head wood screws, secure Parts B and C to Part A. Cut the required 1" x 3"

mortises on Parts A as suggested. Cut a matching tenon on both ends of Part D so that a 32" distance is maintained between shoulder cuts, Parts A, when the stretcher is inserted into the mortises. The spreader tenon should extend past Part A by at least 1¼" on each end. Drill a ½" diameter hole through the tenon where it clears Part A. Secure Part D to Parts A with a ½" diameter hardwood dowel pin through the pre-drilled holes.

3. Lay out and cut the stock for Part E. Cut a chamfer on the front edge to suggest heavy wear. Secure Part E to Parts C by means of several 3½" #10 flat head wood screws.

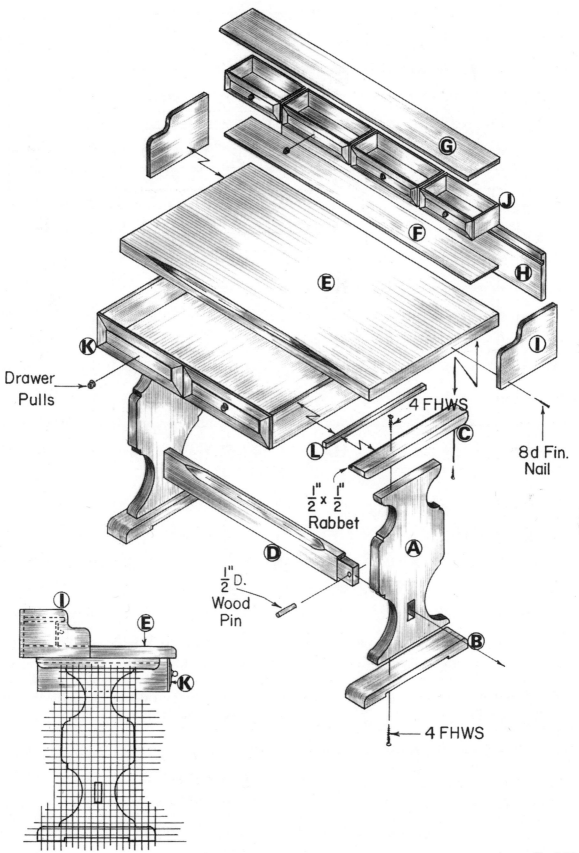

Drawer
Pulls

4 FHWS

8d Fin.
Nail

$\frac{1}{2}" \times \frac{1}{2}"$
Rabbet

$\frac{1}{2}"$ D.
Wood
Pin

4 FHWS

Fig. 5–21.

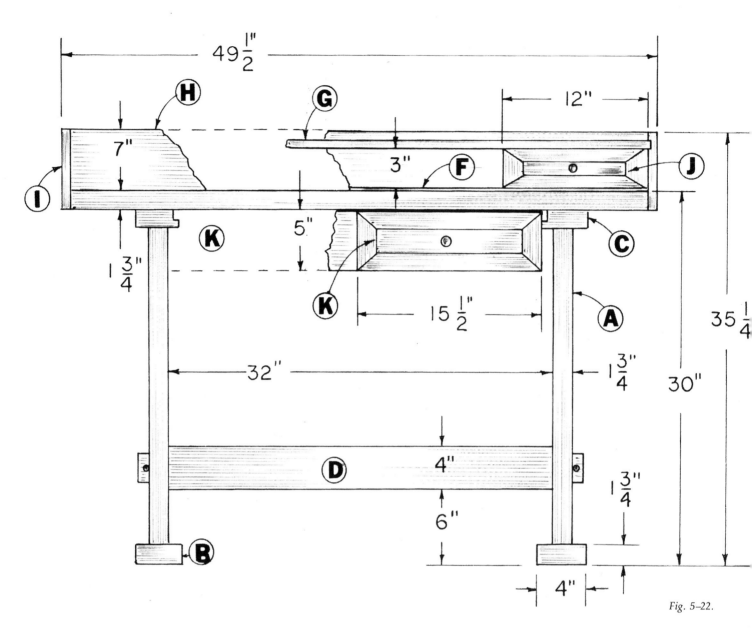

Fig. 5–22.

4. Lay out and cut the stock for Parts F, G, H, and I. Cut the design on Parts I. Cut a ¾" x ⅜" rabbet on Part H. (See Fig. 5–21.) Nail Part F onto Part E, flush with the rear. Nail Part H to the rear of Part E. Nail Part I to edges of Part E and into Part H. Nail Part G into Parts I and the rabbet on Part H. Insert three ⅜" spacer blocks between Parts F and G to divide the area into four equal parts for the small drawers, Parts J.

5. Make four small raised panel drawers, Parts J, to fit the openings. (See *Section One* for drawer construction details.) Insert the finished drawers into the openings.

6. Make a 5" x 32" double raised panel drawer unit, Part K, to fit the opening between Parts A, under Part E. Nail the ½" x ½" drawer guides, Parts L, to the sides of the finished drawer unit. Guides will fit into the ½" x ½" rabbets precut into Parts C.

FINISH

Set and fill all nail holes. Sand the entire desk smooth. Stain, and cover with several coats of lacquer. Rub with pumice and lemon oil. Finish with paste wax.

Squire's Desk

This desk, as in the case of the chest of drawers, evolved from the early colonial chest or trunk. Valuables and personal belongings were kept in a till-like affair on the side of the chest. The earliest desks were very small portable affairs, with slanted tops for writing or for using the family Bible, and the interiors contained small compartments. Sometimes secret compartments were built into false drawers or dividers. This type of desk eventually was placed upon a low table or frame of its own. The natural evolution of this piece soon became a free-standing desk.

The squire's desk is based upon colonial styles: plain round legs, a slant-topped section, and large work drawers on the right-hand side.

Material List

Part		Number	Size	Material
A	Sides	2	18¼" x 28" x ¾"	Pine
B	Skirt	1	18" x 3" x ¾"	
C	Stiles	2	1¾" x 25" x ¾"	
D	Rails	4	1¾" x 14½" x ¾"	
D-1	Back	1	17" x 28" x ¼"	Plywood
E	Footrest	1	9" x 33" x ¾"	
F	Spreader	1	2½" x 23" x ¾"	
G	Legs	2	2" dia. x 28"	Fir
H	Leg Cleat	1	4" x 23" x 1¾"	
I	Lower Drawer Guide	1	1¾" x 23" x ¾"	
J	Top	1	24" x 55½" x 1¾"	
K	Drawer Riser	1	5½" x 41¼" x ⅜"	
L	Drawer Spacer	5	5½" x 3" x ½"	
M	Shelf	1	6¼" x 41¼" x ¾"	
N	Top Side	1	7" x 25" x ¾"	
O	Shelf Backer	1	7" x 41¼" x ¾"	
O-1	Bin Backer	1	11" x 14¼" x ¾"	
P	Bin (Outside)	1	11" x 25" x ¾"	
Q	Bin (Inside)	1	9¼" x 24" x ¾"	
R	Bin Top	1	12" x 13½" x ¾"	
S	Bin Door	1	13½" x 13½" x ¾"	
T	Bin Front	1	3" x 15" x ¾"	
U	Top Drawers	4	3" x 10" x 5"	
V	Side Drawer	1	5" x 10" x 19"	
W	Drawer Guides	8	1¾" x 18" x ¾"	
X	Work Drawers	4	4½" x 14½" x 18"	

Hardware

Four ½" diameter porcelain pulls.
Four 1" diameter porcelain pulls.
One ¾" diameter porcelain pull.
One set 1½" x 1½" brass butt hinges.

CONSTRUCTION

1. Lay out and cut the stock for Parts A, B, C, D, and D-1. Cut a ⅜" x ⅜" rabbet at the rear inside edges of Parts A. Cut out the suggested design on Parts A and B. Nail Part B to Parts A. Nail Part C to Parts A and B. Nail Part D to Part C. Insert Part D-1 into the rabbets and nail firmly into Parts A.

Note: Parts W, the drawer guides, may be screwed to Parts A at this time if desired.

2. Lay out and cut the stock for Parts E, F, G, H, and I. Cut a ½" x ½" rabbet in Parts H and I. (See Fig. 5–25.) Drill two 2" diameter holes in Part H for the legs. Cut a ¾" x 2½" mortise in Parts G. (See Fig. 5–26.) Glue and nail Parts G into the pre-drilled holes. Insert Part F into the mortise and nail or pin it in place. Secure Part E to the drawer unit assembly with a scab, and secure the other end of Part E into Part F with wood screws covered with wooden plugs.

3. Glue up the stock for Part J. Secure the drawer assembly to Part J with wood screws. Secure Parts H and I to Part J with screws.

4. Lay out and cut the stock for Parts K, L, M, N, and O. Nail Part N to Part J flush with the bottom. Nail Part K to Part J flush with the rear edge. Nail Part O to Part J and Part N. Glue in Parts L to make four equal drawer openings. Nail Part M into Parts L, N, and O.

5. Lay out and cut the stock for Parts O-1, P, Q, and R. Nail Part P to the left-hand edge of Part J flush with the bottom. Nail Part O-1 into Parts J

Fig. 5–23. Desk from **The Pine Furniture of New England** *(1929), by Russell Hawes Kettell, Dover Publications, Inc., reprinted by permission of the publisher.*

Fig. 5–24. Squire's desk project.

and P. Nail Part Q into Parts J and O-1. Lay out and cut the stock for Parts S and T. Nail Part T into Parts J, P, and Q. Adjust Part S to fit the opening if needed. Secure Part R onto the bin top opening and nail into Parts P, Q, and O-1. Attach Part S to Part R with a pair of butt hinges.

6. Make four small drawers, Parts U. The raised panel fronts are optional. (See *Section One* for drawer construction details.) Slide the finished drawers into the openings.

7. Construct a 5″ x 10″ x 19″ drawer unit, Part V. Attach ½″ x ½″ drawer guide flush with the drawer top on the sides. This drawer unit fits between Parts H and I.

8. Make four large drawer units, Parts X, for the right-side drawer assembly with a ⅜″ x ⅜″ lap-over all around. Raised panel fronts are optional. Insert the finished drawers.

FINISH

Set and fill all nail holes. Cover all screw heads with hardwood plugs. Sand the entire project smooth. Locate and install hardware. Remove all hardware and apply stain. Cover with several coats of lacquer. Hand rub the desk with pumice and lemon oil. Finish with paste wax. Re-install all hardware.

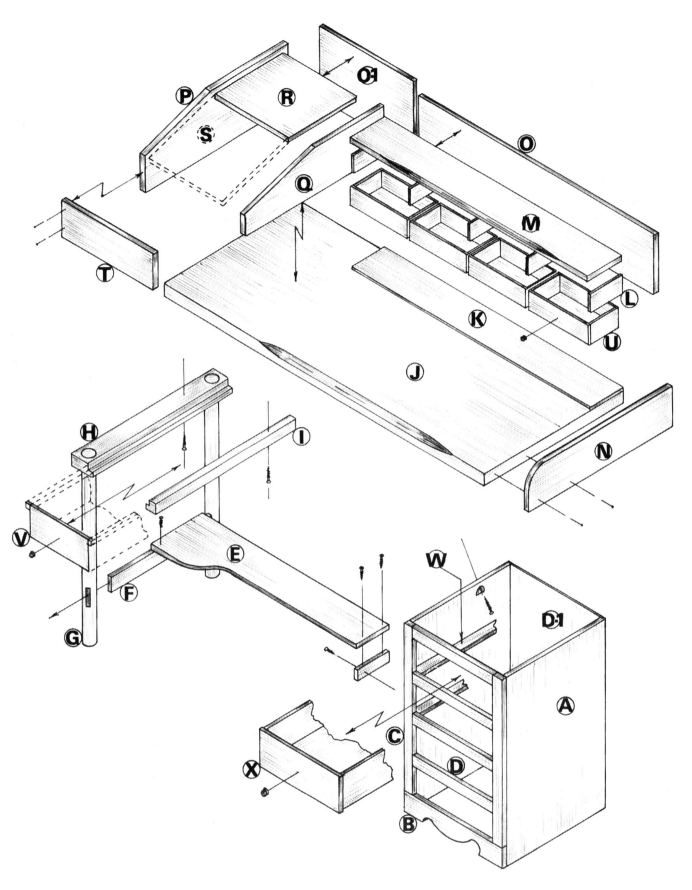

Fig. 5–25.

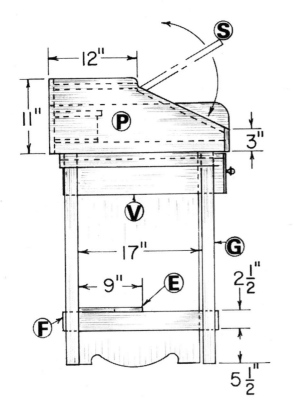

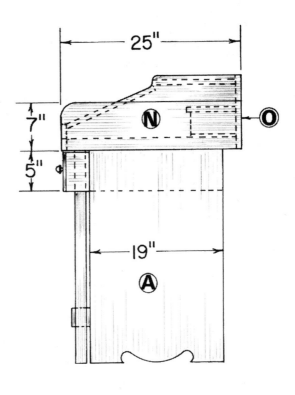

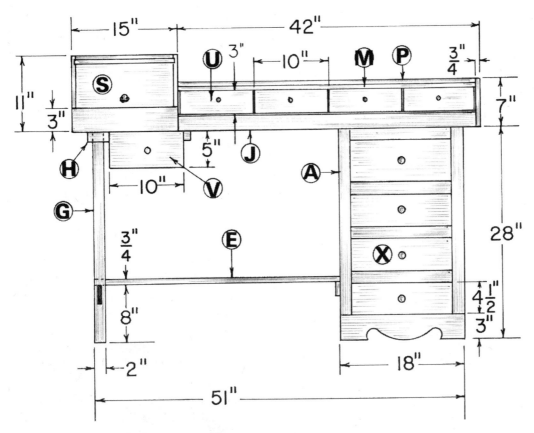

Fig. 5–26.

Captain's Desk

Desks had small interior sections, large working or writing areas, and many had large drawers down one side.

This project is called a captain's desk because it contains features often found in ship's cabins. The turned balusters supporting a railing around the desk top held papers or maps in place on a rolling ship. The small drawers over the map or work area kept small items close at hand, and the larger drawers were mainly for storage. The original ship's desk was often built right into a bulkhead. In order to adapt this desk as a functional home furnishing, add a trestle type of leg with a foot rest or a spreader.

Material List

Note: The drawer assembly is made of raised panels fit-ted into a frame. (Study Figs. 5–29 and 5–30.)

	Part	Number	Size	Material
A	Stiles	6	3" x 28" x 1¾"	Pine
B	Side Skirts	2	4" x 10" x 1¾"	
C	Top Rails	2	3" x 12" x 1¾"	
		1	3" x 10½" x 1¾"	
D	Raised Panels	2	11" x 22" x ¾"	
		1	9½" x 22" x ¾"	
E	Front Skirt	1	4" x 14½" x ¾"	
E-1	Drawer Rails	3	1¾" x 14½" x ¾"	
F	Drawer Guides	8	2" x 13¼" x ¾"	
G	Foot Rest	1	6" x 27" x 1¾"	
H	Trestle Leg	1	10" x 24½" x 1¾"	
I	Shoe	1	3½" x 16" x 1¾"	
J	Plate	1	3½" x 16" x 1¾"	
K	Top	1	22¼" x 47¼" x 1¾"	
L	Drawer Riser	1	4" x 26" x ⅜"	
M	Drawer Back	1	7" x 27" x ¾"	
N	Drawer Sides	1	7" x 10" x ¾"	
		1	5¼" x 10" x ¾"	
O	Drawer Top	1	6" x 47" x ¾"	
P	Balusters	8	1¾" dia. x 4"	
Q	Finial	1	1¾" dia. x 2"	
R	Small Drawers	4	3" x 6½" x 4"	
S	Large Drawers	3	6" x 15" x 14"	
T	Writing Drawer	1	¾" x 15" x 14"	

Hardware

Five ½" diameter, porcelain drawer pulls.
Three 1" diameter, porcelain drawer pulls.

Note: Parts P and Q may be lathe-turned, or if a wood lathe is not available pre-made turnings can be purchased from local lumberyards. See Section Eight for list of suppliers.

CONSTRUCTION

1. Lay out and cut the stock for Parts A, B, and C. Cut a ½" x ¾" dado lengthwise down the center of Parts A. (See Figs. 5–29 and 5–30.) Cut a ½" x ¾" tenon on each end of Parts B and C. Cut a ½" x ¾" dado in the center of these parts to match the dado cut in Part A. Cut in the skirt design on Parts B.

2. Lay out and cut the stock for the insert raised panels, Parts D. Allow for a ½" x ¾" tenon all around. Sand the raised panels at this time and stain them. (If the panels shrink, they will not show because they will be stained through the complete tenon, or ¾" both ways.) Glue and nail Parts B to Parts A. Insert the finished raised panels, Parts D, into the dados and glue and nail Parts C to Parts A, locking in the panels. Do not use glue on the panels. Screw the assembly sections together to form a ''U''. This assembly has two sides and a back.

3. Lay out and cut the stock for Parts E and E-1. Cut in the suggested design in Part E. Nail Part E to the ''U'' box assembly. Cut a ¾" notch in one piece of Part E-1 to receive the writing drawer, Part T. Nail Parts E-1 to the finished assembly making three equal spaces for the large working drawers. Screw on the drawer guides, Parts F, at this time.

4. Lay out and cut the stock for Parts G, H, I, and J. Cut a 4" diameter rounded tenon on one end of Part G. Cut the suggested shape on Parts H, I, and J. Cut a 1¾" x 4" mortise on Part H. (See Fig. 5–29.) Screw Parts I and J to Part H. Insert Part G into the mortise and lock it in with a ½" diameter hardwood pin. Screw Part G to the finished large drawer assembly. Cover all screw heads with hardwood plugs.

5. Glue up the stock for Part K. When dry, lay out and cut Park K. Secure Part K to the drawer assembly and Part J with several 3" #10 flat head wood screws.

6. Lay out and cut the stock for Parts L, M, N, and O. Nail Part L to Part K flush with the right

Fig. 5–27. Desk from *The Pine Furniture of Early New England* (1929), by Russell Hawes Kettell, Dover Publications, Inc., *reprinted by permission of the publisher.*

Fig. 5–28. Captain's desk project.

hand side and back edge. Cut a ⅜″ x ¾″ rabbet on Parts N. Nail Parts N to Parts K. Nail Part M into the rabbets on Parts N and into Part K. Cut Part O to the suggested shape with a hand or electric jigsaw. With a router, cut in a molded edge where Part O narrows down to become a railing. (See Fig. 5–29.) Drill the required ¾″ diameter holes, 4″ on centers on the lower side of Part O. These holes will receive Part P. Drill matching holes into Part K.

7. Lathe-turn Parts P and Q to the suggested shape, or purchase the turnings pre-made. (See *Section Eight* for list of suppliers.) Glue Parts P into the pre-drilled holes and secure Part O in place, nailing the other end into Parts M and N. Glue Part Q into place. (See Figs. 5–29 and 5–30.) Cut a trough for pens and pencils into the top right-hand side of Part O using a router and core box bit.

8. Make four small raised panel drawer units, Parts R, to fit the openings on the desk top, with a ¼″ lap-over all around, except for the top edge.

9. Make three raised panel drawers, Parts S, to fit the lower unit openings with a ⅜″ lap-over all around. Make a writing drawer, Part T, to fit the opening in Part E-1.

FINISH

Set and fill all nail holes. Cover all screw heads with hardwood plugs. Sand the entire project smooth. Stain. Cover with several coats of varnish or lacquer. Hand-rub the project with pumice and lemon oil until a high satin sheen develops. Finish with paste wax.

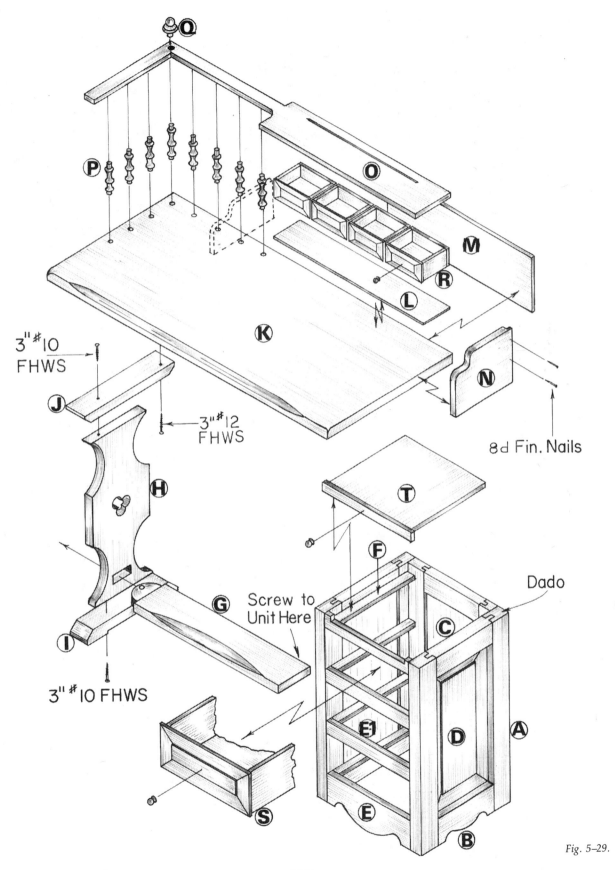

3"#10
FHWS

3"#12
FHWS

3"#10 FHWS

Screw to
Unit Here

8d Fin. Nails

Dado

Fig. 5–29.

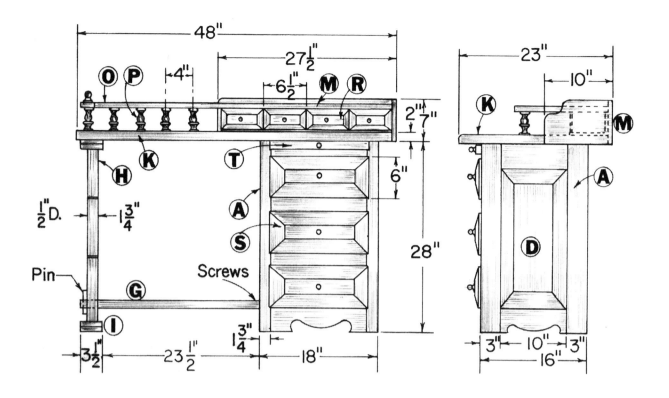

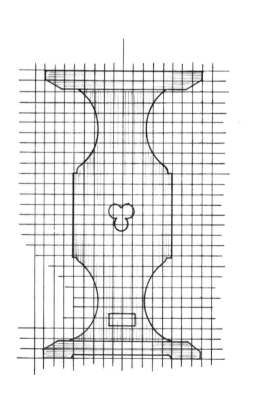

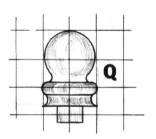

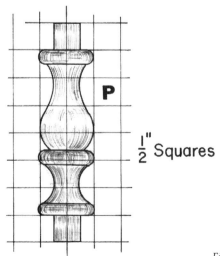

Fig. 5–30.

Mirror
(Courting Glass)

The first mirrors to be had in the colonies were imported. So scarce were these looking glasses that even broken pieces were sold and used. Wood frames were placed around some mirrors to make them appear as pictures, and to protect the expensive glass. Later, very ornate frames with delicate scrollwork topped off with an eagle or turned finial became the vogue.

This mirror, with a slightly scrolled pine frame, is designed very much like one of the early copies of old-world styles.

Fig. 5–31. Early American mirror, gift of Mrs. Russell Sage, Metropolitan Museum of Art, New York, N. Y.

Material List

Part	Number	Size	Material
A	1	8″ x 20″ x 1½″	Pine
B	1	4″ x 20″ x 1½″	
C	2	3″ x 19″ x 1½″	
D	1	15″ x 16″ x ¼″	Mirror

CONSTRUCTION

1. Lay out and cut the top and bottom pieces, Parts A and B. See Figure 5–33 for the suggested shape. Lay out and carve in relief a small eagle at the top center of Part A. The eagle's wings form part of the cyma scrollwork.

2. Cut a ship-lap rabbet in Parts A and B on both sides to take Parts C. The ship-lap joint should be ¾″ deep or one-half the stock thickness. Cut a rabbet in the back of all the pieces for the mirror. (Rabbet suggested: ¼″ x ½″.)

3. Cut the side pieces, Parts C, to the required size. Cut a matching rabbet to complete the ship-lap joint with the top and bottom pieces. Cut a ¼″ x ½″ rabbet for the mirror.

4. Glue the side pieces, Part C, to the top and bottom pieces, Parts A and B. Put two ⅜″ dowel pins through each ship-lap joint.

FINISH

Distress, if desired, and sand the entire frame smooth. Cover with several coats of lacquer. Install the mirror into the pre-made rabbets with several glazier's points or small strips of wood. Install two screw-eyes and a wire for hanging.

Fig. 5–32. Mirror (courting glass) project.

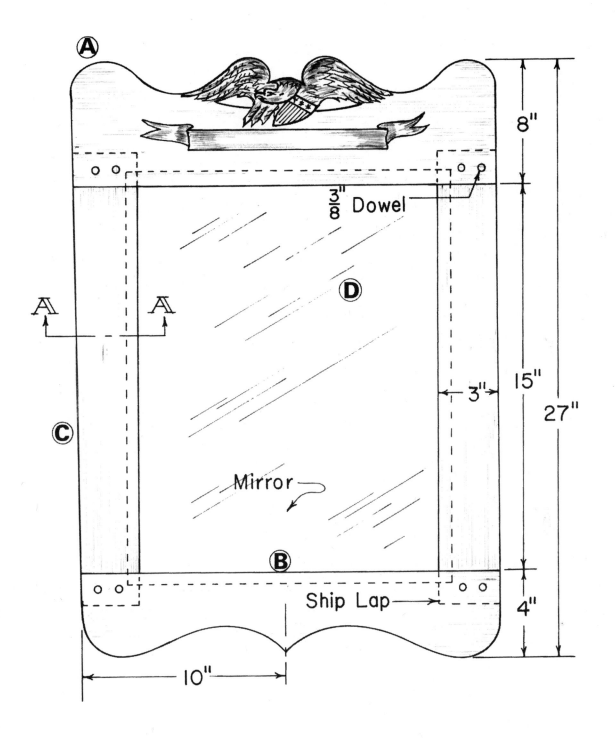

Ⓐ

8"

$\frac{3}{8}$" Dowel

Ⓐ   Ⓐ

Ⓓ

3"   15"   27"

Ⓒ

Mirror

Ⓑ

Ship Lap →   4"

10"

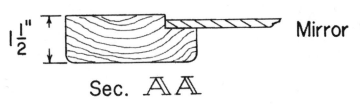

$1\frac{1}{2}$"   Mirror

Sec. 𝔸𝔸

Fig. 5–33.

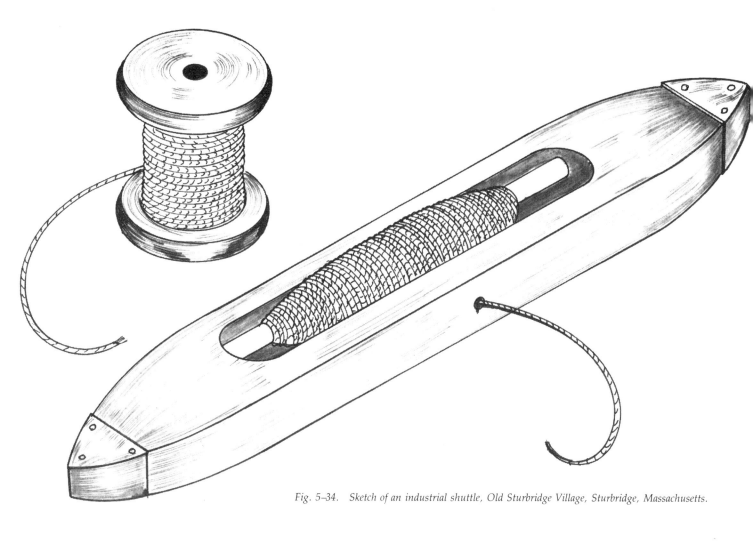

Fig. 5–34.   *Sketch of an industrial shuttle, Old Sturbridge Village, Sturbridge, Massachusetts.*

Wall Sconce

One of the main sources of interior lighting in early American homes was candlelight. The candles were held in sconces, often made from discarded objects. The wall sconce shown here is a composite of a basic design found in weavers' shuttles and some jack stands. Holes are drilled in the side of the shuttle so that the candleholder can be adjusted for height.

Material List

Part	Number	Size	Material
A	1	3″ x 22″ x 1½″	Pine
B	1	3½″ x 4¼″ x 1½″	
C	1	Dish, 2″ diameter	Sheet Metal
D	1	Socket, ¾″ dia. x 1″	Sheet Metal
E	1	¼″ dia. x 4″	Dowel

174

CONSTRUCTION

1. Lay out the suggested shape on Part A and cut it out (See Fig. 5–36). Drill a ¾" hole, 3" down from the top and another 3" up from the bottom. Cut a slot between these two holes. Drill six evenly spaced ¼" diameter holes through the side edge of Part A. (Suggested: 2" on centers.)

2. Optional edging: With a Roman ogee router bit, cut a molded edge all around the outside edges of Part A.

3. Lay out and cut the candle holder, Part B (See Fig. 5–36.) Cut the back edge down to a ¾" wide tenon to fit into the slot cut into Part A. This should leave a ⅜" shoulder on both sides of the holder. Drill two ¼" diameter holes 2" apart to match the holes drilled in the side of Part A.

4. Cut a 2" diameter dish from sheet metal and drill a 3/16" diameter hole dead center, Part C. Cut a sheet metal strip 1" wide by 3" long and bend it into a tube to act as a candle socket, Part D. Solder the tube socket to the dish and screw the dish to Part B.

Note: A wood dish and socket may be used if desired. Cut a 2" diameter circle from 1½" pine and lathe-turn this circle into a dish and candle socket. (See detail drawing in Fig. 5–36 for the shape.)

5. Attach Part B to Part A with the hardwood dowel pin.

FINISH

Distress if desired; sand all parts smooth. Stain or paint and cover with several coats of lacquer.

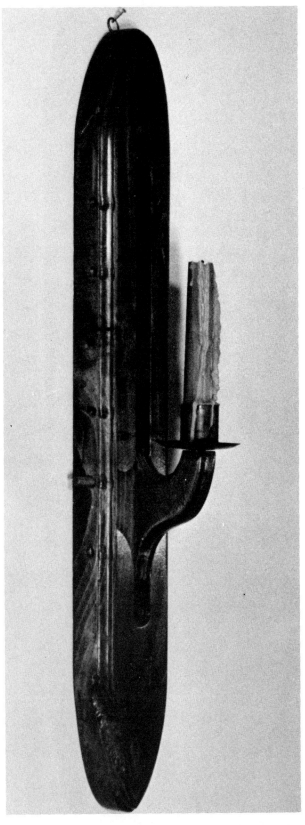

Fig. 5–35. Wall sconce project.

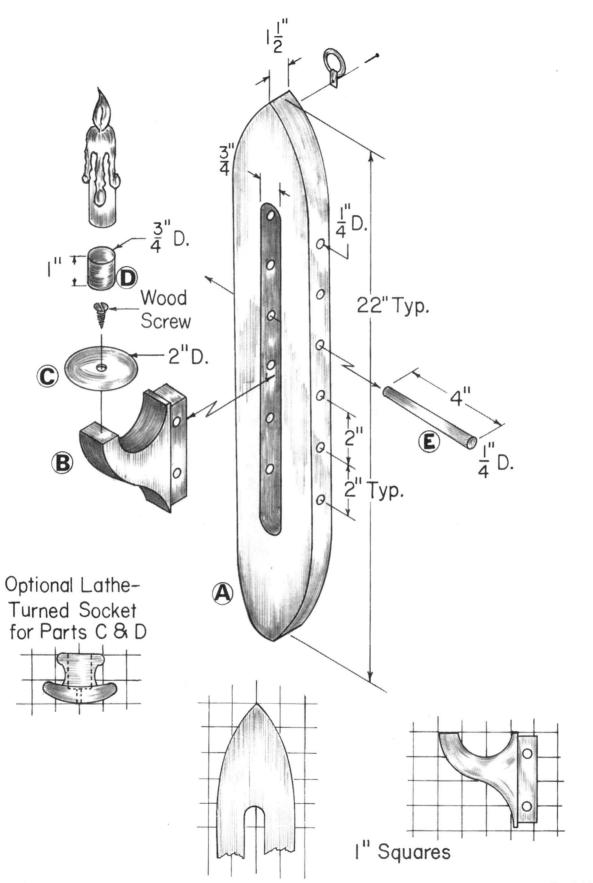

$1\frac{1}{2}$"

$\frac{3}{4}$"

$\frac{3}{4}$"D.

$\frac{1}{4}$"D.

22" Typ.

2"

2" Typ.

4"

$\frac{1}{4}$"D.

Ⓔ

3"
$\overline{4}$"D.

1"

Ⓓ

Wood
Screw

2"D.

Ⓒ

Ⓑ

Ⓐ

Optional Lathe-
Turned Socket
for Parts C & D

1" Squares

Fig. 5–36.

176

SECTION SIX

Folk Art

This section was developed in order to create small wall pieces that would fit in with early American decor. Unique but authentically designed wall objects or accessory pieces are difficult to locate. It is these small items that blend furnishings into a totality of design. Modern mass-production makes only so many styles or designs, and duplications abound.

The decorative items shown here have been based upon authentic pieces; with imagination, new and different pieces can be created. Some are composites of colonial originals, and some have been reduced in scale, but this does not distract from their charm. They can all be made from small pieces of stock and require only a few evenings to complete.

Fig. 6–1. Butcher's signboard,
Index of American Design, Washington, D. C.

Fig. 6–2. Nautical merchant's sign,
Index of American Design, Washington, D. C.

Fig. 6–3.   Colonial Williamsburg, Williamsburg, Virginia.

179

Wolfe Tavern
Signboard

Because many colonists were illiterate, a unique method of identification was developed by means of a "signbord." Limners painted large pictures of famous people or things on large wood planks, thereby making colorful landmarks for taverns, tradesmen, or professional offices. Overlarge boots, eyeglasses, anchors, or profiles soon dotted the settlements. The General Wolfe tavern sign hung in Newburyport, Massachusetts, from 1762 until 1950, and is one of the oldest tavern signs in continuous use in America.

	Material	
One piece	16″ x 24″ x ¾″	Pine

CONSTRUCTION

Glue up the stock to the required width (See Fig. 6–5). When the glue has dried, cut the board into an oval.

DESIGN

Lay out the design on paper. Transfer the design to the board.

FINISH

1. Paint in the design with water-based paints. (Suggested: border, blue; background, light yellow; lettering, green; Wolfe's coat, black; hair, brown).

2. Distress the signboard and cut in deep age cracks. Finish the signboard with a glaze and several coats of lacquer.

Wolfe Tavern

James Wolfe Esq.

1762

3/4"
Border

Age
Cracks

1" Squares

Fig. 6–5.

Fig. 6–6. *Three Crowns signboard project.*

Three Crowns Signboard

This sign represented English authority and dependence, and was erected by a Loyalist tavern owner. When the Revolutionary War broke out, the colonies were split by political sentiments. Some young colonial soldiers wanted to kill the Tory owner, but settled instead for shooting at his signboard; it still carries the bullet holes. After the shooting incident, the owner reassessed his position and the tavern's name was changed to the Waterloo Tavern.

Material

One Piece   14″ x 24″ x ¾″   Pine

CONSTRUCTION

Glue up the stock to the required size (see Fig. 6–7). Lay out and cut when the glue has dried.

DESIGN

Lay out a crown on paper. Transfer the crown drawing to the board, three times.

FINISH

1. Paint the design with water-based colors. (Suggested: border, dark blue; background, white; crowns, gold; felt inside crowns, red; jewels, green, red, yellow, and blue.)

2. Distress the signboard and drill in the simulated bullet holes three-fourths of the way through the board. Cut the edges of the bullet holes with a knife to make them look splintered. Wipe the distressed board down with a black glaze, and finish with several coats of lacquer.

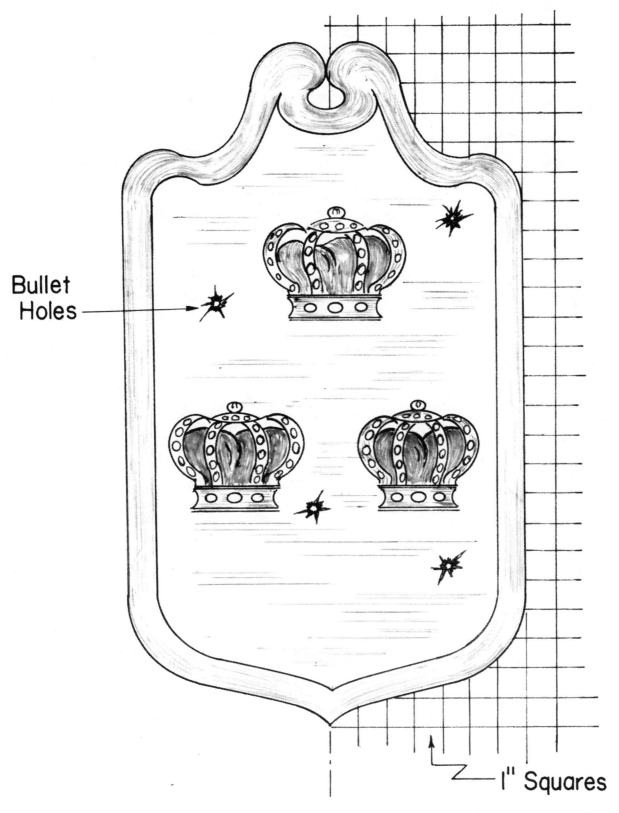

Bullet
Holes

1" Squares

Fig. 6–7.

183

Fig. 6–8. Ship Tavern Signboard, Shelburne Museum, Shelburne, Vermont.

Ship Signboard

Sailing ships were the lifelines of colonial America, and the majestic ships soon appeared on tavern signs, beckoning sailors in for grog and fare.

The ship motif was also used as trade boards for craftsmen connected with the sailing trade. The ship signboard is a composite of many found in the seacoast towns.

Material

One piece	16″ x 23″ x ¾″	Pine

CONSTRUCTION

1. Glue up stock to the required size (see Fig. 6–10).

2. Lay out and cut the board to the suggested shape.

DESIGN

Lay out a picture of a ship on tracing paper and

transfer the picture to the board. (Ship pictures can be found in magazines or libraries.)

FINISH

1. Paint the ship design with water-based paints. (Suggested: border, red or blue; background, gray; sea, blue and green; ship's hull, brown or black; sails, off-white; and the lettering, if used, black.)

2. Distress the signboard and wipe down with a black glaze. Finish with several coats of lacquer.

Fig. 6–9. Ship signboard project.

8"

22$\frac{1}{2}$"

1"

Ship's Inn

1" Squares

Fig. 6–10.

Fig. 6–11. Liberty signboard project.

Liberty Signboard

This signboard was developed from the design used on colonial money, carrying the same message: Unite or live under English domination. The colonies are represented by thirteen heavy chain links (suggesting strength), around a Continental soldier. A picture of General Washington might be substituted in the center.

Material List

Part	Number	Size	Material
A Board	1	10" x 16" x ¾"	Pine
B Rails	2	1¾" x 24"	
C Top	2	2" x 10" x ¾"	
Bottom			

CONSTRUCTION

1. Lay out and cut the stock for Parts A, B, and C. Lathe-turn Parts B to the suggested shape and design. (Note: pre-turned parts may be purchased in lumber or hardware supply outlets.) Drill ¼" diameter holes for the dowel pins where marked in Figure 6–12.

2. Cut the center board, Part A, into an oval. Drill matching ¼" dowel holes in this board.

3. Lay out and cut Part C to the suggested shapes as shown in Figure 6–12. Drill matching ¼" holes for the dowel pins.

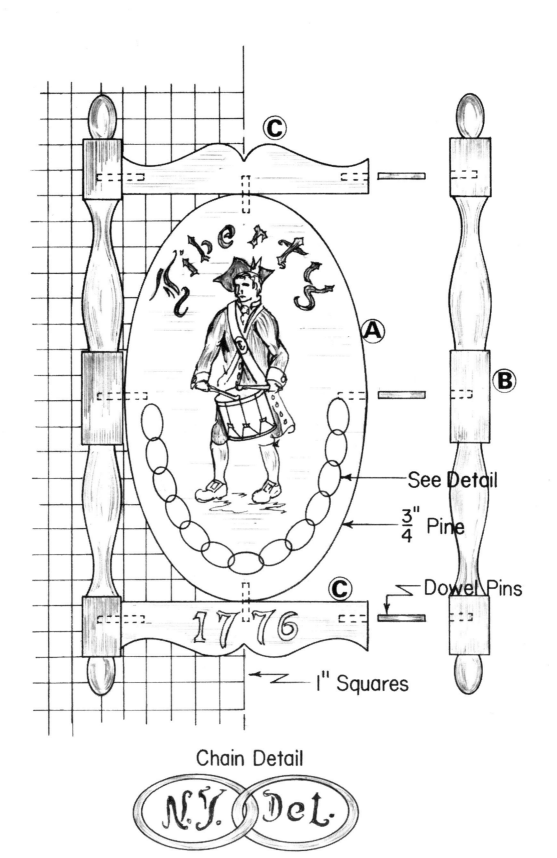

See Detail

$\frac{3}{4}$" Pine

Dowel Pins

1" Squares

Chain Detail

N.Y. Del.

13 Colonies in Links

Fig. 6–12.

Fig. 6–13. *Eagle sign from the Red Lion Inn, Index of American Design, Washington, D. C.*

4. Glue the dowel pins into the signboard. Attach the top and bottom pieces, Parts C, to the pins. Attach the turned side pieces, Parts B, to the pins in Parts A and C.

DESIGN

Lay out the motif on paper and transfer the design to the signboard.

FINISH

Paint the design and signboard pieces with water-based paints. (Suggested: turned side rails, blue; top and bottom rails, red; sign background, light green; soldier's coat, blue with red trim; drum straps, white; pants, brown; stockings, white; chain links, black; lettering, black.)

Distress the signboard and wipe down with a black glaze. Finish with several coats of varnish or lacquer.

Additional Suggestions

Signboards make an interesting wall decoration, and several signboards grouped together make a most interesting wall for the living room or family room. Original one-of-a-kind designs can be adapted from any interesting idea. A family name may be used in place of the tavern name and almost any symbol may be used for the motif. The tavern signboard may also be used for an exterior name or street number sign. If it is made for outdoor purposes, use water-proof paints and finishes.

Fig. 6–14. "Bell-in-Hand" signboard, Index of American Design, Washington, D. C.

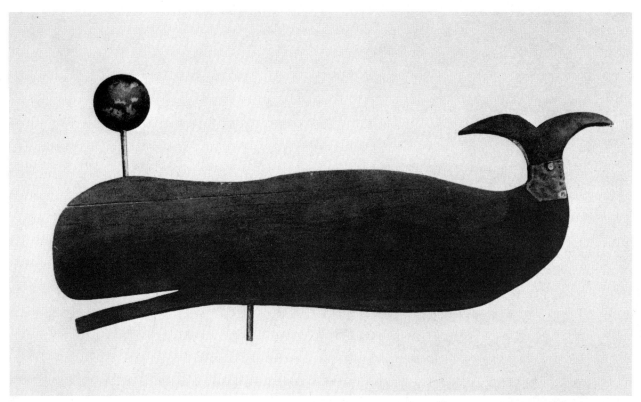

Fig. 6–15. Whale weathervane, Index of American Design, Washington, D. C.

Whale Weathervane Plaque

Carpenters, sailors, farmers, tinkers, whitesmiths, and blacksmiths all made weathervanes, resulting in a wide variety of materials and many different symbols and shapes.

Whales and their harvesting were very important economic factors in many seacoast towns. Often whale oil and candles were the town's main industry, and the whale became a popular symbol to the townspeople. As a result, whales appeared in many different shapes and sizes on weathervanes.

The whale weathervane has a harpoon as a pointer in place of the customary arrow.

Material List

Part	Number	Size	Material
Whale	1	10″ x 18″ x 2″	Pine
Harpoon (handle)	1	3″ x 6″ x ¾″	
(spear)	1	2″ x 4″ x ¾″	
	1	¼″ dia. x 16″	Dowel
Stem	1	2″ x 2″ x 10″	

CONSTRUCTION

1. Lay out the suggested whale design on the 2″ pine boards; cut. Round over and shape the whale, leaving the back section plain and flat.

191

Fig. 6–16. *Whale weathervane plaque project.*

Using a ½" gouge chisel, cut gouges in the entire surface of the whale.

2. Lathe-turn the stem to the suggested shape leaving a ¾" x 1¼" tenon on the top. Lathe-turn the harpoon handle. (See Fig. 6–17).

3. Cut out the harpoon point and gouge it to match the whale.

4. Clamp a piece of scrap wood to the back side of the whale and drill a ¾" hole in the center bottom so that one half of the hole is in the whale and one half of the hole is in the scrap wood. Drill a ¼" hole through the stem where indicated in Figure 6–17, and drill a ¼" hole partway through the harpoon point and handle.

5. Cut the stem and harpoon handle in half. Glue the ¼" piece of doweling into the hole in the stem and glue on the point and handle. Glue the stem into the "half" hole in the whale.

FINISH

Paint the entire vane with a water-based paint. (Light green or blue is suggested.) Wipe with a glaze. Cover with several coats of varnish or lacquer.

192

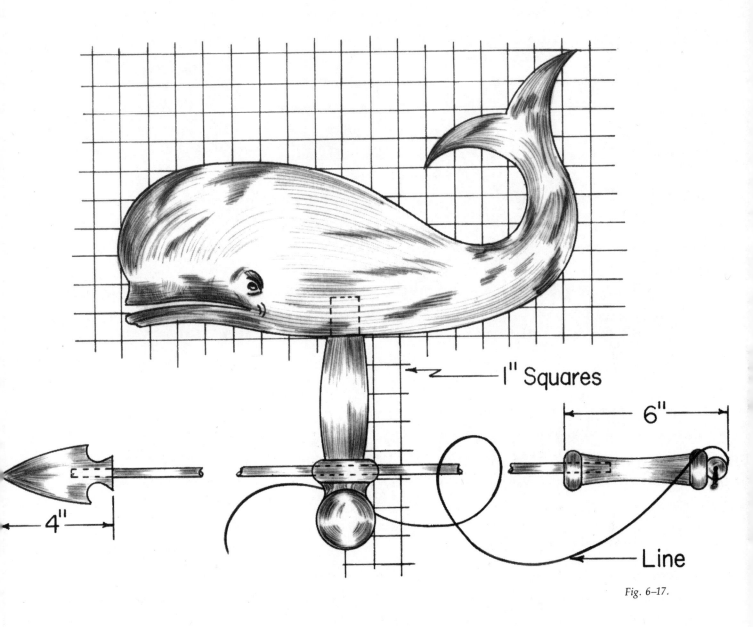

1" Squares

6"

4"

Line

Fig. 6–17.

Fig. 6-18   *Horse vane made of zinc and sheet copper, Index of American Design, Washington, D. C.*

Horse Weathervane Plaque

Horses were always popular as motifs for weathervanes, perhaps because many were crafted by blacksmiths.

Material List

Part	Number	Size	Material
Horse	1	8″ x 10″ x ¾″	Pine
Pointer	2	2″ x 3″ x ¾″	
	1	¼″ dia. x 12″	Dowel
Stem	1	1½″ dia. x 10″	

CONSTRUCTION

1. Lay out the horse design suggested on ¾″ clear pine and cut it out. With a sharp knife or chisel, round out the legs and cut in the details of the face and mane in relief. Cut in the hair lines on the mane and tail. (This work requires extra care because of the thinness of the legs and tail and the grain direction on these features.)

2. Clamp a piece of scrap stock to the center back of the finished horse and drill a ¾″ hole so that one half of the hole is cut into the horse, the other half in the scrap wood.

3. Cut out the arrow point and tail. Lathe-turn the stem to the suggested shape leaving a ¾″ diameter tenon on the top.

4. Drill a ¼″ hole through the stem as suggested in Figure 6–20 and part way through the arrow point and tail piece. Cut the finished stem in half and glue the ¼″ dowel into the ¼″ hole drilled in the center. Glue on the arrow point and tail. Glue the stem to the horse weathervane.

FINISH

Paint the entire project with a water-based paint (light yellow is suggested). Wipe on a black glaze and cover with several coats of lacquer.

Fig. 6–19. Horse weathervane plaque project.

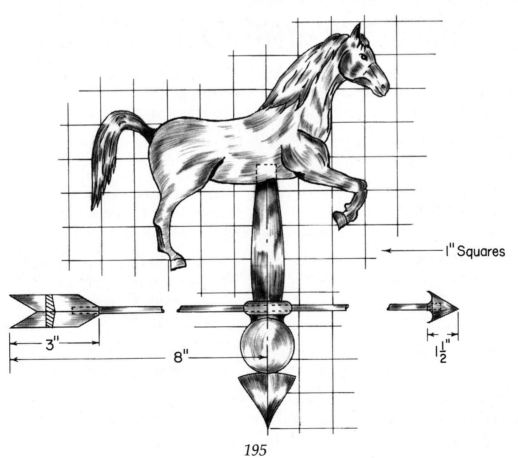

1" Squares

3"

8"

1½"

Fig. 6–20.

195

Fig. 6–21. Wood rooster from a weathervane, Shelburne Museum, Shelburne, Vermont.

Rooster Weathervane Plaque

Many astonishing creatures and motifs topped off weathervanes, from large grasshoppers to dragons. One of the most widely used was the rooster, whose popularity was rooted in religion as well as the agrarian nature of the colonies. Many farmers carved their own vanes and they chose motifs that were important to them.

Material List

Part	Number	Size	Material
Rooster	1	12″ x 14″ x 1½″	Pine
Pointer	1	2″ x 10″ x ¾″	
	1	¼″ dia. x 10″	Dowel
Stem	1	3″ dia. x 10″	Pine

CONSTRUCTION

1. Lay out the suggested rooster motif on the 1½″ stock and cut it out. With a sharp knife, round off all edges and cut the head, feet, and feathers in relief. (Extreme care must be taken when cutting the feet and tail feather detail be- cause of the thinness of the stock and the grain direction.)

2. Clamp a piece of scrap stock to the back bottom center of the rooster and drill a ¾″ hole 1¼″ deep so that one half the hole is bored into the rooster.

3. Lathe-turn the stem to the suggested shape. Make a ¾″ x 1¼″ tenon at the top of the stem to fit the hole in the rooster. Drill a ¼″ hole through the stem as suggested in Fig. 6–23 for the pointer.

4. Cut out the pointer tail and arrow. Drill a ¼″ hole partway through these two parts.

5. Cut the stem in half. Glue the ¼″ doweling into the pre-drilled hole. Glue on the pointer arrow and tail. Glue the stem into the rooster.

FINISH

Paint the entire rooster with a water-based paint (bright red suggested). Wipe down with a black glaze, and finish with several coats of lacquer.

196

Fig. 6–22. Rooster weathervane plaque project.

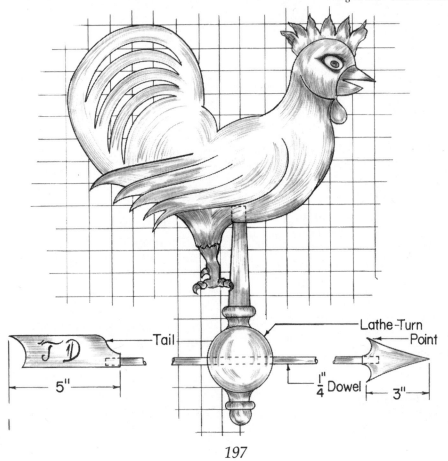

Tail

Lathe-Turn
Point

$\frac{1}{4}$" Dowel

5"

3"

Fig. 6–23.

197

*Fig. 6–24. Carved eagle from the **Enterprise**, Index of American Design, Washington, D. C.*

Carved Eagle

The large carved eagles first came from the sterns of sailing ships. Retired sea captains often hung the eagles over the doors of their land homes, as an open invitation to seafaring men to stop in and have a little grog and friendly talk.

All of the early eagles were hand-carved, and many examples still hang over customs houses, federal courts, and private homes. In modern colonial-styled homes, this eagle may be hung over the fireplace or over the front door as a sign of hospitality, as well as an indication of national pride.

Material List

Part	Size	Material
1 Piece	20″ x 48″ x 2″	Clear Pine

CONSTRUCTION

1. Glue up stock to the suggested thickness, using clear pine without knotholes.

2. Lay out the eagle shape on a large piece of paper. Transfer the design to the stock. Cut out the basic outline of the eagle. From the scrap stock (cut away from the main piece), draw and then cut out the head, neck, and the claws. Glue the raised head, neck, and the claws to the places indicated on Figure 6–26. It is suggested that these blocks be glued on with the grain running in the direction of the intended carvings.

3. With a router, taper the thickness of the main piece from 2″ at the top of the wings to about 1″ at the bottom of the wings. The shield remains 2″ thick. (See detail, Fig. 6–26.)

4. Lay out the feather details on the main piece. Cut the feather lines with a sharp razor knife or chisel. Cut in the details of the eyes and beak with

the knife. Sand the outside edges (top) of the feathers and shoulders round. Sand the bottom edges of the head round and smooth. Sand the lower neck to blend in with the main piece and blend between the shoulders. Cut in the details of the claws and arrow. Sand the entire eagle smooth.

FINISH

The eagle may be stained, or painted gold. The arrow may be stained, or painted brown. The stripes on the shield should be red and white, with a blue chief and white stars.

Optional Eagle
Name Sign

Cut the surname sign from 2" stock in the suggested shape and size. Cut in the end flows with a razor knife and cut in the surname with a chisel or knife. Finish the name sign the same as the eagle.

Fig. 6–25. Carved eagle project.

199

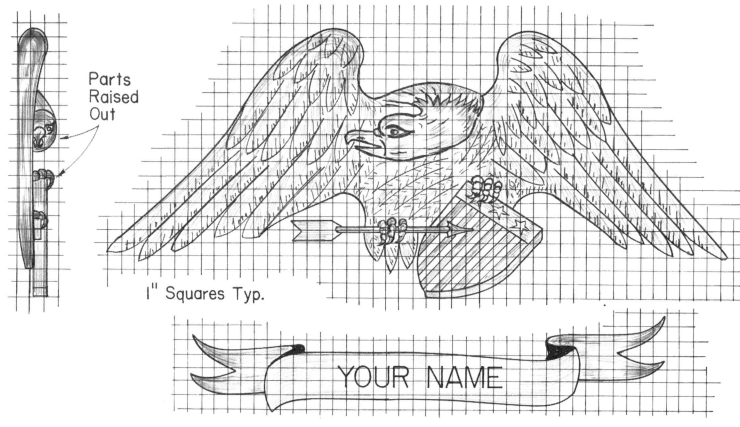

Parts
Raised
Out

1" Squares Typ.

YOUR NAME

Note: scale may be reduced by making squares $\frac{3}{4}$" or $\frac{1}{2}$".

Fig. 6–26.

Fig. 6–27. *Shorebird, Index of American Design, Washington, D.C.*

Decoys
(Ducks, Geese, and Shorebirds)

The early settlers found an abundance of wildfowl and game; in fact, a flock of wild geese helped the Plymouth settlement to survive their first harsh winter.

The flocks were so plentiful that for the first few years, wildfowl could be harvested without difficulty; however, wild game soon learned to fear the new hunter and his far-reaching gun. In order to add fresh meat to the colonial table, the settlers had to employ deception in the form of duck, goose, and shorebird decoys.

The use of decoys was a European practice developed because hunting pressures made game birds wary. The purpose of the decoy is to give a high-flying wild flock the impression that the calm, placid body of water below them is serene and devoid of humans; if any intruders were nearby, that flock of ducks feeding and sleeping on the water's surface would not remain there.

Some enterprising hunters used trained live birds for their decoys. The tame ducks or geese, tied to poles, called to the wild flocks overhead,

Fig. 6–28. Mallard decoy, the Kidas, Chester, Massachusetts.

Fig. 6–29. Carved wood duck, the Kidas, Chester, Massachusetts.

202

luring them within range of guns or traps. But live decoys had to be fed all year long, and when times were poor, the live decoy frequently ended up in the cooking pot. The best solution seemed to be wooden decoys that could be stored when not in use.

There is evidence that confidence decoys were used by the Egyptians in ancient times and by American Indians as well. The simplest way to form a decoy was to wrap a fowl's skin around a bunch of reeds.

It was the early American settler who perfected the art form of the wooden decoy. The first wooden decoys were crude blocks painted to somewhat resemble a duck. Little attention was paid to detailing because the purpose of the wood block was to bring the flock within gun's range. They had to deceive for only a little while.

As the migrating flocks became more shy of humans, the decoys became more sophisticated. Individual decoys were carved in different positions—sleeping, stretching, feeding, and preening. Feather and wing details appeared and great care and time was spent to match the coloring and characteristics of different species. The first crude wooden blocks had evolved into folk art and shortly thereafter many decoys were carved to exact perfection. These became the "show" decoys, never meant to feel water's surface. The plans shown here were developed from several different antique decoys found in restoration settlements and some private collections. In general, most ducks have the same basic shape and line except for the head; feather coloring varies greatly. These drawings give a generalized body shape and a selection of head shapes. Most often

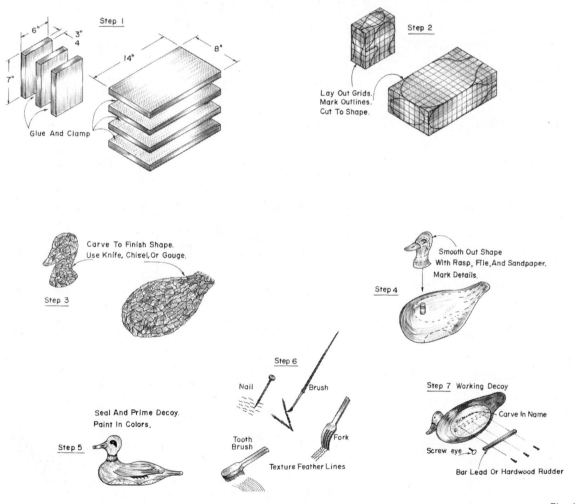

Fig. 6–30.

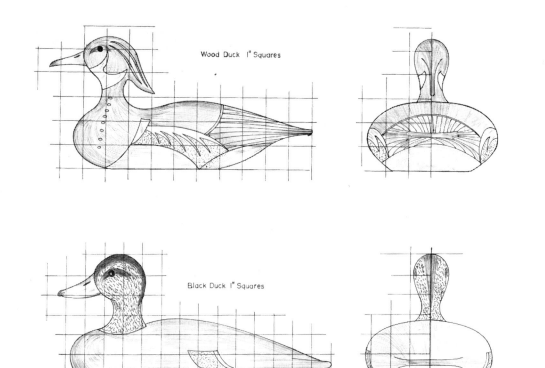

Wood Duck 1" Squares

Black Duck 1" Squares

Fig. 6-31.

Canada Goose 1" Squares

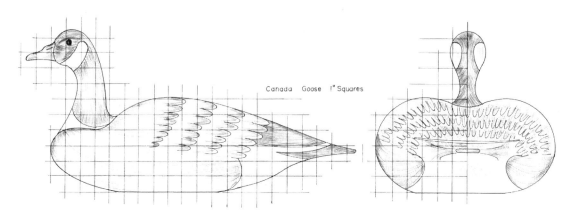

Pintail Duck 1" Squares

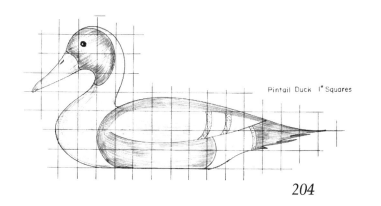

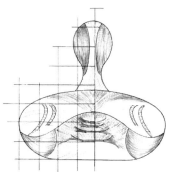

Fig. 6-32.

wooden decoys were made oversize so that they could be seen readily from the air. The decoys may be made full-size or half-scale, if preferred.

Material List

Most decoys were made from a few pieces of scrap wood. Many expert carvers prefer straight-grain mahogany because this type of wood will hold a fine line. In general, decoys may be made from any clear wood, hard or soft.

CONSTRUCTION

(See Fig. 6–30.)

1. Cut selected clear stock to size. Glue and clamp the stock together to achieve the desired thickness. Allow the block to set overnight.

2. Lay out one-inch-grid marks on the glued block. Mark in the desired duck profile and head shape. Make a rough cut along the lines with a sabre, jigsaw, or band saw.

3. Carve to a semi-finished shape with a knife, chisel or gouge.

4. Smooth out the decoy to a final shape with a wood rasp, file, and sandpaper. Fit the decoy's head to the body with a piece of dowel and blend the two parts together.

FINISH

1. Seal and prime the decoy with two coats of waterproof paint. Pencil in the wing, eye, and coloring detailing. An excellent source of feather detailing and coloring can be obtained from wildlife books, encyclopedias, or nature study books.

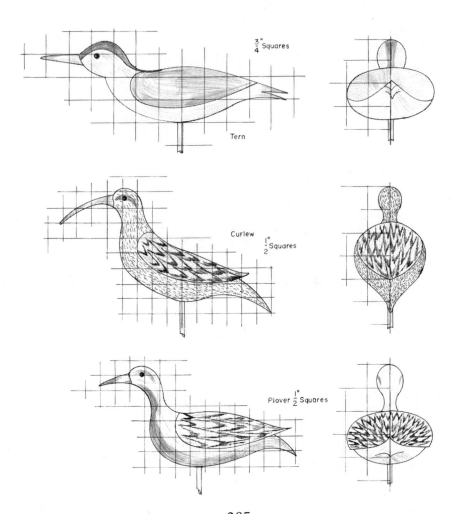

$\frac{3}{4}''$ Squares

Tern

Curlew $1\frac{1}{2}''$ Squares

Plover $1\frac{1}{2}''$ Squares

Fig. 6–33.

2. Paint in the feather and wing details. Several methods may be employed to achieve this detailing. When a two-tone color is desired, paint the decoy with the lighter color and allow this coat to dry. Paint the area with a darker color and while the second coat is still wet, cut in feather details with a sharp nail, fork, or toothbrush. Any of these tools will cut through the still wet top coating. To reveal traces of the lighter undercoat. Another method would be to paint the darker color first and while this coat is still moist, blend in a lighter color with an artist's brush.

Balance

To finish a "working" decoy, test float it in order to find its center. (Most blocks are front heavy because of the added head weight.) Attach a strip of bar lead to the bottom to level the decoy and to act as a rudder. Carve in your name and date and attach a screw-eye for the anchor line.

Several mail order companies sell decoy eyes, anchor lines, bar lead rudders, and mixed decoy paints for different species of ducks or geese; also, local sporting goods stores frequently stock these items.

Fig. 6–34.

Miniatures

The early colonial youngster had very little in the form of toys or playthings. All of the parents' time and efforts were devoted to building a home, clearing farmland, planting crops, and housekeeping chores. Toys were a luxury few could afford. Once the bitter first years were surmounted and life became more orderly, some leisure time was possible and toys and playthings appeared in homes.

Some authorities claim that miniatures, or child-size furnishings, evolved from prototypes made by European craftsmen. In Europe a craft journeyman was expected to complete a master-piece or example of his best effort and skill. Most towns could not support several such craftsmen, thus the new journeyman took to the open road seeking fame, fortune, and a town of his own. Full-size furnishings were difficult to carry, and the idea of a scale model became popular. The smaller version was easily carried about and it served to display the craftsman's talents. Some parents purchased these scale models for their children, and the idea of building child-size or miniature furnishings soon became part of the craftsman's offerings.

Pennsylvania Dutch fathers made chests and furnishings for older daughters and the original *puppethouzen* is believed to have been perfected in central Europe. The German fairy tale, folk art, and toys came to American shores with these people, and then like all things good, spread to the other colonies.

There are as many different scales of furnishings and toys as there are people making them. Some furnishings were half-scale or child-size. Some furnishings were designed for a certain size doll, thus beds, cradles, tables, and chairs were made for 6-, 9-, or 12-inch dolls.

The smallest furnishings were expressly designed for the dollhouse, often on a one-inch-equals-one-foot scale. Most of the reduced size furnishings were made as carefully as their full-size counterparts. The task of construction is not reduced with the size, but rather made more difficult because of the stock size and the tools available for the work.

Fig. 7–1. Miniature collection, Old Sturbridge Village, Sturbridge, Massachusetts.

The plans offered for building miniatures have been developed from authentic colonial pieces. Some drawings have several dimensions given so as to allow for building those projects in different sizes. The first dimension given is for dollhouse furnishings at a one-twelfth scale; These are items designed specifically for the dollhouse. Some drawings have a second dimension for a certain size of doll, so that pieces may be made for other uses, and not only as dollhouse furnishings. A note is made alongside the dimensions for the particular size of doll.

Many of these pieces have not been duplicated in other printed works and are perfect examples of colonial art forms.

Some drawings have notes on dimensions for full-size furniture. The reverse is also true. Any plans offered in this book can be made in dollhouse size furnishings by dividing the stated measurements by twelve. An easy example is the *Family Dining Table* in *Section Three*. Whereas the full-size drawings call for 30″ high legs, and a 5′ x 7′ oval top, the dollhouse size converts to 2½″ high legs with a 5″ x 7″ oval top. With this formula in mind, any article in the other sections can be made for the dollhouse.

The offered dollhouse was developed from the Fenno House in old Sturbridge Village. The original house was built in 1704. It was considered perfect for a dollhouse plan because of the simple two up and two down, four-room layout. Many of the furnishings in this section were taken from the Fenno House or surrounding homes of the same period.

Both the dollhouse and the furnishings can be made with simple hand tools and a table saw. Some pieces call for turned legs, and this small stock problem can be solved by using a small electric drill as a lathe. The drill chuck will hold even the smallest dowel, and all the turning or shaping is completed with a file and sandpaper; *No cutting tools* are needed. It is best to lock the drill in a vise, or clamp it to a work bench so that the work extends over an open area.

Most often mortise and tenons are not used on small pieces because of stock size. Glue is the most common fastener, again because nails or brads often will split the small-size stock used for miniature furnishings.

*Fig. 7–2. Dollhouse-size table developed from full-size table in **Section Three**.*

Fig. 7–3. Fenno House, Old Sturbridge Village, Sturbridge, Massachusetts.

Fenno House Dollhouse (¹/₁₂ Scale)

The Fenno House in Old Sturbridge Village is a perfect example of colonial living. The house was built around its center section that contains the gang fireplaces, central stairway, closets, and kitchen pantry. This home was considered small, however, in colonial times new rooms were often added as they were needed. In this respect, the Fenno House can be described as a starter dwelling, with the idea that as the family grew, so too would the home.

The plan has been changed only slightly to allow for miniaturization. The original house had two windows on the front right side and the lap boards had mitered corners. Because of the reduced scale, the drawings call for corner boards with the lap boards butting into this trim.

An interesting feature in the Fenno House is the "gun-stock" corner posts that support the main framing beams. The gun-stock corner posts resemble inverted firearm stocks with the widest butt section at the ceiling line. The main support beams meet at the corners.

Fig. 7–4.   *Fenno House dollhouse (1/12 scale), project.*

Fig. 7–5.   *Dollhouse interior.*

Fig. 7–6. Dollhouse room detail.

Fig. 7–7. Dollhouse fireplace detail.

Fig. 7–8. Dollhouse roof shingle detail.

Rake Trim

Front Roof Board
$\frac{1}{4}$" Plywood

Chimney

Rear Roof Board

Shingles

Cornice

Scale Wallpaper

Wall "C"

Wall "D"

Wall "A"

Ceiling $\frac{1}{4}$" Plywood

Paint Off White

Rake Trim

2nd Floor
Paint Brown

1st Floor, Paint Brown

Corner
Board

Wall "B"

Stairs

Plywood
Front Wall

Paint 1st Floor Walls Off-White,
Woodwork Barn Red.

Plywood Wall

Lap Boards

Batten Door

Window Unit

Lap Boards

Corner
Board

Fig. 7–9. Dollhouse assembly.

Material List

Each individual piece is not listed; instead, the board footage needed to make certain pieces is given.

Wood: One, 4' x 8' sheet of ⅜" plywood (A.C.) will make all of the exterior walls, floors, ceiling, and roof panels. (See Fig. 7–10 for suggested layout.)

Ten board feet (1" x any size), of clear pine will make all the window and door framing, casing, and trim; all interior walls, corner boards and exterior trim, beams, lap-siding, and roof cornice.

Four board feet of 1" clear cedar will make the roof shingles.

Fasteners: ⅛ pound of ½" bank pins (sometimes called sequin pins, available at craft shops), one package of small ½" brads.

Detailing: Fireplace bricks were made with drywall joint cement. Coloring, staining, and paints are ordinary supplies found in any paint or hardware outlet. Scale-size wallpaper can be purchased. (See list of suppliers, *Section Eight*.)

Hinges: Strap hinges were made of belt leather, however, scale-size hinges can be purchased. (See list of suppliers, *Section Eight*.)

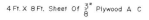

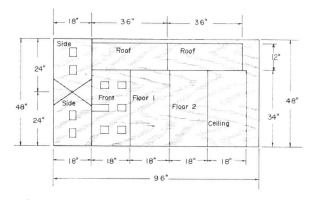

Fig. 7–10. Material layout, dollhouse.

CONSTRUCTION

1. Lay out and mark the plywood sheet for the walls, floors, ceiling board, and roof requirements. (See Fig. 7–10.) Cut out the marked pieces. With a jigsaw or saber saw, cut out the openings as shown in Figure 7–10. Paint all interior areas with two or more coats of off-white paint. Do not assemble parts at this time.

2. Make the window sash of wood or plastic. (See Fig. 7–14.) On the single wall sections, cut the window frame and exterior casing stock on a table saw. Frame each window as suggested in Figure 7–14. Secure the exterior trim to the frame and the plywood sides with pins. Insert the premade window sash and apply the interior trim or casing. (It is best to stain the window frames and interior casing before installing.) Make a frame and casing for the main entrance. Make a door from thin clear pine and secure the door to the frame. (See Fig. 7–13.)

3. Carefully mark locations on each wall section for the beams and interior walls. It is suggested that if wallpaper is to be used it be applied at this time.

4. Lay out the first and second floor boards. Cut the stair opening (well) as shown in Figure 7–9 and in the floor plan, Figure 7–11. Make a small railing of ⅛" doweling and install this rail on the second floor. Paint both floor boards with two coats of brown paint.

5. Assemble the front and side wall sections around the first floor board. Nail the walls to the first floor and to each other.

6. Lay aside the main house and cut out stock for the bottom center interior wall section, walls A and B. See details in Figure 7–11. Cut openings for the fireplaces and box in these areas. Mark out the brick areas and attach temporary forms to the walls. Apply a thin first coat of drywall joint cement. Allow this coat to dry. Apply a thin second coat, and while the cement is still wet, score the area into small-scale bricks with a knife. Mix colors of model paint to achieve a "brick red" paint; paint each brick individually. While the red paint is still wet, tone each brick with flat black paint. (See Fig. 7–17.) When the fireplaces are completed, build the stairway in the front section of

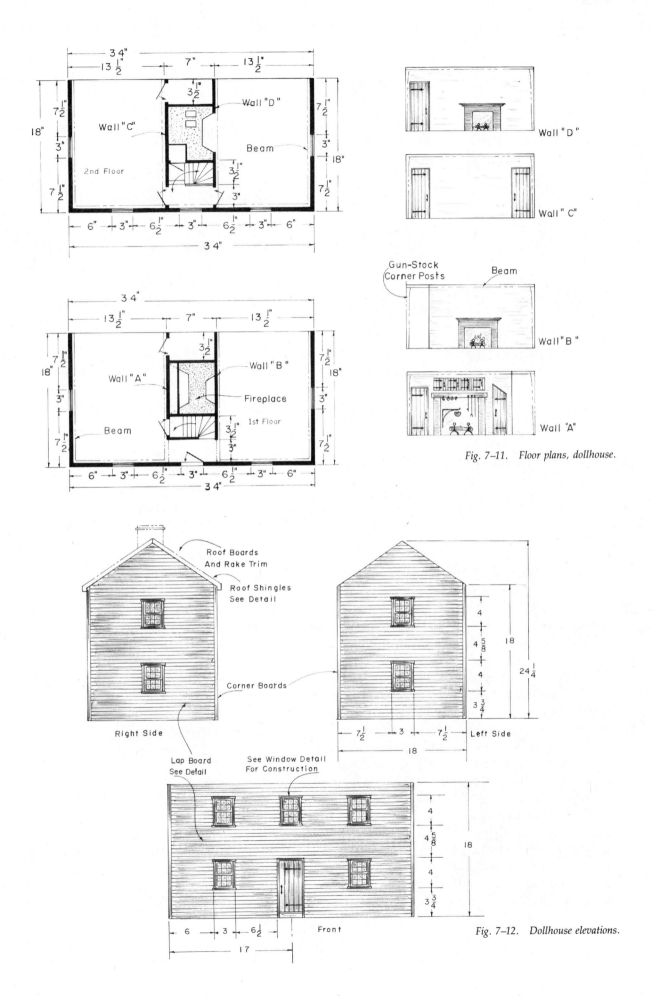

Fig. 7–11. *Floor plans, dollhouse.*

Fig. 7–12. *Dollhouse elevations.*

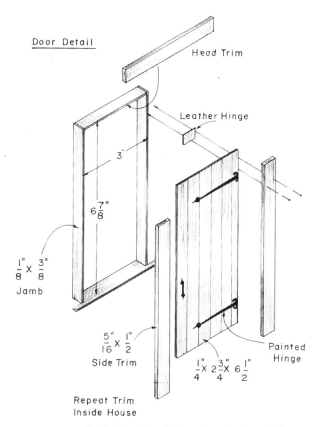

Door Detail

Head Trim

Leather Hinge

3"

6 7/8"

1/8" x 3/8"
Jamb

5/16" x 1/2"
Side Trim

1/4" x 2 3/4" x 6 1/2"

Painted Hinge

Repeat Trim
Inside House

Fig. 7–13. Door detail and construction, dollhouse.

the interior walls. (The stair risers will be higher than normal because dollhouses have extra high ceilings to allow for viewing and access to the interiors.) Complete the interior wall section with a pantry door and false cabinet doors. It is recommended that the gun-stock corner posts and master header beams be installed at this time (See Fig. 7–17.) Install this first floor center wall section temporarily on the floor board and mark out for the fireplace floors and hearth. Again, make bricks within the marked areas. (See Fig. 7–17.)

7. Cut the gun-stock corner posts and master header beams to size. Cut with a knife to resemble hand hewed timers. Stain and allow beams to dry. Install the header beams and corner posts on the first floor. Install the first floor interior wall/ fireplace section. Install the pre-made and pre-painted second-floor board. Nail the second floor into the center wall section and the master header beams.

8. Cut the stock for the second floor interior wall section, walls C and D. (See Fig. 7–11.) Cut the door openings, and frame and trim them. Make the required doors and attach to the frames with leather hinges. Make the bedroom fireplace in the same manner as the lower fireplaces. Fit the second floor interior wall section in place and mark out the fireplace floor and hearth. Make bricks within this area. Wallpaper the interior wall at this time. Make the second floor corner posts and header beams and stain them. Install them on the second floor. Install the interior wall section. Nail this section into the second floor. Paint the ceiling board off-white. Install the ceiling board by nailing it into the master beams and the center wall section.

9. Cut and fit the roof boards. A center roof support is recommended. Nail the roof boards in place. Make a chimney from 2" x 4" stock. Make bricks in the method outlined for the fireplaces. Secure the finished chimney to the roof.

10. Cut the stock for the cornice, rake trim, and corner boards. (See Figs. 7–12 and 7–16.) Secure the cornice, rake trim, and corner boards with small brads or bank pins. Cut the clear pine board into 1/8" strips. Sand each strip slightly to remove any saw marks. Attach the lap siding strips to the plywood sides with a 1/2" exposure to the front and sides. (See Fig. 7–15.)

Make strips to cover the exposed plywood at the rear of the dollhouse. Attach these strips with glue and brads. Remove any excess glue. Stain the entire exterior of the house. The exterior window and door trim is painted barn red.

11. To make roof shingles, cut the cedar board into 1½" cross-sections. (See Figs. 7–16 and 7–8.) Secure a cut block to a work bench with a clamp and split off 1/16" thick chips. Any sturdy, sharp instrument will slice them.

Attach the roof shingle chips to the roof boards with a 1/2" to 3/4" exposure, nailing each one so that the next row will cover the pin or nail heads. The shingles may be stapled to the roof with 1/4" or 3/8" staples if desired. The shingles are not stained or painted. The top rows of shingles are finished with a "ridge cap" made of 1/8" x 3/8" strips of cedar nailed or glued together to form a right angle and this right angle secured to the peak of the roof.

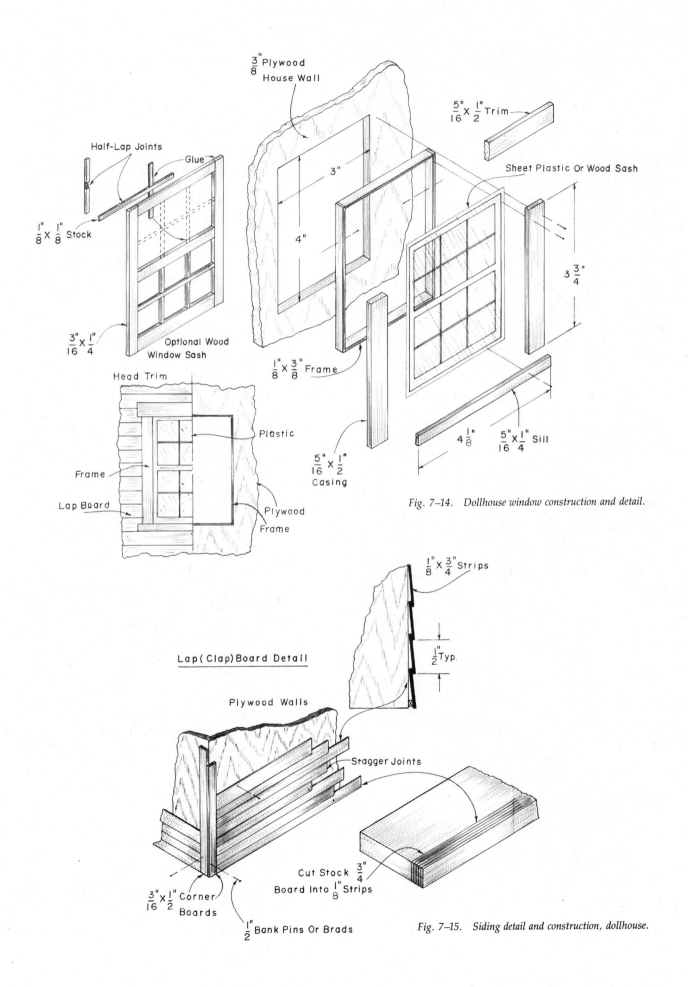

$\frac{3}{8}$" Plywood House Wall

Half-Lap Joints

Glue

$\frac{5}{16}$" X $\frac{1}{2}$" Trim

$\frac{1}{8}$" X $\frac{1}{8}$" Stock

Sheet Plastic Or Wood Sash

3"

4"

$3\frac{3}{4}$"

$\frac{3}{16}$" X $\frac{1}{4}$"

Optional Wood Window Sash

$\frac{1}{8}$" X $\frac{3}{8}$" Frame

Head Trim

Plastic

Frame

$\frac{1}{8}$" X $\frac{3}{8}$" Frame

Lap Board

Plywood Frame

$\frac{5}{16}$" X $\frac{1}{2}$" Casing

$4\frac{1}{8}$"

$\frac{5}{16}$" X $\frac{1}{4}$" Sill

Fig. 7–14.   Dollhouse window construction and detail.

$\frac{1}{8}$" X $\frac{3}{4}$" Strips

$\frac{1}{2}$" Typ.

Lap(Clap)Board Detail

Plywood Walls

Stagger Joints

$\frac{3}{16}$" X $\frac{1}{2}$" Corner Boards

$\frac{1}{2}$" Bank Pins Or Brads

Cut Stock Board Into $\frac{1}{8}$" Strips

$\frac{3}{4}$"

Fig. 7–15.   Siding detail and construction, dollhouse.

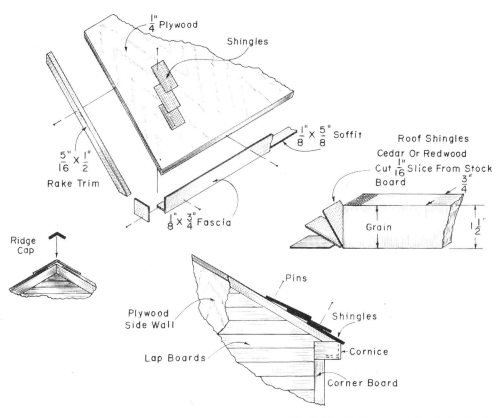

$\frac{1}{4}$" Plywood

Shingles

$\frac{1}{8}$" X $\frac{5}{8}$" Soffit

$\frac{5}{16}$" X $\frac{1}{2}$"
Rake Trim

$\frac{1}{8}$ X $\frac{3}{4}$" Fascia

Ridge
Cap

Roof Shingles
Cedar Or Redwood
Cut $\frac{1}{16}$" Slice From Stock
Board

$\frac{3}{4}$"

$1\frac{1}{2}$"

Grain

Pins

Shingles

Plywood
Side Wall

Cornice

Lap Boards

Corner Board

Fig. 7–16.   Dollhouse roof shingle detail and roof construction.

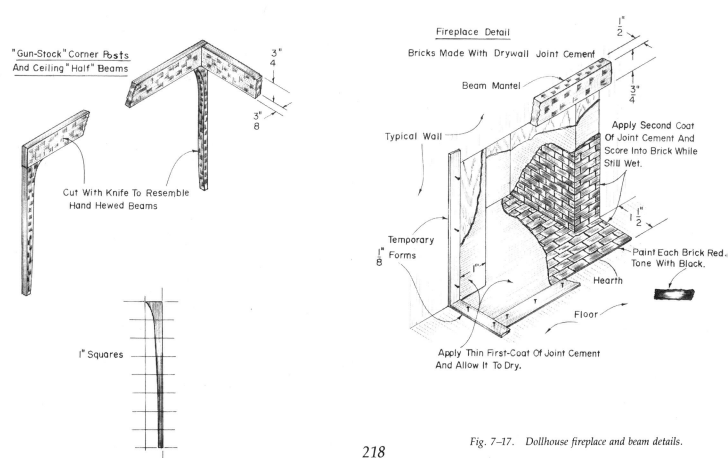

"Gun-Stock" Corner Posts
And Ceiling "Half" Beams

$\frac{3}{4}$"

$\frac{3}{8}$"

Cut With Knife To Resemble
Hand Hewed Beams

1" Squares

Fireplace Detail

Bricks Made With Drywall Joint Cement

$\frac{1}{2}$"

$\frac{3}{4}$"

Beam Mantel

Typical Wall

Apply Second Coat
Of Joint Cement And
Score Into Brick While
Still Wet.

Temporary
Forms

$\frac{1}{8}$"

$1\frac{1}{2}$"

1"

Paint Each Brick Red
Tone With Black.

Hearth

Floor

Apply Thin First-Coat Of Joint Cement
And Allow It To Dry.

218

Fig. 7–17.   Dollhouse fireplace and beam details.

Dollhouse Accessories

Every home, colonial or modern, needs many items for proper operation and for storage. Fireplace tools, andirons, brooms, canisters, and baskets are only a few of such items needed by homemakers for daily living. These items and others—the various things that transform a house into a home—are offered on a scale suited for the dollhouse.

Firetools and Andirons

The principal material used for construction of these tools is a heavy wire coat hanger, cut into straight lengths. Sand the wire to remove its protective paint coating.

Make a paper pattern from the suggested sizes and shapes shown in Figure 7–18, lower left. Bend the coat hanger wire to match the pattern, and solder the pieces together. When completed, paint the firetools flat black.

Hearth Broom

Cut a ⅛" dowel 2¾" long. Temporarily secure (with a rubber band), a small bunch of straw cut from an old broom or brush, and insert the dowel into the center. Lash the straw permanently to the dowel with a brightly colored thread or string; remove temporary band.

Cheese Box

The cheese box can be cut from scrap ¾" pine stock or made from a large dowel. The "wrap around" effect is painted on.

Chest

The travel chest can be made from solid wood or from ⅛" x ¾" strips. If solid wood is used, merely cut the stock to size and shape it with a file and sandpaper. The hardware is painted on.

If thin strips are used, make a hollow box to the suggested size. Cut the half-circle tops and glue on thin strips for the top.

Hinges this small are difficult to locate, but strips of leather glued on will act as serviceable hinges.

Butter Churn

Lathe-turn (or carve) a section of 1" dowel to the suggested shape and size. Drill a ⅛" hole in the top. Insert a 1¾" piece of ⅛" dowel into the hole as a handle.

Canister Set

Several of these canister sets of different diameters may be used in the kitchen and pantry. Pieces of different size dowels can be shaped on a lathe, drill press, or hand drill and a file and sandpaper. Small pins or brads will serve for handles. (Suggested diameters: ¼", ⅜", ½", ⅝", ¾".)

Produce Basket

Baskets are made by drilling out the centers of various size dowels. These pieces are then shaped on a lathe or drill press (or carved).

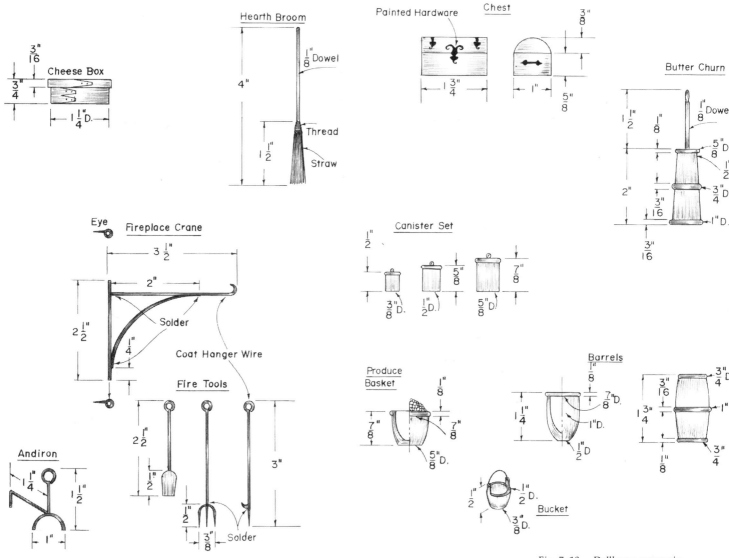

Fig. 7–18. Dollhouse accessories.

Water Bucket

The bucket is drilled-out doweling that is shaped oversize in height. The handle section is made by cutting down on both sides to make a small extension. A thin wire or twine is inserted to make the bail handle.

Barrels

Colonists stored everything in barrels, from spirits to rainwater. The barrels can be made hollow by lathe-turning both the interior and exterior, or they can be made of solid wood by shaping a section of 1″ dowel.

All of the accessories are stained and waxed as a finish.

Fig. 7–19. *Wall shelf, Tavern Room, Old Sturbridge Village, Sturbridge, Massachusetts.*

Sturbridge Wall Shelf

The wall shelf plan shows three different sets of dimensions. The first set is on a dollhouse scale, the second set is designed for a large doll or miniature size, and the third set was included for a full-size shelf.

Material List

	Part	Number	Size	Material
A	Sides	2	7/8″ x 2½″ x 3/16″	Pine
B	Shelf	1	½″ x 2″ x 1/8″	
C	Shelf	1	5/8″ x 2″ x 1/8″	
D	Shelf	1	9/16″ x 2″ x 1/8″	

221

Full Size = 1" Squares

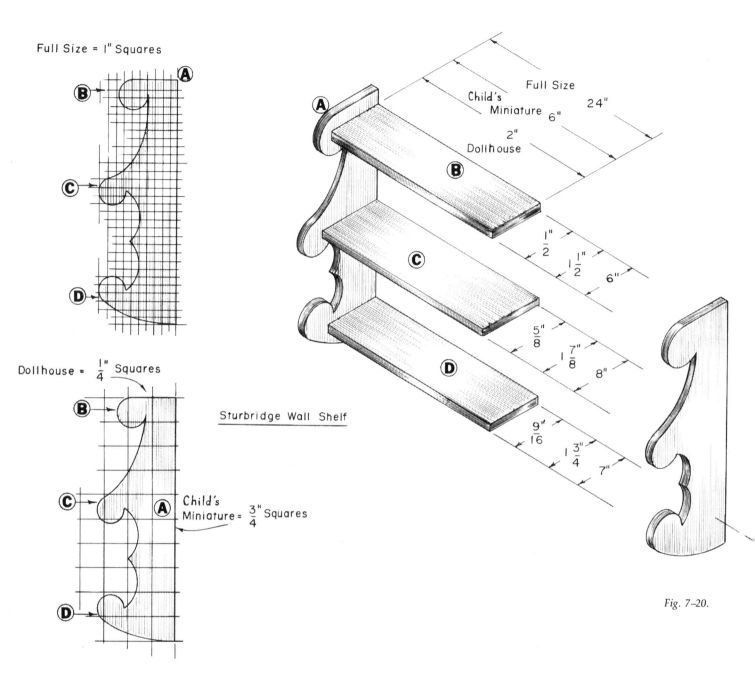

Dollhouse = $\frac{1}{4}$" Squares

Sturbridge Wall Shelf

Child's
Miniature = $\frac{3}{4}$" Squares

Full Size   24"
Child's
Miniature 6"
2"
Dollhouse

$\frac{1}{2}$" $1\frac{1}{2}$" 6"

$\frac{5}{8}$" $1\frac{7}{8}$" 8"

$\frac{9}{16}$" $1\frac{3}{4}$" 7"

Fig. 7–20.

CONSTRUCTION

1. Lay out and cut Parts A to shape and size. (See Fig. 7–20.)

2. Lay out and cut the stock for Parts B, C, and D. Glue and pin Parts A into Parts B, C, and D.

FINISH

Sand entire project smooth. Set and fill all nail heads. Stain or paint. Cover with several coats of lacquer or similar finish. Apply paste wax.

Fig. 7–21. Ladder-back chair, Old Sturbridge Village, Sturbridge, Massachusetts.

Ladder-back Chair

The chair is dimensioned for dollhouse furnishings. If a miniature or large doll-size chair is desired, multiply all dimensions by three. If a full-size chair is desired, multiply the given size by twelve.

Material List

Part	Number	Size	Material
A	2	3¾″ x ³/₁₆″	Dowel
B	2	1¾″ x ³/₁₆″	Dowel
C	2	1⅛″ x ⅛″	Dowel
	2	1⁷/₁₆″ x ⅛″	Dowel
	6	1½″ x ⅛″	Dowel
D	3	⅜″ x 1″ x ⅛″	Birch

CONSTRUCTION

1. Lay out and cut the stock for Parts A and B. Mark out and drill ⅛″ diameter holes for Parts C where indicated in Figure 7–23. Parts B have a wider spread than do Parts A, therefore the drilled holes will be on a slight angle.

2. Lay out and cut Parts C. Glue Parts C into the pre-drilled holes on Parts A and B. Lay out and glue Parts D between Parts A as shown in Figure 7–23.

FINISH

Sand entire chair smooth. Paint or stain the chair at this time. Cover with several coats of lacquer. When dry, wind carpet yarn or heavy string over the top Parts C front to back. Weave the yarn or string side to side and over and under the front to back material. Coat the yarn seat with lacquer if desired.

It is suggested that several such chairs be made for the dollhouse. Four or more chairs will be used at the table in the kitchen area, and one or two chairs may be used in the living room area or bedrooms.

Fig. 7–22.   Ladder-back chair project.

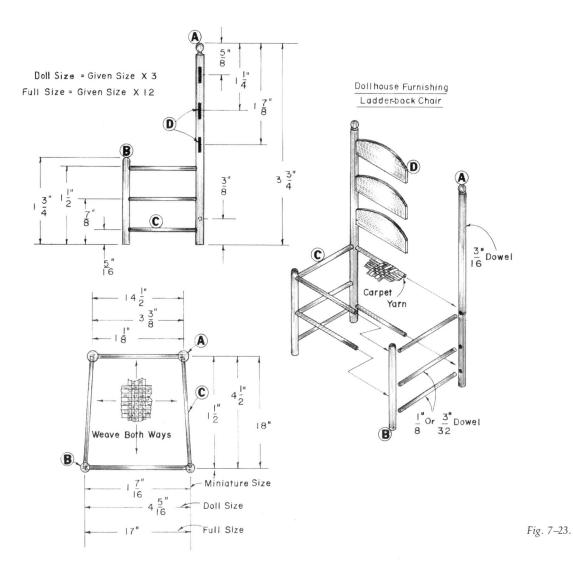

Doll Size = Given Size X 3
Full Size = Given Size X 12

Dollhouse Furnishing
Ladder-back Chair

$\frac{3}{16}$" Dowel

Carpet
Yarn

Weave Both Ways

$\frac{1}{8}$" Or $\frac{3}{32}$" Dowel

Miniature Size

Doll Size

Full Size

Fig. 7–23.

Fig. 7–24. Drover's bench, Old Sturbridge Village, Sturbridge, Massachusetts.

Drover's Bench

This bench was the colonial equivalent to a modern hide-a-bed. The original bench had a fixed seat and the front panel opened to reveal a straw mattress for unexpected overnight visitors. Often benches of this type were kept in the local tavern, to be used when all of the beds were occupied.

This plan was changed slightly to provide a storage area. A full-size bench can be made (by multiplying the given dimensions by twelve), providing an excellent place to store children's playthings or storm wear.

CONSTRUCTION

1. Lay out and cut Parts A to shape and size. Cut the stock for Parts B, C, and D. Nail (using brads), Parts A into Parts B and C. Nail Part D into Parts B and A.

2. Lay out and cut the stock for the seat brace Part E, and the seat braces (scabs) Parts F. Glue and nail Parts F into Part C, and glue and nail Part E to Parts F and C.

3. Cut the stock for Part G. Hinge Part G to the seat brace, Part E. Hinges may be doll-size brass hinges or leather strap hinges. Cut out six small block feet, Parts H. Glue and nail Parts H to the bottom of Part B.

FINISH

Set and fill all nail heads. Sand the bench smooth. Paint or stain. Cover with several coats of lacquer or similar material. Finish off with paste wax.

Material List

	Part	Number	Size	Material
A	Sides	2	1⅜″ x 2½″ x ³/₁₆″	Pine
B	Base	1	1⅛″ x 6″ x ³/₁₆″	
C	Back	1	2⅛″ x 6″ x ³/₁₆″	
D	Front	1	1¼″ x 6″ x ⅛″	
E	Brace	1	⅛″ x ³/₁₆″ x 6″	
F	Scab	3	³/₁₆″ x ¼″ x ³/₁₆″	
G	Seat	1	1¼″ x 6″ x ⅛″	
H	Feet	6	¼″ x ¼″ x ⅛″	

225

Fig. 7–25.   Drover's bench project.

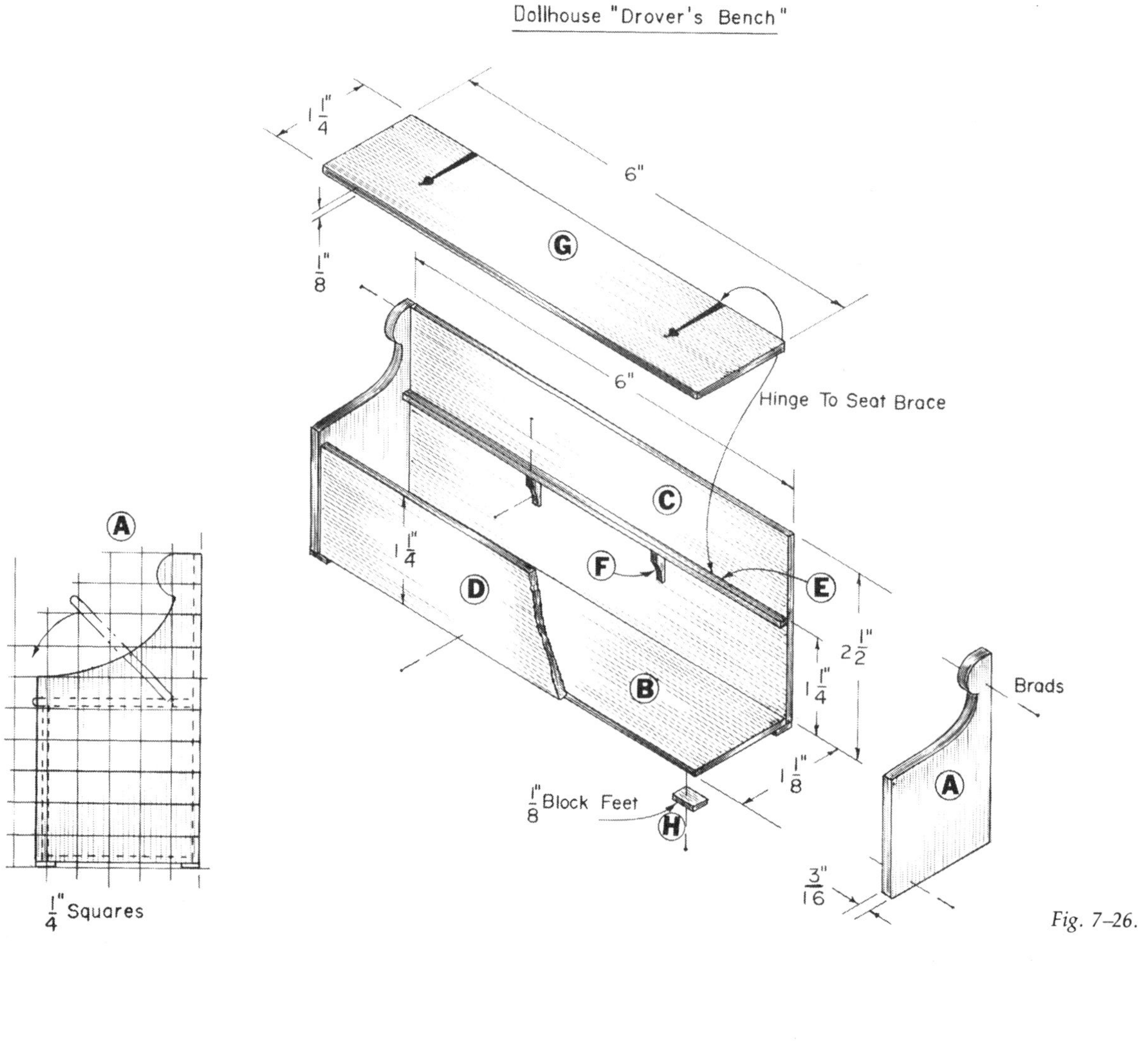

Dollhouse "Drover's Bench"

$1\frac{1}{4}$"

6"

G

$1\frac{1}{8}$"

6"

Hinge To Seat Brace

A

C

$1\frac{1}{4}$"

D

F

E

$\frac{1}{4}$" Squares

B

$2\frac{1}{2}$"

$1\frac{1}{4}$"

Brads

A

$\frac{1}{8}$" Block Feet

H

$1\frac{1}{8}$"

$\frac{3}{16}$"

Fig. 7–26.

Fig. 7–27. Chest, Old Sturbridge Village, Sturbridge, Massachusetts.

Chest of Drawers

This chest of drawers was developed from a Sturbridge Village antique. The sizes given are one-twelfth the actual size. A larger scale chest can be made for doll clothes by multiplying the given dimensions by three.

Material List

Part		Number	Size	Material
A	Sides	2	1³⁄₈″ x 2½″ x ³⁄₁₆″	Pine
B	Bottom	1	1¼″ x 3⅛″ x ³⁄₁₆″	
C	Back	1	2½″ x 3⅛″ x ⅛″	
D	Guides	8	⅛″ x ⅛″ x 1⅛″	
E	Dividers	4	⅛″ x ⅛″ x 3⅛″	
F	Skirt	1	³⁄₈″ x ³⁄₁₆″ x 3⅛″	
G	Top	1	1⁵⁄₈″ x 4″ x ³⁄₁₆″	
H	Drawer	1	⁵⁄₁₆″ x 3⅛″ x 1¼″	
I	Drawer	3	½″ x 3⅛″ x 1¼″	

CONSTRUCTION

1. Lay out and cut the stock for Parts A, B, and C to size. Nail (using brads), Parts A into Part B. Nail Part C to Parts A and B.

2. Lay out and cut the drawer guides, Parts D. Glue Parts D to Parts A. (See location and suggested drawer size in Fig. 7–29.) Lay out and cut Parts E, the drawer dividers. Glue Parts E to Parts D.

3. Lay out and cut the skirt, Part F. Glue and nail Part F to Parts A and B. Cut the stock for Part G. Glue and nail Part G to Parts A, C, and the top D, and E.

4. Make four drawers, Parts H and I, to fit the openings. (See *Section One* for construction details.) Insert the drawers into the openings and adjust if needed.

FINISH

Set and fill all nail heads. Sand entire project smooth. Stain or paint. Cover with several coats of lacquer or similar material. Finish with a coat of paste wax.

Fig. 7–28. *Chest of drawers project.*

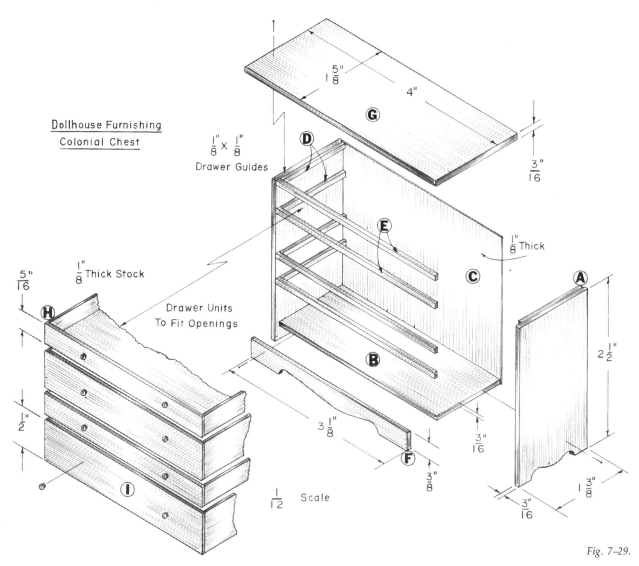

Dollhouse Furnishing
Colonial Chest

$\frac{1}{8}" \times \frac{1}{8}"$
Drawer Guides

$1\frac{5}{8}"$

4"

G

$\frac{3}{16}"$

D

E

$\frac{1}{8}"$ Thick

C

A

$\frac{5}{16}"$ $\frac{1}{8}"$ Thick Stock

H

Drawer Units
To Fit Openings

$2\frac{1}{2}"$

$\frac{1}{2}"$

B

$3\frac{1}{8}"$

F

$\frac{3}{16}"$

$\frac{3}{8}"$

I

$\frac{1}{12}$ Scale

$\frac{3}{16}"$

$1\frac{3}{8}"$

Fig. 7–29.

Fig. 7–30. Tavern Table, Old Sturbridge Village, Sturbridge, Massachusetts.

Tavern Side Table

Many colonial homes had several small side or wall tables. Some held the family Bible, and others served in various ways. The tavern side table was found in Old Sturbridge Village near the Fenno House. The table legs may be round dowels if preferred, or turned legs as suggested in Figure 7–31.

CONSTRUCTION

1. Lay out and cut Parts A. Lay out and cut Parts B and C. Glue Parts B and C to Parts A.

2. Lay out and cut the top, Part D, into an octagon. Glue and nail Part D to Parts B.

FINISH

Remove all traces of glue. Sand entire table smooth. Stain or paint. Cover with several coats of lacquer or similar finish. Apply a coat of paste wax.

Material List

Part		Number	Size	Material
A	Legs	4	3/8″ dowel x 2¾″	Dowel
B	Top	4	3/8″ x 1″ x 1/8″	Pine
C	Bottom	4	¼″ x 1″ x 1/8″	
D	Table top	1	1⅝″ x 1⅝″ x 3/16″	

229

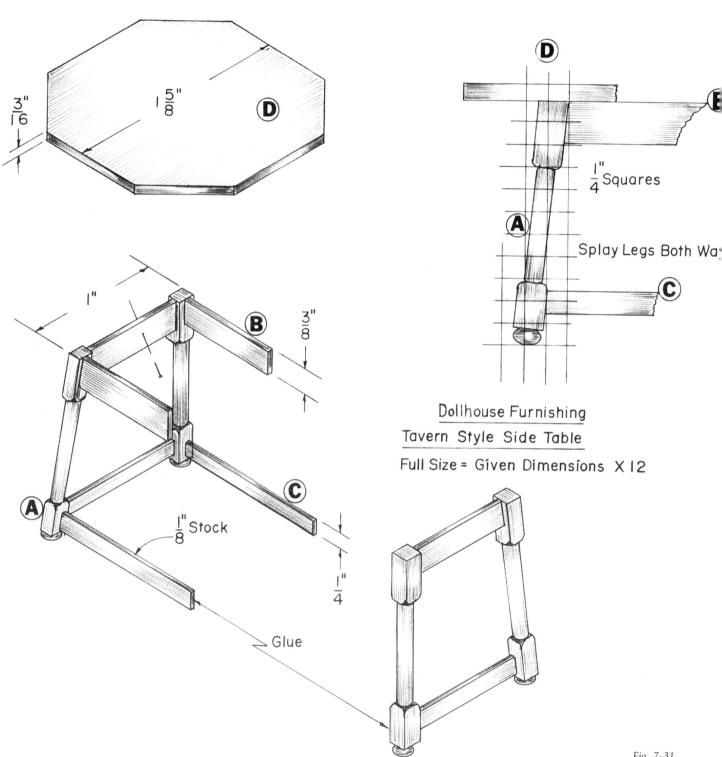

$\frac{3}{16}$"

$1\frac{5}{8}$"

D

D

B

$\frac{1}{4}$" Squares

A

Splay Legs Both Way

C

Dollhouse Furnishing

Tavern Style Side Table

Full Size = Given Dimensions × 12

$\frac{3}{8}$"

B

C

A

$\frac{1}{8}$" Stock

$\frac{1}{4}$"

Glue

Fig. 7–31.

Fireside Settle

Fig. 7–32. Settle. Fenno House, Old Sturbridge Village, Sturbridge, Massachusetts.

In colonial times the only heat came from fireplaces. This meant that the portion of the body turned toward the fire was hot, while the side turned away from the fire was cold. To help eliminate this discomfort, the high backed settle was developed.

The very high sides and solid back caught the fire's heat and helped prevent drafts. The settle is given with three full sets of dimensions: A dollhouse furnishing size, a size suited for an eight-inch doll, and full-size.

CONSTRUCTION

1. Lay out and cut Parts A to suggested size and shape. Cut the stock for Parts B, C, and D. Nail (using brads), Parts A into Part B. Insert Part C at the suggested height and nail Parts A and B into Part C. Glue and nail the brace, Part D, under Part C.

FINISH

Set and fill all nail heads. Sand entire reproduction smooth. Stain or paint. Cover with several coats of varnish or similar finish.

Material List

Part		Number	Size	Material
A	Sides	2	1³⁄₈″ x 4″ x ³⁄₁₆″	Pine
B	Back	1	4″ x 4″ x ³⁄₁₆″	
C	Seat	1	1³⁄₈″ x 4″ x ³⁄₁₆″	
D	Brace	1	³⁄₈″ x 4″ x ³⁄₁₆″	

231

Fig. 7–33. Fireside settle project.

Fireside Pine Settle

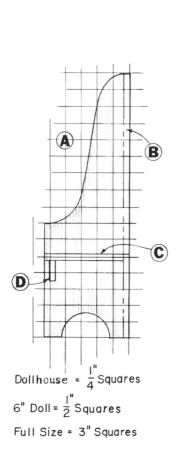

Dollhouse = $\frac{1}{4}$" Squares

6" Doll = $\frac{1}{2}$" Squares

Full Size = 3" Squares

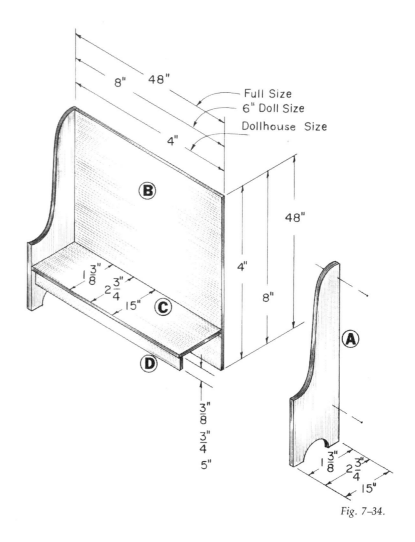

8" 48"

Full Size
6" Doll Size
Dollhouse Size

4"

B

48"

4"

$1\frac{3}{8}$"

$2\frac{3}{4}$"

15" C

8"

D

A

$\frac{3}{8}$"

$\frac{3}{4}$"

5"

$1\frac{3}{8}$"

$2\frac{3}{4}$"

15"

Fig. 7–34.

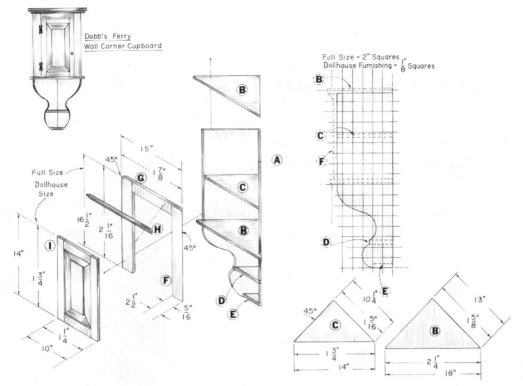

Dobb's Ferry
Wall Corner Cupboard

Full Size = 2" Squares
Dollhouse Furnishing = ⅛" Squares

Fig. 7–35.

Corner Wall Cupboard

The hanging wall cabinet was developed from several different antiques. The corners of most rooms are often considered wasted space because very few furnishings fit there. Perhaps that is why so many different types of corner cabinets were developed and made for early American homes. This corner cupboard was designed to utilize the corner space, yet not be as large as some full standing corner china cabinets.

Two sets of dimensions are included in the drawing, a dollhouse size and full-size. What served the colonials could well serve modern homemakers, and the uniqueness of this piece is not limited to dollhouses.

Material List
(Dollhouse Size)

Part		Number	Size	Material
A	Side	2	1⅜" x 4" x 3/16"	Pine,
B	Top	2	1⅝" x 2¼" x 3/16"	Cherry,
	Bottom			Maple
C	Shelf	1	1 5/16" x 1¾" x ⅛"	
D	Shelf	1	⅝" x ⅝" x ⅛"	
E	Shelf	1	7/16" x 7/16" x ⅛"	
F	Frame	2	5/16" x 2 1/16" x ⅛"	
G	Header	1	5/16" x 1¼" x ⅛"	
H	Mold	1	3/16" x 2"	
I	Door	1	1¼" x 1¾" x ⅛"	

CONSTRUCTION

1. Lay out and cut Parts A. One Part A should be made a board thickness wider so that the two parts may be joined at a right angle. Nail (using brads), Parts A together.

2. Lay out and cut the stock for Parts B, C, D, and E. It is recommended that these parts be cut a little oversize and "fitted" into Parts A as suggested in Fig. 7–35. Nail Parts A into Parts B, C, D, and E.

3. Lay out and cut the stock for Parts F, G, and H. Cut a 45° angle on Parts F. Nail Parts F into Parts A and C. Glue Part G between Parts F and B. Glue on the molding, Part H.

4. Make a raised panel door to fit the opening, Part I. (See *Section One* for construction details.) Secure Parts I to Part F with hinges.

FINISH

Set and fill all nail heads. Sand entire project smooth. Paint or stain. Cover with several coats of lacquer or similar material. Finish with paste wax.

Flat Wall Cupboard

This hanging wall cupboard was developed from the preceding wall corner cupboard, designed for a flat wall where gunstock corner posts interfere with corner cabinets. Two sets of dimensions are provided, one for the dollhouse size and the other for full-size.

Material List

Part		Number	Size	Material
A	Sides	2	$1^{7}/_{16}$" x 3" x $^{1}/_{8}$"	Pine
B	Shelf	1	$1^{3}/_{4}$" x $1^{3}/_{4}$" x $^{1}/_{8}$"	
C	Shelf	1	$1^{7}/_{16}$" x $1^{3}/_{4}$" x $^{1}/_{8}$"	
D	Shelf	1	$^{3}/_{4}$" x $1^{3}/_{4}$" x $^{1}/_{8}$"	
E	Shelf	1	$^{5}/_{8}$" x $1^{3}/_{4}$" x $^{1}/_{8}$"	
F	Top	1	$1^{3}/_{4}$" x $2^{3}/_{8}$" x $^{1}/_{8}$"	
G	Frame	2	$^{5}_{16}$" x $2^{1}/_{8}$" x $^{1}/_{8}$"	
H	Header	1	$^{5}/_{16}$" x $1^{5}/_{16}$" x $^{1}/_{8}$"	
I	Mold	1	$^{3}/_{16}$" x $2^{1}/_{8}$"	
		2	$^{3}/_{16}$" x $1^{3}/_{4}$"	
J	Door	1	$1^{13}/_{16}$" x $1^{5}/_{16}$" x $^{1}/_{8}$"	

CONSTRUCTION

1. Lay out and cut Parts A. Cut Part B and notch for the over extension. Nail (using brads), Parts A into Part B. Cut Parts C, D, and E. Nail Parts A into these shelves as shown in Fig. 7–37. Cut the stock for the top, Part F. Nail Part F into Parts A.

2. Cut the stock for Parts G and H. Nail Parts G into Parts A and Part C. Glue Part H between Parts G and Part F. Make a molding, Part I. Make 45° miters on the corners. Glue Parts I to Parts F, G, and H.

3. Make a raised panel door to fit the opening, Part J. (See *Section One* for construction details.) Secure Part J to Part G with hinges.

FINISH

Set and fill all nail heads. Sand entire cupboard smooth. Stain or paint. Cover with several coats of lacquer or similar coating. Finish with paste wax.

Fig. 7–36. Flat wall cupboard project.

234

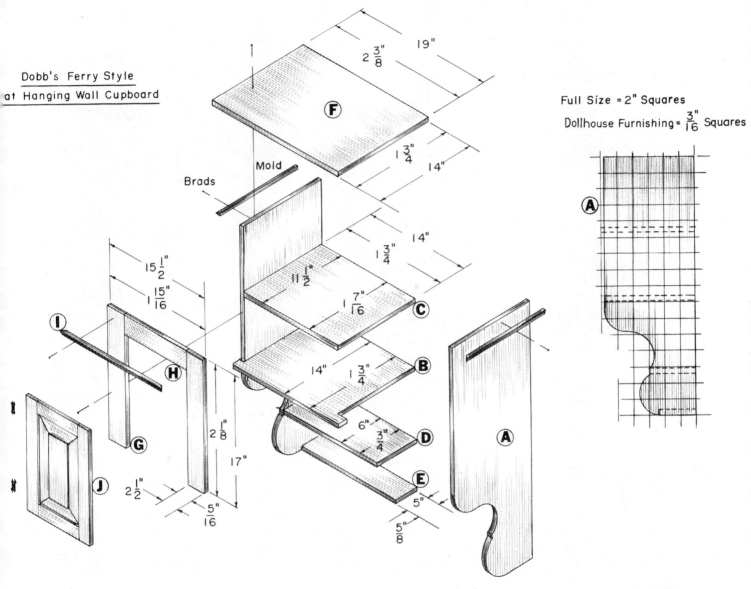

Dobb's Ferry Style
at Hanging Wall Cupboard

Mold

Brads

$2\frac{3}{8}''$ 19"

$1\frac{3}{4}''$ 14"

14"

$1\frac{3}{4}''$

$11\frac{1}{2}''$

$1\frac{7}{16}''$ C

$15\frac{1}{2}''$

$1\frac{15}{16}''$

I

H

G

J

14" $1\frac{3}{4}''$ B

6" $\frac{3}{4}''$ D

E

$2\frac{1}{8}''$

17"

$2\frac{1}{2}''$ $\frac{5}{16}''$

$\frac{5}{8}''$ 5"

A

Full Size = 2" Squares

Dollhouse Furnishing = $\frac{3}{16}''$ Squares

A

Fig. 7–37.

235

Small Gateleg Table

Fig. 7–38. *Gateleg table, Fenno House, Old Sturbridge Village, Sturbridge, Massachusetts.*

Space was a problem in colonial homes. The house was often small, but empty space represented waste. In order to best utilize the space they had, furnishings were designed to fold, drop, or tilt out of the way when not in use. This table from Old Sturbridge Village is a perfect example of utility when used, and conservation when not in use.

Material List
(Dollhouse Size)

Part		Number	Size	Material
A	Sides	2	5/8" x 2¾" x ⅛"	Of Choice,
B	End	2	¾" x 5/8" x ⅛"	Pine,
C	Frame	2	5/8" x 2" x ⅛"	Cherry,
D	Frame	2	5/8" x 1¼" x ⅛"	Birch
E	Legs	4	¼" x 2½" x ¼"	
F	Top	1	3½" circle x 3/16"	

CONSTRUCTION

1. Lay out and cut the stock for Parts A and B. Nail these Parts together to form a simple box. Cut the stock for Parts C and D. Make finger mortise and tenons as shown in Figure 7–40. Drill a hole through the mortise and tenon for the swing pin. (A brad will serve as a drill, and the same size brad will act as the pivot pin.)

2. Make four legs, Parts D. Glue Parts C and D to the separate legs. When hinged together they will form a side the same size as the simple box of Parts A and B. Glue and nail Parts C to Parts A. This will allow Parts D (complete with a leg, Part F), to swing free.

3. Cut the stock for Part F, the table top. Cut the circle into drop leaves. Secure each leaf to the center section with small-scale hinges. Glue the center Part F to Parts A and B. When the leaves are needed, swing one of the legs out and under for support.

FINISH

Set and fill all nail heads. Sand entire table smooth. Stain or paint. Cover with several coats of lacquer or varnish. Finish with paste wax.

Fig. 7–39. *Small gateleg table project.*

Dollhouse Gateleg Side Table

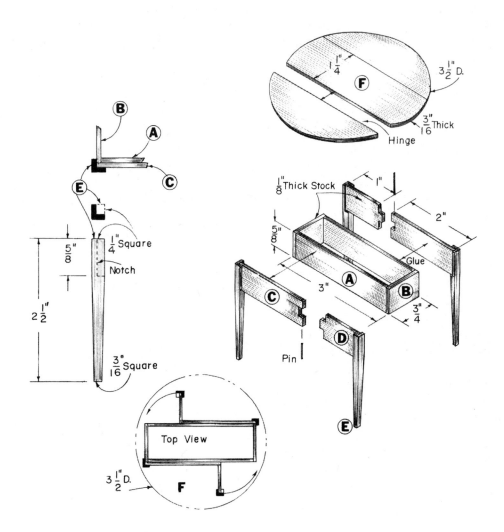

Fig. 7–40.

Rocking Settee (Mammy Bench)

Fig. 7-41. Mammy bench, Greenfield Village Museum, Dearborn, Michigan.

There were several different styles of rocking settees or "Mammy Benches." Without the rockers the benches resemble "Deacon Benches," and this one may be made either way.

Material List
(Dollhouse Size)

Part		Number	Size	Material
A	Bench	1	1³⁄₈" x 4¼" x ³⁄₁₆"	Cherry,
B	Legs	4	¼" dowel x 1"	Birch,
				Maple
C	Stretcher	2	¼" x 3½" x ⅛"	
D	Stretcher	2	⅛" dowel x 1¼"	
E	Rockers	2	⁵⁄₁₆" x 2" x ³⁄₁₆"	
F	Back	2	¼" dowel x 1½"	
G	Back	1	⁵⁄₁₆" x 3¾" x ³⁄₁₆"	
H	Arms	2	³⁄₁₆" dowel x 1³⁄₈"	
I	Dowels	11	⅛" dowel x 1¼"	
J	Dowels	8	⅛" dowels x 1"	
K	Guard	2	³⁄₁₆" dowels x 1"	
		3	³⁄₁₆" x 1½" x ⅛"	

CONSTRUCTION

1. Lay out and cut the stock for Part A. Drill ⅛"diameter holes ⁵⁄₁₆" on centers on the back edge and sides. Cut and shape Parts B, the legs. Cut Parts C, D, and E. Drill holes in Parts E to take Parts B. Drill holes in Parts B to take Parts D. Glue Parts C and D to Parts B, and glue Parts B to Parts E. Drill mount holes in the bottom of Part A and glue the tops of Parts B into Part A.

2. Cut and shape Parts F. Drill holes in Part F to take Part H. Cut and drill Part G to match the holes in Part A. Cut the ⅛" dowels to size, Parts I. Glue Parts I into Part G. Glue the finished Part G between Parts F. Glue Parts F and I to Part A.

3. Cut and drill Parts H. Cut and glue Parts J to Parts H. Glue Parts H to the holes in Part F and the bottoms of Parts J into the side holes in Part A.

4. Make the child guard, Part K, by gluing slats between shaped dowels. Mark and drill holes in Part A to receive the dowels. Part K drops into these mount holes.

FINISH

Remove all traces of glue. Sand entire bench smooth. Stain or paint. Cover with several coats of lacquer or similar covering. Finish with paste wax.

Fig. 7–42. Rocking settee (Mammy bench), project.

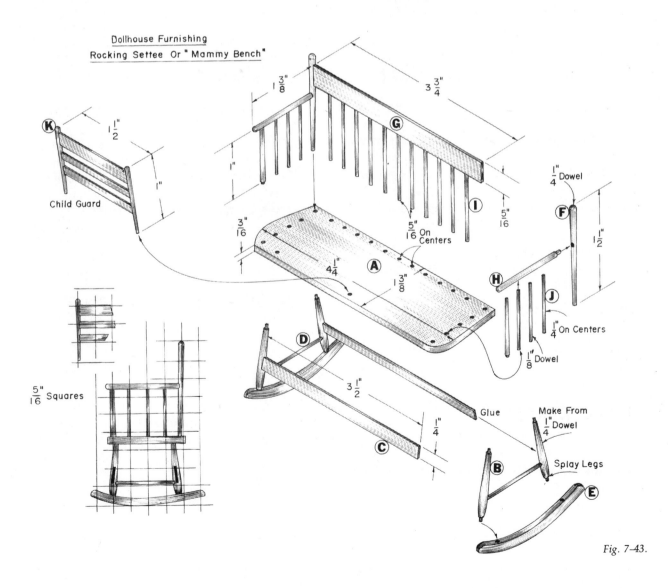

Dollhouse Furnishing
Rocking Settee Or "Mammy Bench"

Child Guard

K   1½"   1"

1⅜"   3¾"   G

¼" Dowel   F

5/16 On Centers   I   5/16   1½"

3/16   A   4¼"   1⅜"   H   J   ¼" On Centers

⅛" Dowel

5/16" Squares   D   3½"   ¼"   C   Glue

Make From ¼" Dowel

B   Splay Legs

E

Fig. 7–43.

Trestle-Leg Cradle

The trestle-leg cradle was developed from a simple cradle and a trestle leg, found on many colonial styled tables. The dimensions given are on a dollhouse scale. However, a larger size cradle can be made by increasing the grid size and dimensions. (See notation in Fig. 7–45.)

Material List

Part		Number	Size	Material
A	Leg	2	3/8" x 5/16" x 2 5/8"	Cherry,
B	Base	2	1/2" x 3/16" x 2"	Maple,
C	Stretcher	1	3/16" x 5/16" x 3 1/2"	Birch,
D	Sides	2	1 5/8" x 3" x 1/8"	Pine
E	Head	1	1 3/4" x 1 7/8" x 1/8"	
F	Foot	1	1 3/4" x 1 7/8" x 1/8"	
G	Bottom	1	1 3/4" x 3" x 1/8"	

CONSTRUCTION

1. Lay out and cut the stock for the trestle legs, Parts A, and the leg base, Parts B. Shape Parts A with a file and sandpaper. Glue Parts A to Parts B. Cut the suggested mortise for the stretcher (Part C) into each trestle leg. Glue Part C between Parts A with a 3 1/8" inside spacing.

2. Lay out and cut Parts D, E, F, and G to suggested size and shape. Glue Parts D to Parts F, E, and G. (Small pins or brads may be used if desired.)

3. Drill matching holes into Parts A, E, and F for a 1/8" dowel pin. Suspend the finished cradle between the trestle legs with these pins. One trestle leg has a second 1/8" pin to lock the cradle in place. (See Fig. 7–45.)

FINISH

If brads were used, set and fill all nail heads. Sand entire project smooth. Stain or paint. Cover with several coats of lacquer. Finish with paste wax.

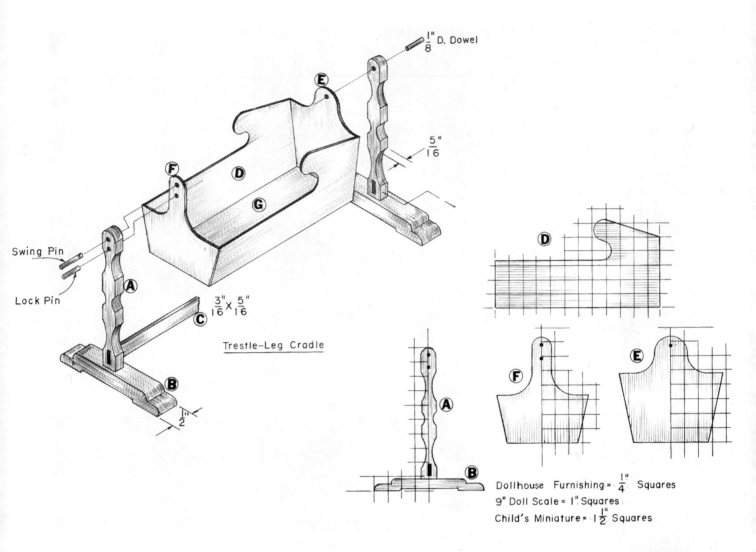

$\frac{1}{8}''$ D. Dowel

E

$\frac{5}{16}''$

F

D

G

Swing Pin

A

Lock Pin

$\frac{3''}{16} \times \frac{5''}{16}$

C

Trestle-Leg Cradle

B

$\frac{1}{2}''$

D

A

B

F

E

Dollhouse Furnishing = $\frac{1}{4}''$ Squares
9" Doll Scale = 1" Squares
Child's Miniature = $1\frac{1}{2}''$ Squares

Fig. 7–45.

Tall Poster or Canopy Bed

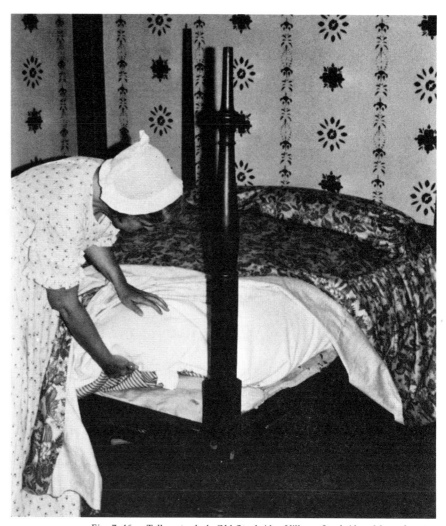

Fig. 7-46. Tall poster bed, Old Sturbridge Village, Sturbridge, Massachusetts.

The tall poster bed often had a canopy frame which was put up each fall to conserve heat for the master and his wife. A sure sign of spring and warm weather was when the canopy was removed and stored until the first frost of October.

The plan for this four-poster evolved from designs of several tall poster beds found in museums and restoration settlements. The size given is for the master bedroom in the dollhouse. If a single or separate bed is desired for a larger doll, double all dimensions. If a larger sized bed is desired, multiply the given dimensions by three or even four.

A full-size bed can be made by multiplying all dimensions by twelve. If a full-size bed is contemplated, then the exact size of the proposed box-spring and mattress should govern the length and width of the bed proper. Slats should be used in place of the ropes.

Material List
(Dollhouse Size)

	Part	Number	Size	Material
A	Head	1	2¾" x 4½" x ³/₁₆"	Pine,
B	Posters	4	⅜" x ⅜" x 6"	Cherry,
C	Foot	1	¾" x 4½" x ³/₁₆"	Maple
D	Sides	2	¾" x 6½" x ³/₁₆"	
E	Frame	2	¾" x 7" x ³/₁₆"	
F	Frame slats	8	³/₁₆" x ³/₁₆" x 5"	

242

CONSTRUCTION

1. Lay out and cut the stock for the headboard, Part A. Drill the ⅛" diameter rope holes. (See Fig. 7–48.)

2. Lay out and cut the squares for the four posters, Parts B. Shape on a lathe, drill press, or hand electric drill with a file and sandpaper. Cut the footboard, Part C. Glue Part A between two Parts B, and glue Part C between the remaining Parts B. (Small dowel tenons may be used for these joints if desired. The dowel tenons are recommended for the larger sizes.)

3. Lay out and cut the side boards, Parts D. Glue Parts D between the head and foot boards. Drill the required rope holes. (See Fig. 7–48.) String heavy duty mason's line through the holes.

4. *Canopy frame.* Lay out and cut Parts E to suggested shape and size. These pieces are extremely fragile and extra care should be taken in construction. Notch Parts E for the canopy slats, Parts F. Cut Parts F to fit into the notches in Parts E. Fasten the ends of Parts E to the tops of Parts B with small steel pins and a finial. Lay the slats between the canopy frame. Make a cotton canopy to fit.

5. The original bed, Figure 7–46, had a straw mattress to be laid upon the ropes, and a feather tick. Dollhouse scale blankets, comforters, counterpanes, or quilts may be purchased (see the list of suppliers, *Section Eight*), or can be made from scraps of material.

FINISH

Sand all parts smooth. Remove any trace of dried glue. Stain or paint. Cover with several coats of lacquer or similar material. Finish with paste wax.

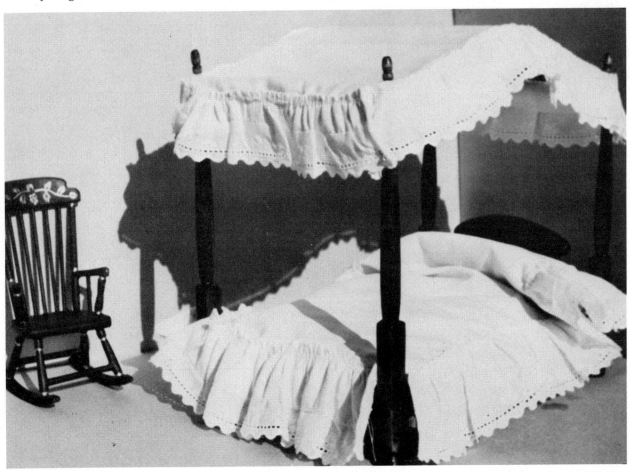

Fig. 7–47.   Tall poster or canopy bed project.

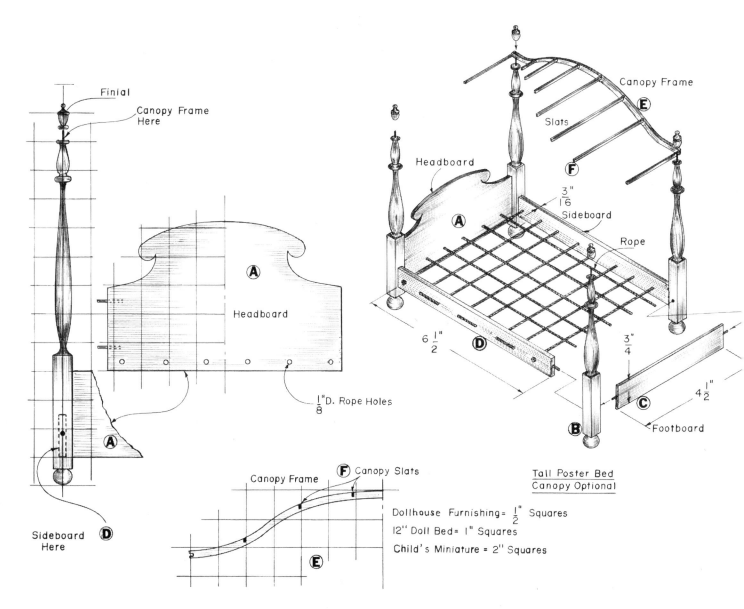

Finial

Canopy Frame
Here

(A)

Headboard

Headboard

Canopy Frame

Slats

(E)

(F)

$\frac{3}{16}$"

Sideboard

(A)

Rope

$\frac{1}{8}$"D. Rope Holes

(A)

(D)

6$\frac{1}{2}$"

$\frac{3}{4}$"

(C)

4$\frac{1}{2}$"

(B)

Footboard

Sideboard
Here

(D)

Tall Poster Bed
Canopy Optional

Canopy Frame

(F) Canopy Slats

Dollhouse Furnishing= $\frac{1}{2}$" Squares

12" Doll Bed= 1" Squares

Child's Miniature = 2" Squares

(E)

Fig. 7–48.

244

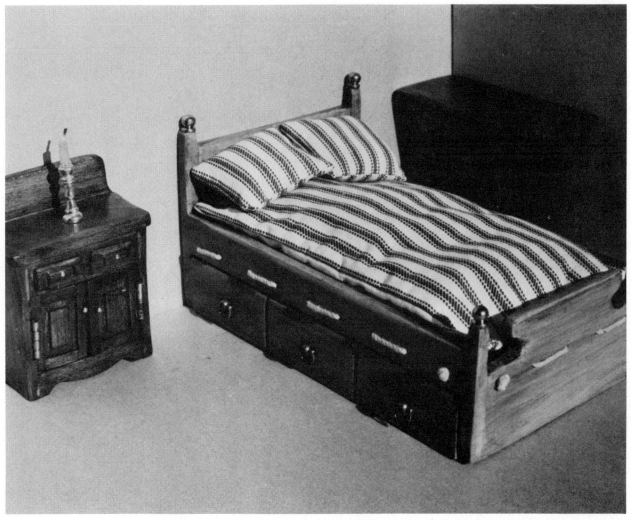

Fig. 7-49. Child's trundle bed project.

Child's Trundle Bed

Trundle beds have a lower section that rolls out from under the mattress and frame. Sometimes this section contains another mattress to make into a second bed, and some styles of beds have storage drawers. These beds were developed to conserve space; similar beds were used aboard sailing ships.

This plan was developed by combining designs of several antiques. Bed slats and a slat rest are used in place of the rope spring. However, rope may be used if desired.

Material List
(Dollhouse Size)

	Part	Number	Size	Material
A	Top posts	2	¼" sq. x 3½"	Pine
B	Bottom posts	2	¼" sq. x 2⅜"	
C	Head Board	1	3" x 3½" x ³/₁₆"	
D	Foot Board	1	2" x 3½" x ³/₁₆"	
E	Side	1	2" x 6¾" x ³/₁₆"	
F	Side	1	1" x 6¾" x ³/₁₆"	
G	Rest	2	¼" x 6¾" x ⅛"	
H	Slats	6	¼" x 3½" x ⅛"	
I	Drawer Sides	2	1" x 6⅝" x ⅛"	
J	End	2	1" x 3¼" x ⅛"	
K	Bottom	1	3¼" x 6⅝" x ⅛"	

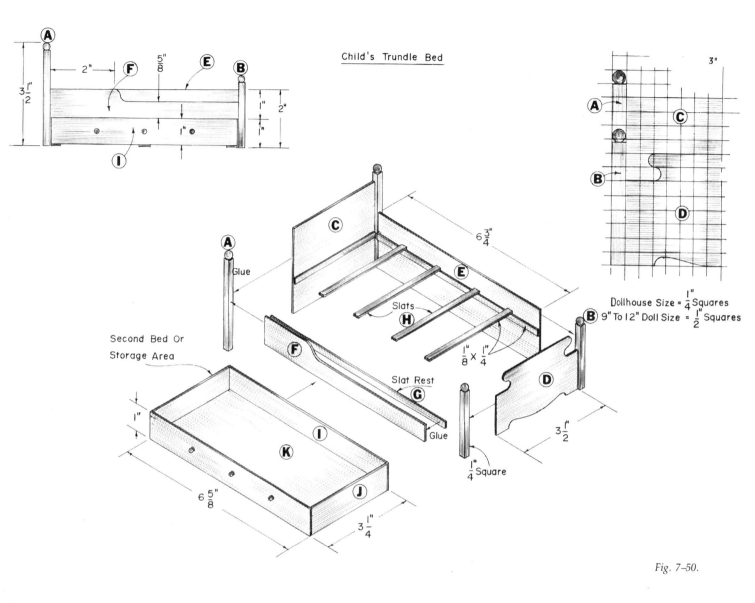

Child's Trundle Bed

Dollhouse Size = $\frac{1}{4}$" Squares
9" To 12" Doll Size = $\frac{1}{2}$" Squares

Fig. 7–50.

CONSTRUCTION

1. Lay out and cut the stock for the head and foot posts, Parts A and B. (See Fig. 7–50.) Cut the stock for Parts C and D. Glue Part C between Parts A. Glue Part D between Parts B.

2. Lay out and cut the stock for Parts E and F, the two side boards. Cut the slat rests, Parts G. Glue Parts G to Parts E and F. Glue Parts E and F to the foot and head board assemblies. Cut the bed slats, Parts H. Drop Parts H onto the slat rest, Parts G.

3. Lay out and cut the stock for Parts I, J, and

K. Make a large drawer unit from these parts. (See *Section One* for construction details.) The finished drawer unit slides under and flush with Part F on the bed proper. Adjust the drawer unit if needed.

FINISH

Sand entire bed smooth. Remove any trace of dried glue. Stain or paint. Cover with several coats of lacquer or similar material. Finish with paste wax.

List of Suppliers

IN TWO PARTS

PART A: SUPPLIERS FOR BUILDING FURNITURE AND FOLK ART

PART B: SUPPLIERS FOR BUILDING MINIATURES

Many of the plans suggest the use of certain materials, fasteners, and decorative hardware. At times such items may prove difficult to obtain.

Check first for retail availability in the immediate area. Most often suitable materials or possible substitutions can be found locally.

To provide insurance that specified materials are available, a list of suppliers has been included. Many of these companies have catalogs available, and will send them upon request. All of the companies will sell and ship small orders, and all of them are very reliable.

In some projects, such as building clocks, it would be best to have the parts and supplies on hand before starting the actual project. Part sizes may vary depending upon the supplier, and any needed adjustments can be made before the work is started.

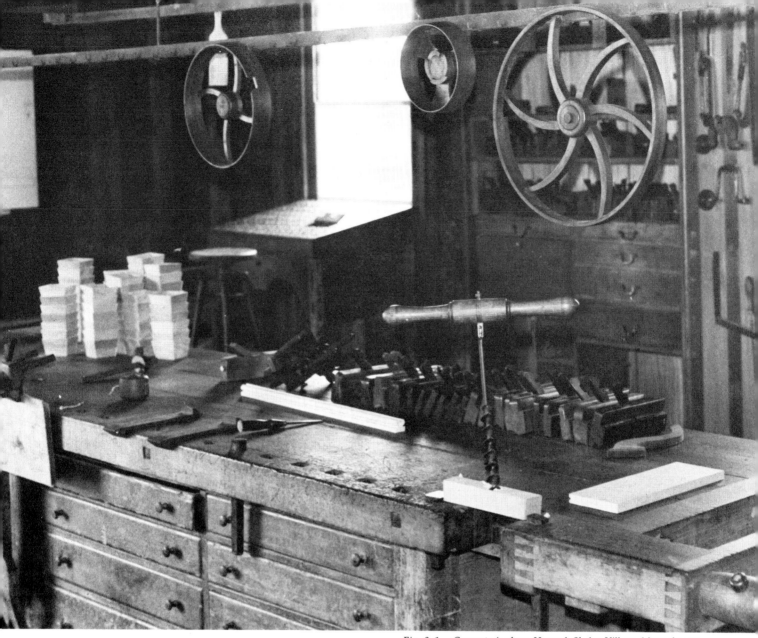

Fig. 8–1. Carpenter's shop, Hancock Shaker Village, Massachusetts.

PART A: SUPPLIERS FOR BUILDING FURNITURE AND FOLK ART

*A comprehensive catalog listing nearly anything needed for the projects in this book is that of Albert Constantine; see **LUMBER** listing for address.*

CLOCKS (movements, dials, and hands)

Mason and Sullivan
Osterville, MA 02655

Jeweler's Service
60 Eighth Street
New Bedford, MA 02740

School Products Co., Inc.
East 23rd Street
New York, NY 10010

Emperor Clock Company
Fairhope, AL 36532

FASTENERS (screws, nails, and glue)
Most local hardware stores and lumberyards will have ordinary items in stock. For handmade, colonial types of nails:

Tremont Nail Co.
P. O. Box 111
Wareham, MA 02571

FOLK ART DESIGNS (early American and Pennsylvania Dutch)
For information, write:

Spanninger's (no catalog)
2809 Bergey Road
Hatfield, PA 19440

GLASS
Ordinary window glass may be found in local lumber, hardware, or glass outlets. Single-strength or double-strength glass or non-reflective glass may be purchased.
For duplication of the old glass (with bubbles and imperfections), as well as bull's eye glass:

S. A. Bendheim (catalog)
122 Hudson Street
New York, NY 10013

HARDWARE
Door pulls, drawer pulls, and hinges in colonial styles, and drawer guides are available in local lumber and hardware outlets.
Decorative and colonial styled hardware:

Minnesota Woodworkers Supply Co.
  (catalog available)
925 Winnetka Ave.
Minneapolis, MN 55427

Amerock Corp.
Rockford, IL 61105

Ball and Ball (catalog and
  custom orders)
463 W. Lincoln Highway
(Sales Showrooms and Museum)
Exton, PA 19341

Hand-wrought hardware is available from:

Robert Bourdon, Blacksmith
Skunk Hollow Road
Greensboro, VT 05841

Old Smithy Shop
P. O. Box 236
Powers Street
Milford, NH 03055

LUMBER (special types)
Local lumberyards will stock one-inch #2 or clear (C-select) pine. Many outlets stock 5-quarter (1¼") or 6-quarter (1½") thicknesses along with some hardwoods. Plywoods and hardboards are also normal stock items. If unable to locate, write:

Albert Constantine and Sons
2050 Eastchester Road
Bronx, NY 10461

Woodcraft Supply Corp.
313 Montcale Avenue
Woburn, MA 01801

PAINTS, STAINS, AND FINISHES
Local outlets carry a full range of oil- or water-based paints and stains. Sandpapers, fillers, wax, lemon oil, steel-wool, and pumice are also stock items. Finish shellac, varnish, and lacquers are normal stock items or they may be ordered with little trouble.
For special finishes:

Yield House
Conway, NH 03860

Minnesota Woodworkers Supply Co.
925 Winnetka Avenue
Minneapolis, MN 55427

Deft, Inc.
411 Keystone Street
Alliance, OH 44601

PRE-MADE PARTS (turnings or legs)
Many local outlets have displays of pre-made legs or wood turnings.
To order:

Royal Oak Industries, Inc.
Box 125
Marion, VA 24534

Minnesota Woodworkers Supply Co.
925 Winnetka Avenue
Minneapolis, MN 55427

Albert Constantine and Sons
2050 Eastchester Road
Bronx, NY 10461

Emco Specialties, Inc.
P. O. Box 864
Des Moines, IA 50304

**SPECIAL WOODWORKING TOOLS
AND SUPPLIES**

Brookstone Co.
Brookstone Building
Peterborough, NH 03458

Woodcraft Supply Corp.
313 Montcale Avenue
Woburn, MA 01801

PART B: SUPPLIERS FOR BUILDING MINIATURES

(Dollhouse Suppliers)

Barnstable Originals **(accessories)**
50 Harden Avenue
Camden, ME 04843

Chestnut Hill Studio **(accessories)**
Box 38
Churchville, NY 14428

Connoisseur Studio, Inc. **(hardware)**
P. O. Box 7187
Louisville, KY 40207

Cunningham Art Products, Inc. **(hardware)**
Stone Mountain, GA 30083

Craft Patterns **(patterns)**
Elmhurst, IL 60126

Eastern Findings **(findings)**
19 West 34th Street
New York, NY 10001

Lox-Box, Inc. **(hardware)**
Heirloom Mini-Hardware
Boxwood Lake Road
York, PA 17402

Rombin's Nest Farm **(accessories)**
Fairfield, PA 17320

The Miniature Mart and Peddlers Shop
  (wood products)
Dept. NN
883 Thirty-Ninth Avenue
San Francisco, CA 94121

This'N'That Shop **(hardware)**
P. O. Box 131
Columbia, IL 62236

Fig. 8–2. Miniature trestle dining table shown using miniature accessories.

Glossary

Apron Horizontal stock to join legs and support table tops.

Baluster A small turned pillar used to support a railing. See also Spindles.

Bar clamp Adjustable clamps set upon long bars (pipes) in order to clamp wide pieces of stock.

Bellows valve Bellows project. A flap of flexible material used to act as a flap valve, allowing air intake yet retarding air exhaust.

Bevel See Chamfer.

Bezel The rounded glass cover and ring used to cover small clock faces.

Board Any piece of lumber less than two inches thick. (Pieces over two inches thick are referred to as planks.)

Board foot Unit of measurement. One board foot is a piece of stock 12 by 12 inches by 1 inch thick.

Butt joint A plain simple edge or right angle joint where boards come together plain.

Butterfly Small double dovetail shaped inserts (tenons) installed into surface mortise holes of the same shape and size.

Butterfly hinge A small cabinet-type hinge that resembles a butterfly's wing.

Butterfly wing Braces. The table top brace that swings out from the apron to support a drop leaf.

Candle socket A wooden or metal member made to hold and support a wax candle.

Carved inlay Small ornate carving inserted into the surface of furniture.

Cedar lining Aromatic red cedar, ¼″ thick and in various widths and lengths used to line closets.

Center drawer guides Wood members to guide drawer movement and support the drawer in the center of its opening.

Chamfer To cut away the edge of a board on an angle.

Clamps Any threaded tool used to bring pressure by means of the screw principle.

Clamps, C Metal clamps resembling a large C. Used to clamp glued stock.

Clock strike Tone bars which are struck by clock movement to sound the hour.

Concave To arch inwards or thin out in the center.

Convex To arch outwards or thicken at the center.

Copper back The name given first quality plate glass mirrors.

Corner posts Reinforcement members erected in the corners of furniture or dwellings.

Counterbore Where a larger hole is drilled over a smaller hole so as to enable a screw or bolt head to be recessed below the surface.

Countersink To cut the edges of a hole so as to fit the slope of a flathead screw and enable the screw head to fit flush or below the surface. Most often 60°.

Countersink bit A cutting tool designed to cut the countersink angle. Used in a bit brace or electric drills.

Cross-buck See Sawbuck.

Cross nailing When nails can be driven two different ways into a joint, thus forming right angles.

Cyma curve A shape or profile made from part concave and part convex curves. Design of colonial foot or toe boards. Basic design of crown molding.

Dado A recess or "U" shaped groove cut into one board so as to receive and support another board at a right angle.

Dado, blind A recess or "U" shaped groove cut into a board stopping short of the board's edge(s).

Dado saw   A combination of two circular saw blades and assorted cutter/spacers used to plough out various width dados.

Deft   A trade name of a lacquer-based finish.

Dentil (mold)   A molding resembling small wooden blocks that project like a row of teeth.

Diameter   A straight line passing through the center of a circle and ending at the circumference. Abbreviated: Dia. or D.

Dish slot   A small dado-like trough cut into a board to hold the edges of dishes. Most often used on hutch cupboard tops.

Distressing   To intentionally mark and gouge furniture to suggest years of wear.

Door, flush   Any cabinet door fitting flush or even with the rails and stiles.

Door frame   The wooden members forming a door opening or the door members which contain a panel insert.

Door pull   The handle used to open and close the door.

Dovetails   Triangular male tenons that fit into a similar female mortise making a locking joint. Several dovetail tenons are used on each joint.

Dowel joint   The joint where hardwood dowels are used to reinforce and support the joint.

Drawer guides   Members used to contain drawer movement and provide drawer support.

Drawer pulls   The handles installed on drawers.

Drill press   An upright drilling power tool, the drill being pressed against the stock by hand or machine power. Usually electrically powered, it has the virtue of drilling holes more accurately than can usually be done by hand. Cutting attachments other than drill bits can also be used in the tool.

Fasteners   Any materials that join two pieces together; nails, screws, bolts, pegs, glue, solder, pins, etc.

Felt buttons   Small self-sticking felt fiber buttons placed on furniture to prevent scuffing and marking.

Fill   To cover the "set" head of a nail with wood putty or plastic wood.

Finger hole   A hole drilled to act as a handle.

Finial   The turned or carved ornament used between pediment breaks or as a high point to molded planes.

Finish nail   A series of nails that have a small head which can be driven in (set) below the surface of the wood and their surface indentations filled.

Five quarter   Lumber that is 1¼" thick.

Gauge   A term used to denote screw thickness.

Glazier's points   Steel triangles or pins used to hold glass in a frame. Most often they are covered with putty.

Glue blocks   A wooden block glued to a spot in order to reinforce and support that area.

Grid   A series of small squares to aid in the layout of irregular shapes.

Half-columns   A lathe-turning or column cut in half lengthwise and mounted as a relief.

Hide glue   A glue made from the bones, hoofs and hides of animals.

Hinge   A device consisting of two parts and a pin forming a movable joint, as in allowing doors to swing.

Hood (Clock)   The top section for a tall clock which houses the movement and strike.

I.P.S.   Iron pipe series of standard threading. ⅛" I.P.S. means a ⅜" outside diameter.

Joinery   The various techniques for joining two pieces of wood together. "Joiners"—Colonial name for expert woodworkers.

Jorgensen clamps   Name given wooden clamps with two threaded handles used to clamp glued wood.

Lamp cord   Sometimes called "zip-cord". A number 18-gauge plastic-coated electrical feed wire used to convey energy from a plug-in socket to lamps and small electrical appliances.

Lap joint   A large group of joints where one member overlaps a second member making a flush joint. Examples: End-lap, edge-lap, center-lap, middle or T-lap, ship-lap, half-lap.

Leaf support   That member that pulls or swings out to support a table or desk top.

Lemon oil   Oil commercially made from lemons, used to polish furniture.

Lineal foot   Meaning length only, with no reference to width or thickness; as distinguished from board foot or cubic foot.

Maple leaf bail pull   A door or drawer pull (handle) made in the shape of a maple leaf supporting a thin handle.

Miter joint   An angle cut joint where two members join each other. Most often 45°. Used to join two irregular shapes such as moldings.

Molded edge   A design put on the edge of boards by a router or shaper cutter.

Moldings   Narrow strip of wood shaped to a curved or rounded profile.

Molding, bed   Commonly used in right angle corners.

Molding, cove   Molding with a concave profile.

Molding, crown   Molding with part concave and part convex profiles.

Molding, half-round   Small molding which has the cross-section profile of a half circle.

Molding, rounds   Small molding which has the cross-section profile of a full circle.

Molding, shoe   Small narrow molding with a rounded top.

Mortise   Hole or recess to receive a tenon.

Mortise machine   Machine that cuts a square hole in wooden members to receive tenons.

Nipple   Small section of fully threaded pipe. Used for electrical connections.

On centers   Distance between framing members from center to center. Ex. 16″ O.C. means 16 inches on centers.

Orbital sander   Small electrical hand-held sander that makes very small high-speed orbital rotations.

Pegged   Using hardwood dowels to join wood members. The round ends may be exposed or short pegs used to cover screw holes.

Pigeon holes   Series of compartments inside desks. Till-like.

Pilot holes   The holes drilled to receive screws. Standard rule: Pilot holes on soft woods are 10% less than the root size of the screw. On Hardwood, 7% less than the root size.

Pumice   Finely ground volcanic rock used as a polishing material in oil (Lemon oil).

Rabbet   A recess or "L" shaped groove cut into one board so as to join another board at a right angle.

Rabbet, blind   Where the recess or "L" shaped groove stops short of the board's edge(s).

Radius   A straight line starting at the center of a circle ending at the circumference. Abbreviated: "Rad. R."

Rail   Horizontal pieces of a door, window or cabinet.

Raised panel   A cabinet door made by inserting in the frame a cut panel having a raised center section.

Relief   To remove a section so as to cause a void or indentation. Relief-type legs.

Router   Small hand-held electrical tool which turns at a very high speed, using assorted bits and cutters to make molded edges, rabbets, or mortises.

Rule joint   Used on table leaves. One edge has a "cove" molding and the other edge has a "thumb nail" molding.

Sabre saw   A small hand-held electric saw that moves a knife-like blade at high speed but in short reciprocal strokes and able to make tight turns.

Sawbuck   Sometimes called a "cross-buck". The "X"-like affair of table legs resembling the log holders used in timber sawing.

Scab   A secondary block added to a joint to reinforce and strengthen it.

Scale   A system of designating units of measure, or fixed proportion. Any progressive or graded classification.

Set   To push or depress a nail head below the surface of the wood, usually by employing a nail set tool.

Side drawer guides   To support and contain the action of a drawer along its sides.

Six-quarter   Lumber 1½ inches thick.

Skirts (boards)   A wooden member that creates a border or margin.

Spindles   Small turned columns used to support a railing or gallery. Balusters.

Splay   To spread out; increase angle. The angle of a chair or table leg as it descends from injection point in the top or seat.

Spline joint   A joint that incorporates a double dado held together with a key tenon engaging both dados. A third piece added to a pair of matching dados.

Stile   Vertical side pieces of a door, window or cabinet.

Stretchers   Wooden members used to reinforce and hold two legs at a proper distance.

Strike tone   The tone bars used to strike the hour and activated by clock movement.

Table board   A wide plank put across several trestle legs to serve as a table.

Taper   A gradual decrease in size of an elongated object, usually denoted by fractions per inch or Morse number.

Tenon   In joinery, male projection on the end of a wooden member that fits into a female mortise of similar size.

Terminal(s)   The small screws on electrical equipment for holding wires and making electrical connections.

Toe boards   See Skirt boards.

Trammel   An adjustable hook used to hold pots from a crane over a fireplace.

Trestle legs   An open number of uprights held apart by stretchers supporting a platform or table top.

Truncated   To cut off short. A truncated cone.

Trunnel   Treenail. A hardwood peg used to hold heavy timbers or to act as a hinge pin.

Underwriter's knot   Interlocking loops made in electrical wire(s) to prevent their being pulled through sockets or pipes.

Window glass   Single strength clear glass.

White glue   Polyvinyl or white liquid glue.

Wobble blade   A saw blade mounted with adjustable slanted bushings or washers to offset the blade so that it will wobble and cut a pre-determined, wider than normal cut. Used for dado cuts.

Index

254

684.1   copy 1
Da
Q
Daniele
Building colonial furnishings,
    miniatures, and folk art

DATE DUE